I'M A SAINT IN THE MAKING

By Lisa M. Hendey

Illustrated By
Katie Broussard

 PARACLETE PRESS
Brewster, Massachusetts

2020 First and Second Printing

I'm a Saint in the Making

Text © 2020 by Lisa M. Hendey
Illustrations © 2020 by Katie Broussard

ISBN 978-1-64060-163-5

The Paraclete Press name and logo (dove on cross)
are trademarks of Paraclete Press, Inc.

Library of Congress Cataloging-in-Publication Data
Names: Hendey, Lisa M., author. | Broussard, Katherine, 1982- illustrator.
Title: I'm a saint in the making / Lisa M. Hendey ; illustrated by
Katherine Broussard.
Other titles: I am a saint in the making
Description: Brewster, Massachusetts : Paraclete Press, 2020. | Audience:
Ages 8 | Audience: Grades 2-3 | Summary: "Saints-in-the-making are
ordinary people who can learn from the saints, and choose to share God's
love with everyone they meet"-- Provided by publisher.
Identifiers: LCCN 2020001405 | ISBN 9781640601635 (hardcover)
Subjects: LCSH: Christian saints--Juvenile literature. | Christian
children--Religious life--Juvenile literature.
Classification: LCC BX4653 .H36 2020 | DDC 248.8/2--dc23
LC record available at https://lccn.loc.gov/2020001405

10 9 8 7 6 5 4 3 2

Published by Paraclete Press
Brewster, Massachusetts
www.paracletepress.com

Manufactured by Regent Publishing Services Limited, Hong Kong
Printed December, 2020, in ShenZhen, Guangdong, China

God Has a Mission for Me

I'm a saint in the making. What does that mean?

It means that although I am small, God has an important mission for me.

God loves me so much that long before I was born, he sent his Son, Jesus, to save me and to teach me to love and serve our world.

Guess what: God loves you that much too. That's why you are also a saint in the making.

But how can this be? I mean, how could *I*, an ordinary person, ever be a saint?

Here's what I know: saints in the making are ordinary people like you and me, and even ordinary people are called to live extraordinary lives.

Thea Bowman

Saints have been kings and queens, priests and religious sisters, moms and dads, teachers and doctors, and business owners and workers. Some people were even children when they became saints.

They've all had one thing in common: they are heroes.

Not the kind of heroes who wear capes or have superpowers like flying or X-ray vision. The saints' superpowers are courage, peacemaking, hope, faith, and love.

I can be a hero too.

Every saint is unique. Do you know what that means? Each one was different from the others. Each had his or her own way of being a saint.

But they all shared two important missions.

Role Model and Prayer Champion

Every saint in the past—and every saint in the making—is a **role model** and a **prayer champion**.

Role models set a good example. They teach and help others with words, with actions, and with love. You don't have to be older than someone else to set a good example. You don't even have to be smarter—or faster, or stronger.

I try to set a good example for my brothers and sisters and the other kids at my school. I try to love them as a role model would. I can even teach my parents and my teacher how to love as Jesus did.

Prayer champions love God so much that they speak to God every day in prayer.

You've seen how people become champions in books, games, and movies. Champions don't have to be big, loud, or first in line in order to become champions. They support and defend others with practice, loyalty, and faithfulness. A champion in prayer does that too.

Because we are saints in the making, we try to be prayer champions with practice, loyalty, and faithfulness. We can pray quietly, in our hearts, or with our out-loud words and songs. We can pray alone or invite others to pray with us.

Meet Some Saints Who Came Before Us

I have learned about some saints from long ago. They aren't very different from me.

But some of them were able to walk and work and eat with Jesus when he was living on earth. That must have been amazing!

Jesus' mother and father, Mary and Joseph, held, fed, sheltered, and cared for Jesus. Mary and Joseph were Jesus' parents, but they were also his very first followers. They were saints. It's Mary who taught us that to be saints in the making, we should always say "yes" to Jesus.

Jesus also had a group of followers called his disciples. After Jesus went to heaven, they became leaders in the early church, and they taught everyone they met to know and love Jesus. They were saints.

Peter, John, Paul, Mary Magdalene, Priscilla and Aquila, and many others who we read about in the Bible found different ways to share what they had learned from Jesus. Sometimes, they were very afraid to be Christians. But they found the courage they needed to choose the right path.

Soon, more and more people wanted to know about the lessons that Jesus taught.

The church grew and grew, calling all of us to be saints in the making.

Some saints are so famous that the whole world celebrates them. But sometimes, we might forget the real reason we are celebrating.

I've heard about Saint Nicholas. He was always generous and protective of those in need. Because he gave secret gifts to the poor, we celebrate his memory as a kind and loving saint who shared what he had with others.

Then there's Saint Patrick. He loved God so much that he devoted his whole life to sharing God's love with the people of Ireland. Each year, on Saint Patrick's Day, we wear green to remember the creative ways he shared his faith. We use the image of the shamrock as Saint Patrick did to remember the Holy Trinity: God the Father, Son, and Holy Spirit.

Every saint has what we call a feast day, a day on which we remember the life of that saint.

Saints in the making live in many different places. Some live in cities, some on farms, some in deserts, some in suburbs, and some near water.

Saint Juan Diego was a poor farmer in Mexico who learned to love Jesus and Mary very much.

Saint Therese of Lisieux wanted to travel the world sharing the gospel, but instead lived a quiet life in France as a sister. She found simple little ways to show her love for Jesus and the people around her every day.

Saint Mary MacKillop traveled all over her country of Australia to make sure that poor children had the opportunity to go to school.

Augustus Tolton was born a slave but gained his freedom, was ordained a priest in Rome, and came home to minister to his community in the United States. Father Tolton is on his path to being "canonized"—that's the official way the Church recognizes the life of a saint. Saints come from every corner of the world.

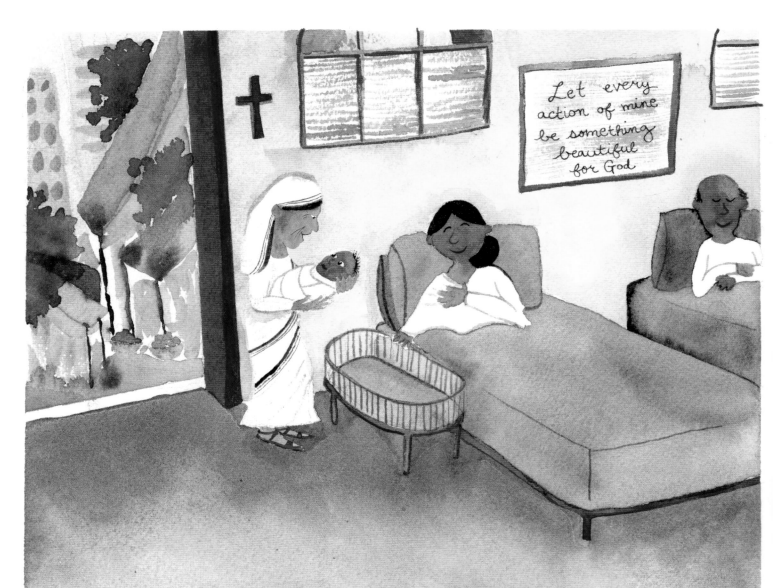

Let every
action of mine
be something
beautiful
for God

Some saints lived many years ago and we learn about them in the Bible or in books.

Many other saints have lived recently. We can see pictures of them or watch videos of them as they were learning to be saints in the making.

Mother Teresa was known around the world for her kindness and love for the poorest of the poor. She was one of the most famous people in the world. She recognized the face of Jesus even in people no one else cared about. Now, she is Saint Teresa of Calcutta.

A young boy named Karol grew up to be a saint named John Paul II.

When Karol was young, he loved playing soccer and acting in plays. When he grew up, he wanted to give his life fully to God. Karol became a priest, a bishop, and then a pope named John Paul II. As pope he led many hearts to Jesus. He did this by writing books, teaching people about God's love, and traveling to every corner of the world to share that love.

One day, a man tried to hurt Pope John Paul II. The pope wanted this man to know the power of God's love so much that he visited him in prison, forgave him, and asked everyone to pray for him. That man came to know and love Jesus too.

St. Dominic Savio

Bl. Chiara Badano

You don't have to be a grown-up to be a saint. I'm not a grown-up yet.

Saint Dominic Savio loved Jesus and Mary so much that he wanted them to be his best friends. He decided to do all of his daily chores with love, turning them into his prayers. "I can't do big things," said Dominic, "but I want everything to be for the glory of God."

Little Saints Francisco and Jacinta and their cousin Lucia were poor shepherds who didn't even know how to read. But God chose to send them a very special message through Jesus' mother, Mary, so that the whole world could know and follow Jesus.

Blessed Chiara Badano loved sports and her family, but she loved Jesus even more. When she became very sick, she helped everyone around her discover that God's beautiful love is always with us, even when life is challenging.

St. Katharine Drexel

Other saints found ways to be missionaries in the neighborhoods where they already lived. They showed God's love to people in many simple ways.

Saint Francis heard God calling him to give away all his riches and help people in his hometown of Assisi to live more peacefully, generously, and lovingly. We saints in the making can do this, too, by opening our hearts and minds to hear what God is asking of us.

Some saints traveled far from their homes to other parts of the world to share their love for Jesus. We call them missionaries.

Saint Katharine Drexel grew up in a wealthy home but had a heart full of love for the poor. After she became a religious sister, she traveled as a missionary to Native American reservations in the United States. Saint Katharine established schools and dedicated her missionary life to sharing God's love with others.

Thea Bowman

So, what should we do?

It's our turn to be saints in the making. In small ways, every day, we have the chance to share God's love with everyone we meet.

love

joy

kindness

patience

faithfulness

self control

gentleness

goodness

Peace

We listen with our ears to hear the cries of someone who is sad.

We look with our eyes to notice a friend who is being treated unkindly.

We speak with our mouths to share words that are just and true.

We touch with our hands to hug a friend who is hurt or feed someone who is hungry.

St. Ignatius

Coat Drive

Being a saint in the making means taking time every day to grow in holiness.

I love to read the stories of saints who came before me and to learn from their examples.

I love to share my love for Jesus with my friends and family.

Do you always like to go to church? Sometimes, we might think it's only a boring place for grown-ups.

But I know that, really, our church is a home for saints in the making. I try to remember that it's not just a place where we go on Sundays, but a special place to visit with Jesus all week long. I love to go inside our church for a few quiet minutes just to say "hi" to Jesus.

God reminds me that prayer is a saint's special way of talking with him, and I can talk with God in prayer any time of day and in any place.

Being a saint in the making also means that I need to keep my body strong and pure.

When I eat healthy meals, sleep well, and exercise, I train my body to be strong so that I'll be ready for any mission God gives me. Caring for the body God gave me means treating my body with respect and love.

God gave me a body to help others.

Being a saint in the making means noticing when someone around me needs help, and acting with generosity.

I help people who may need food or shelter by doing extra chores for my parents or neighbors. I donate the money I earn to charities in my community that provide clothing, groceries, and help to families who need assistance.

Our family makes better choices to buy fewer things so that we will have extra resources to help families in other parts of the world have clean water, good education, and safe homes.

God asks me to share the gifts I have with our world.

Being a saint in the making means caring for God's beautiful creation.

I love to feed my pets and take them for walks in our neighborhood.

Our family recycles and tries to conserve water. We grow vegetables and fruit in our garden and care for the trees in our community.

God made me a caretaker of our world.

Being a saint in the making means looking for special ways to share extra love with those who are hurting or tired or lonely.

Sometimes, loving is easy, but sometimes it takes extra patience and understanding.

I look for the friend in my class who has been bullied and ask him to play with me.

I visit my grandma at her nursing home and draw pictures for her to decorate her walls.

I hug my Dad when he comes home from a long day at work and thank him for taking such good care of our family.

I give an extra smile to the woman I see on the street corner or at the market.

God made my heart big enough to love anyone!

Being a saint in the making means looking for ways to share God's story with everyone I meet.

I learn God's story at church, in the Bible, and by listening to my parents and teachers.

I share my love for God with my words, with songs, or even with dancing and games.

God gave me a huge imagination and special talents to be his storyteller.

Even though I'm a saint in the making, sometimes I make mistakes.

Sometimes I am mean, impatient, or unkind.

Sometimes I don't listen to my parents or I make a bad choice.

If I do something wrong or hurt someone's feelings, I try to make things better and say I'm sorry to God and to the person I have hurt.

God loves me so much that even when I mess up, he always forgives and loves me.

Today and Tomorrow

I try to remember every day when I wake up that I'm on a special mission: a mission to be a saint in the making.

Would you like to be a part of this mission too?

Don't be afraid. Jesus taught us the way, and God has given us every gift we need to live life for him and for others.

I'm a saint in the making and you are too. Our world is waiting for us.

Let's go!

For Teachers, Parents, and Caregivers:

Thank you for walking the ongoing path to sainthood with the children in your care. In visiting classrooms around the United States and internationally, I've learned that children (and the grown-ups who love them!) always enjoy hearing the stories of the saints.

Reading about their lives, considering their legacies, and connecting them to our own faith journey helps us to ponder how we too are called to be saints in the making. I've also learned that children of every age can not only easily identify but also happily embrace the many ways in which they can serve the world around them. Our happy mission as their caregivers is to pray constantly for them and to walk alongside them, accompanying them on their path to know, love, and share Jesus. In doing this, we are blessed by their beautiful witness.

Here are a few ways to discover and follow the legacy of the saints:

1. Research the lives of the saints in books, photos, videos, and movies. When considering the legacy of these holy men and women, help your child identify the virtues that led to their sanctity and make a connection to everyday opportunities in your child's life.

2. Identify your family's patron saints and celebrate your children's feast days. If your child was not named for a saint, simply help them choose a special saintly companion that is meaningful to them or identify the saint whose feast is celebrated on your child's birthday. Choose a special patron saint for your family or classroom and dive into the details of that person's life.

3. Tell your child the stories of "saints" in your family who have gone before you and remember those loved ones in prayer by name.

4. Recognize saints in the making who are a part of your everyday life and discuss with your child what makes these people so special. Help teach the concept of saints as spiritual friends by intentionally pointing out examples of a friend who offers help, support, or encouragement.

5. Discuss intercessory prayer with your child. Invite saintly intercessors into your prayer life and encourage your child to seek the intercession of saintly friends.

6. Look together for ways to serve at home, in your classroom, at church, and in your community. Bridge the connection between service to others and our universal call to holiness.

I pray that this book will be a blessing to you and your saint in the making. As you read the book together, pause to engage with your children. Ask them simple questions that may arise based on the concepts presented—for example, "How can I forgive as Saint John Paul II did?" or "How can I be more loving like Saint Teresa of Calcutta was?" You'll be amazed and delighted by the conversations that ensue as you journey together into friendship with the saints.

I love visiting classrooms virtually and in person—so if you would like to share a story with me or invite me, feel free to connect with me through my website at www.LisaHendey.com or on social media @LisaHendey. May God continually bless you as you live each day with purpose, trust, and love.

Blessings,

Lisa

Access® 2019

for
dummies®

A Wiley Brand

Access® 2019

by Laurie Ann Ulrich and Ken Cook

A Wiley Brand

Access® 2019 For Dummies®

Published by: **John Wiley & Sons, Inc.,** 111 River Street, Hoboken, NJ 07030-5774, www.wiley.com

Copyright © 2019 by John Wiley & Sons, Inc., Hoboken, New Jersey

Published simultaneously in Canada

For general information on our other products and services, please contact our Customer Care Department within the U.S. at 877-762-2974, outside the U.S. at 317-572-3993, or fax 317-572-4002. For technical support, please visit https://hub.wiley.com/community/support/dummies.

Wiley publishes in a variety of print and electronic formats and by print-on-demand. Some material included with standard print versions of this book may not be included in e-books or in print-on-demand. If this book refers to media such as a CD or DVD that is not included in the version you purchased, you may download this material at http://booksupport.wiley.com. For more information about Wiley products, visit www.wiley.com.

Library of Congress Control Number: 2018954128

ISBN: 978-1-119-51326-1

ISBN: 978-1-119-51325-4 (ePDF); ISBN: 978-1-119-51328-5 (ePub)

Manufactured in the United States of America

C10004345_091118

Contents at a Glance

Table of Contents

Introduction

Welcome! Thank you for selecting this book. We assume you've done so because you're hoping it will explain how to use Microsoft Access 2019, and of course, as the authors, we believe this was a wise decision. We, the authors, base this belief on the fact that both of us have been teaching and using Access for a very long time, and we know how to share what we know with our students.

So what was it that made you seek out a book on Access? It might be that you've been asked to use it at work, or perhaps you run your own business or are managing a nonprofit organization. If any of these is the case — or if you're just a regular human with a lot of personal contacts and irons in the fire, you need Access to organize your data. You need it so you can find a name or a transaction in seconds after a few keystrokes, not after minutes spent leafing through your files or swiping apps this way and that on your smartphone. You need it so you can produce reports that make you look like the genius you are. You need it so you can create cool forms that will help your staff enter all the data you've got stacked on their desks — and in a way that lets you know the data was entered properly so that it's accurate and useful. You need Access so you can find little bits of data out of the huge pool of information you need to store. So that's it. You just need it.

About This Book

With all the power that Access has (and that it therefore gives *you*), there comes a small price: complexity. Access isn't one of those applications you can just sit down and use "right out of the box." It's not scarily difficult or anything, but there's a lot going on — and you need some guidance, some help, and some direction to really use it and make it bend to your will. And that's where this book — a "reference for the rest of us" — comes in.

So you've picked up this book. Hang on to it. Clutch it to your chest and run gleefully from the store or click the Add to Shopping Cart button and sit back with an expression of satisfaction and accomplishment on your face, because you've done a smart thing (if we don't say so ourselves). When you get home, or when the book arrives in person (or when you download it to your handheld device), start reading — whether you begin with Chapter 1 or whether you dive in and start with a particular feature or area of interest that's been giving you fits. Just read, and then go put Access to work for you.

Foolish Assumptions

You need to know only a few things about your computer and Windows to get the most out of *Access 2019 For Dummies.* In the following pages, we presume that you:

>> Know the basics of Windows 10 — how to open programs, save your files, create folders, find your files after you've saved them, print, and do basic stuff like that.

>> Have some goals that Access will help you reach. You

- want to build your own databases

    and/or

- want to work with databases that other people have created

>> Want to use and create queries, reports, and an occasional form

>> Have Windows 10

TECHNICAL STUFF

If your computer uses a version of Windows prior to Windows 10, you can't run Access 2019.

Icons Used in This Book

When something in this book is particularly valuable, we go out of our way to make sure that it stands out. We use these cool icons to mark text that (for one reason or another) *really* needs your attention. Here's a quick preview of the ones waiting for you in this book and what they mean.

TIP

Tips are incredibly helpful words of wisdom that promise to save you time, energy, and the embarrassment of being caught swearing out loud while you think you're alone. Whenever you see a Tip, take a second to check it out.

REMEMBER

Some things are too important to forget, so the Remember icon points them out. These items are critical steps in a process — points that you don't want to miss.

TECHNICAL STUFF

Sometimes we give in to the techno-geek lurking inside us and slip some technical babble into the book. The Technical Stuff icon protects you from obscure details by making them easy to avoid. On the other hand, you may find them interesting. (Your inner techno-geek will rejoice.)

WARNING

The Warning icon says it all: *Skipping this information may be hazardous to your data's health.* Pay attention to these icons and follow their instructions to keep your databases happy and intact.

In addition to the content in this book, you'll find some extra content available at the www.dummies.com website:

>> The Cheat Sheet for this book at www.dummies.com/cheatsheet/access2019.

>> Download files for this book: Want to explore the database used in the book or practice importing and updating data? Simply go to www.dummies.com/go/access2019. Here you will find sample files used in Chapters 9 and 17 as well as the Lancaster Food Pantry Access database used throughout the book.

>> Updates to this book, if any, at www.dummies.com/go/access2019fd.

Where to Go from Here

Now nothing's left to hold you back from the thrills, chills, and power of Access. Hold on tight to your copy of *Access 2019 For Dummies* and leap into Access. Not sure where to start? See if you spot yourself in these scenarios:

>> If you're brand new to the program and don't know which way to turn, start with the general overview in Chapter 1.

>> If you're about to design a database, we salute you — and recommend flipping through Chapter 4 for some helpful design and development tips.

>> Looking for something specific? Try the Table of Contents or the index.

1
Basic Training

Contents at a Glance

Chapter **1**

Access 2019 Basic Training

Access 2019, the latest version of the Microsoft Office database application, has always been a powerful program, and this version is no different. Chances are, you're reading this book because all that power makes Access an application that's not so easy to learn on your own. If you're hoping to unleash that power for your data, you'll need us. So, good decision to buy this book!

Now, all that power and the need for our book aside, with the very basic parts of Access, the basic functionality that you'll discover in this book, you'll be able to put Access through many of its most important paces, yet you'll be working with wizards and other onscreen tools that keep you at a comfortable arm's distance from the software's inner workings, the things that programmers and serious developers play with. There. Don't you feel better now?

REMEMBER

You don't have to use every feature and tool and push the edges of the Access envelope. In fact, you can use very little of everything Access has to offer and still create quite a significant solution to your needs for storing and accessing data — all because Access can really "do it all" — enabling you to set up a database quickly, build records into that database, and then use that data in several useful ways. Later on, who knows? You may become an Access guru.

In this chapter, you'll discover what Access does best (and when you might want to use another tool instead), and you'll get a look at what's new and improved in Access 2019 (compared to Access 2016). You'll see how it does what it does, and hopefully you'll begin to understand and absorb some basic terminology.

Now, don't panic; nobody's expecting you to memorize tons of complex vocabulary or anything scary like that. The goal here (and in the next two chapters) with regard to terms is to introduce you to some basic words and general concepts intended to help you make better use of Access — as well as better understand later chapters in this book, if you choose to follow us all the way to its stunning, life-altering conclusion.

What Is Access Good For, Anyway?

What *is* Access good for? That's a good question. Well, the list of what you can do with it is a lot longer than the list of what you *can't* do with it — of course, especially if you leave things like "wash your car" and "put away the dishes" off the "can't do" list. When it comes to data organization, storage, and retrieval, Access is at the head of the class.

Building big databases

Okay, what do I mean by *big* database? Any database with a lot of records — and by *a lot*, I mean hundreds. At least. And certainly if you have *thousands* of records, you need a tool like Access to manage them. Although you can use Microsoft Excel to store lists of records, it limits how many you can store (no more than the number of rows in a single worksheet). In addition, you can't use Excel to set up anything beyond a simple list that can be sorted and filtered. So anything with a lot of records and complex data is best done in Access.

Some reasons why Access handles big databases well are:

>> **Typically, a big database has big data-entry needs.** Access offers not only forms but also features that can create a quick form through which someone can enter all those records. This can make data entry easier and faster and can reduce the margin of error significantly. (Check out Chapter 8 for more about building forms.)

>> **When you have lots and lots of records, you also have lots of opportunities for errors to creep in.** This includes duplicate records, records with misspellings, and records with missing information — and that's just for

openers. So you need an application such as Access to ferret out those errors and fix them. (Chapter 10 lays out how you can use Access to find and replace errors and search for duplicate entries.)

>> **Big databases mean big needs for accurate, insightful reporting.** Access has powerful reporting tools you can use to create printed and onscreen reports — and those can include as few or as many pieces of your data as you need, drawn from more than one table if need be. You can tailor your reports to your audience, from what's shown on the reports' pages to the colors and fonts used.

>> **Big databases are hard to wade through when you want to find something.** Access provides several tools for sorting, searching, and creating your own specialized tools (known as *queries*) for finding the elusive single record or group of records you need.

>> **Access saves time by making it easy to import and recycle data.** You may have used certain tools to import data from other sources — such as Excel worksheets (if you started in Excel and maxed out its usefulness as a data-storage device) and Word tables. Access saves you from reentering all your data and allows you to keep multiple data sources consistent.

Creating databases with multiple tables

Whether your database holds 100 records or 100,000 records (or more), if you need to keep separate tables and relate them for maximum use of the information, you need a *relational* database — and that's Access. How do you know whether your data needs to be in separate tables? Think about your data — is it very compartmentalized? Does it go off on tangents? Consider the following example and apply the concepts to your data and see if you need multiple tables for your database.

The Big Organization database

Imagine you work for a very large company, and the company has data pertaining to their customers and their orders, the products the company sells, its suppliers, and its employees. For a complex database like this one, you need multiple tables, as follows:

>> One table houses the customer data — names, addresses, phone numbers, and email addresses.

>> A second table contains the customers' orders, including the name of the customer who placed the order, the salesperson who handled the sale, shipping information, and the date of the order.

>> A third table contains information on the products the company sells, including product numbers, supplier names, prices, and the number of items in stock.

>> A fourth table contains supplier data — about the companies from which the main organization obtains its inventory of products to resell to customers. The table contains the company names, their contact person, and the address, email, and phone number information to reach them.

>> A fifth table contains employees' data — from the date they were hired to their contact information to their job title — and also contains notes about them, sort of a summary of their resumes for reference.

Other tables exist, too — to keep a list of shipping companies and their contact information (for shipping customer orders), an expense table (for the expenses incurred in running the business), and other tables that are used with the main four tables. The need for and ways to use the main tables and these additional tables are covered later in this book, as you find out how to set up tools for data entry, look up records, and create reports that provide varying levels of detail on all the data you've stored.

TIP

Because you don't have to fill in every field for each record — in any table in the database — if you don't have a phone number or don't know an email address, for example, it's okay to leave those fields blank until you've obtained that information.

Fail to plan? Plan to fail

If you think carefully about your database, how you use your data, and what you need to know about your employees, customers, volunteers, donors, products, or projects — whatever you're storing information about — you can plan:

>> How many tables you'll need

>> Which data will go into which table

>> How you'll use the tables together to get the reports you need

Of course, everyone forgets something, and plans change after a system has already been implemented. But don't worry — Access isn't so rigid that chaos will ensue if you begin building your tables and forget something (a field or two, an entire table). You can always add a field that you forgot (or that some bright spark just told you is needed) or add a new table after the fact. But planning ahead as thoroughly as possible is still essential.

TIP

As part of thorough planning, sketch your planned database on paper, drawing a kind of flowchart with boxes for each table and lists of fields that you'll have in each one. Draw arrows to show how they might be related — it's sort of like drawing a simple family tree — and you're well on your way to a well-planned, useful database.

Here's a handy procedure to follow if you're new to the process of planning a database:

1. **On paper or in a word-processing document, whichever is more comfortable, type the following:**

   - A tentative name for your database

   - A list of the pieces of information you plan on getting from that database on a daily or regular basis

2. **Now, based on that information, create a new list of the actual details you could store:**

   List every piece of information you can possibly think of about your customers, products, ideas, cases, books, works of art, students — whatever your database pertains to. Don't be afraid to go overboard — you can always skip some of the items in the list if they don't turn out to be things you really need to know (or can possibly find out) about each item in your database.

3. **Take the list of fields — that's what all those pieces of information are — and start breaking them up into logical groups.**

   How? Think about the fields and how they work together:

   - For example, if the database keeps track of a library of books, perhaps the title, publication date, publisher, ISBN (*I*nternational *S*tandard *B*ook *N*umber, which is unique for each book), price, and page count can be stored in one group, whereas author information, reviews, and lists of other titles by the same author or books on the same topic can be stored in another group. These groups become individual tables, creating your relational database of books.

   - Figure out what's unique about each record. As stated in the previous point, you need a field that's unique for each record. Although Access can create a unique value for you if no unique data exists for each record in your database, it's often best to have such a field already in place, or to create such a field yourself. Customer numbers, student numbers, Social Security numbers, book ISBNs, catalog numbers, serial numbers — anything that isn't the same for any two records will do.

   With a big list of fields and some tentative groupings of those fields at the ready, and with an idea of which field is unique for each record, you can begin figuring out how to *use* the data.

4. **Make a list of ways you might use the data, including:**

- Reports you'd like to create, including a list of which fields should be included for each report

- Other ways you can use the data — labels for mailings, product labels, catalogue data, price lists, contact lists, and so on

5. **List all the places your data currently resides.** This might be on slips of paper in your pocket, on cards in a box, in another program (such as Excel), or maybe through a company that sells data for marketing purposes.

With this planning done, you're ready to start building your database. The particulars of that process come later in this chapter and in subsequent chapters, so don't jump in yet. Do pat yourself on the back, though, because if you've read this procedure and applied even some of it to your potential database, you're way ahead of the game, and we're confident you'll make good use of all that Access has to offer.

Databases with user forms

When you're planning your database, consider how the data will be entered:

>> If you'll be doing the data entry yourself, perhaps you're comfortable working in a spreadsheet-like environment (known in Access as *Datasheet view*), where the table is a big grid. You fill it in row by row, and each row is a record.

Figure 1-1 shows a table of volunteers in progress in Datasheet view. You decide: Is it easy to use, or can you picture yourself forgetting to move down a row and entering the wrong stuff in the wrong columns as you enter each record? As you can see, there are more fields than show in the window, so you'd be doing a lot of scrolling to the left and right to use this view.

>> You may want to use a *form* (shown in Figure 1-2) instead. A form is a specialized interface for data entry, editing, and viewing your database one record at a time, if:

- Someone else will be handling data entry

- Typing row after row of data into a big grid seems mind-numbing

The mind-numbing effect (and inherent increased margin for error) is especially likely when you have lots of fields in a database, and the user, if working in Datasheet view, has to move horizontally through the fields. A form like the one in Figure 1-2 puts the fields in a more pleasing format, making it easier to enter data into the fields and to see all the fields simultaneously (or only those you want data entered into).

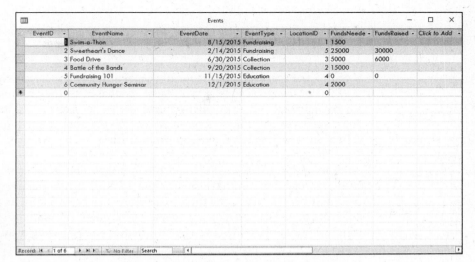

You find out all about forms in Chapter 8. If your database is large enough that you require help doing the data entry, or if it's going to grow over time, making an ongoing data-entry process likely, Access is the tool for you. The fact that it offers simple forms of data entry/editing is reason enough to make it your database application of choice.

Databases that require special reporting

Yet another reason to use Access is the ability it gives you to create customized reports quickly and easily. Some database programs, especially those designed for single-table databases (known as *flat-file* databases), have some canned reports built in, and that's all you can do — just select a report from the list and run the same report that every other user of that software runs.

If you're an Excel user, your reporting capabilities are far from easy or simple, and they're not designed for use with large databases — they're meant for spreadsheets and small, one-table lists. Furthermore, you have to dig much deeper into Excel's tools to get at these reports. Access, on the other hand, is a database application, so reporting is a major, up-front feature.

An example? In Excel, to get a report that groups your data by one or more of the fields in your list, you have to sort the rows in the worksheet first, using the field(s) to sort the data, and then you can create what's known as a *subtotal report*. To create it, you use a dialog box that asks you about calculations you want to perform, where to place the results, and whether you're basing a sort and/or a subtotal on more than one field. The resulting report is not designed for printing, and you have to tinker with your spreadsheet pagination (through a specialized view of the spreadsheet) to control how the report prints out.

In Access? Just fire up the Report Wizard, and you can sort your data, choose how to group it, decide which pieces of data to include in the report, and pick a visual layout and color scheme, all in one simple, streamlined process. Without you doing anything, the report is ready for printing. Access is built for reporting — after all, it is a database application — and reports are one of the most (if not *the* most) important ways you'll use and share your data.

Because reports are such an important part of Access, you can not only create them with minimum fuss but also customize them to create powerful documentation of your most important data:

>> Build a quick, simple report that just spits out whatever is in your table in a tidy, easy-to-read format. (See Figure 1-3 for an example.)

>> Create a customized report that you design step-by-step with the help of the Report Wizard. (See Figure 1-4.) The report shown in the figure has the volunteers sorted by their last names. These options were easily put to work with just a few clicks.

>> You can really roll up your sleeves and design a new report, or play with an existing one, adding all sorts of bells and whistles. Figure 1-5 shows this happening in Design view. Note that the report's title (Volunteers List by Status) is selected: It has a box around it and tiny handles on the corners and sides of the box, which means you can reformat the title, change the font, size, or color of the text, or even edit the words if a new title is needed.

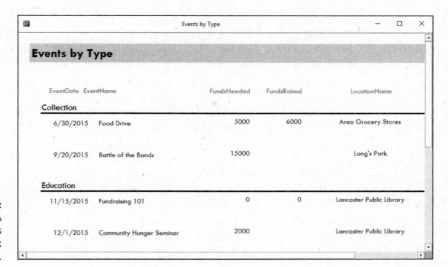

So, you can create any kind of custom report in Access, using any or all of your database tables and any of the fields from those tables, and you can group fields and place them in any order you want:

>> With the Report Wizard, you can choose from several preset layouts for your report, and you can customize all of it row by row, column by column.

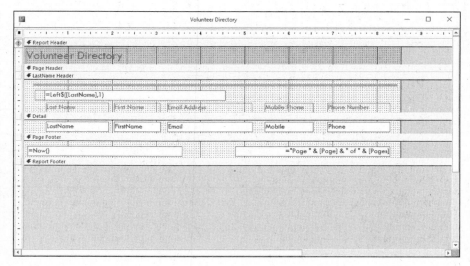

>> You can easily add and remove fields after creating the report, should you change your mind about what's included in the report. If you want to place your personal stamp on every aspect of your report, you can use Design view to do the following:

- Add titles, instructional or descriptive text boxes, and graphics.

- Set up customized headers and footers to include any information you want to appear on all the report's pages.

If all of this sounds exciting, or at least interesting, then you're really on the right track with Access. The need to create custom reports is a major reason to use Access; you can find out about all these reporting options in Chapters 18 through 21. That's right: This chapter you're reading plus three more — that's four whole chapters — are devoted to reporting. It *must* be a big feature in Access!

What's New in Access 2019?

For users of Access 2007, 2010, 2013, or 2016, Access 2019 won't seem like a big deal. Of course, if you're coming from 2003, the biggest changes are found in the interface. Gone are the familiar menus and toolbars of 2003 and prior versions, now replaced by a Ribbon bar divided into tabs that take you to different versions of those old standbys. It's a big change, and it takes some getting used to. In this book, however, we're going to assume you already got your feet wet with 2007, 2010, 2013, or 2016, and aren't thrown by the interface anymore.

Reach Out with SharePoint

What the heck is SharePoint? Even if your company isn't using it yet, you've no doubt been seeing the product name and hearing how it provides the ability to see and use your Access data from anywhere — using desktop applications, a web browser, or even your phone. And in truth, it's Microsoft's software product that does all that and more, helping you manage your documents and collaborate with coworkers via the company network. Simply click the Save Database As command in the Access File tab's panel (see Figure 1-6), and you're on your way to publishing your database to SharePoint, which means you can access it from pretty much everywhere, including that beach in Maui. Of course, if you or your company doesn't have a SharePoint server, you won't be able to make use of this, and you don't need to concern yourself with this section.

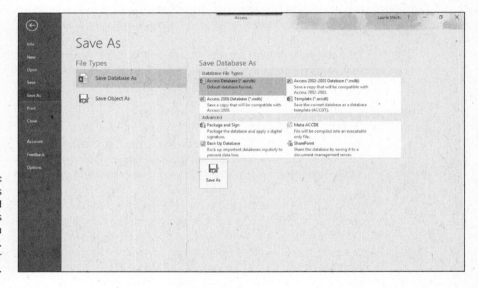

FIGURE 1-6: The Save As command offers choices for . . . you guessed it . . . saving your database.

As shown in Figure 1-6, the Save As options include regular old Save Database As, to save your existing database with a new name or in some format other than as an Access database; and Save Object As, to save a table, form, query, or report with a new name. You can also choose from several Advanced options to save the database as a package (to distribute your Access applications) or as an executable file (a single file that when run by the recipient, opens a database application), to back up the database, and to use the aforementioned SharePoint.

How Access Works and
How You Work with It

When you look at all the applications in Microsoft Office — Word, Excel, Power-Point, Outlook, and of course, Access — you'll see some features that are consistent throughout the suite. There are big differences, too, and that's where books like this one come in handy, helping you deal with what's different and not terribly obvious to a new user.

Access has several features in common with the rest of the applications in the Microsoft Office suite. You'll find the same buttons on several of the tabs, and the Quick Access Toolbar (demonstrated in Chapter 2) appears in all the applications.

TIP

If you already know how to open, save, and print in, say, Word, you're probably ready to do the same things in Access without any difficulty.

To make sure you're totally Access-ready, here's a look at the basic procedures that can give you a solid foundation on which to build.

Opening Access

Access opens in any one of several ways. So, like a restaurant with a very comprehensive menu, some people will love all the choices, and others will say, "I can't decide! There are just too many options to choose from!"

Now, you'll run into situations in which one of the ways is the glaringly best choice — hands down, and that one will be the way to go. But what if you've never heard of it? You'll be trying to find my phone number (I'm unlisted — ha!) so you can give me a piece of your mind. So to acquaint you with *all* your choices (so you'll be ready for any situation), here are all the ways you can open Access:

>> Windows 8.1 users can utilize any of several methods to start an application — click the lower left corner of the screen to display the Start icon, press the Windows key on the keyboard, or if you have a touchscreen, tap the Start button. Once the Start screen appears, tap the Access application tile.

TIP

If you've recently used Access, you'll see it in the list on the left side of the Start menu. Just choose Start ➪ Microsoft Access 2019, and Access opens.

>> Double-click any existing Access database file on your desktop or in a folder (as shown in Figure 1-7). Access opens automatically.

TIP

Good news: Access 2019 will open database files you created with previous versions of Access, and should support whatever features are employed within those database files. All your tables should open properly, and reports, forms, and queries should all work fine, too.

» If some helpful person has added Access to the Quick Launch toolbar (on the taskbar), you can click the Access 2019 icon (it looks like an A on the cover of a book), and there you go. Access opens for you right then and there.

Double-click to open

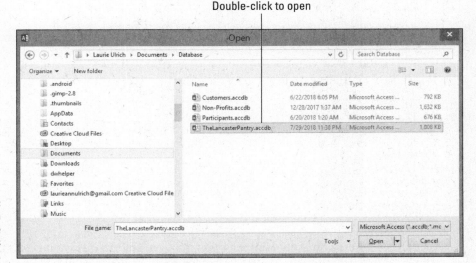

FIGURE 1-7:
Double-click an Access database file, and Access opens right up.

Selecting a starting point

So Access is open, and (assuming you opened it from the Start menu or from the Quick Launch portion of the taskbar) you're staring at the Access interface. You may see features whose purposes elude you or that you don't yet know how to use. Hey, don't worry; that's why you're reading this book!

You can find out more about all the tabs and buttons, panels and menus, and all that fun stuff in Chapter 2. For now, just look at the ways Access offers you to get started with your database, be it an existing one that needs work or a new one you have all planned out and ready to go.

Opening an existing database

Well, this is the easy one. If a database already exists, you can open it by clicking the File tab (at the upper left of the workspace) and choosing Open from the list of commands that appears. As shown in Figure 1-8, a panel opens, displaying the types of files you can open (just to the right of the long red File panel) and the databases you've most recently used. Click the word *Recent* in the list to the near left and then click the database in the Recent list, and it opens, listing its current tables, queries, reports, and forms on the far left side of the window.

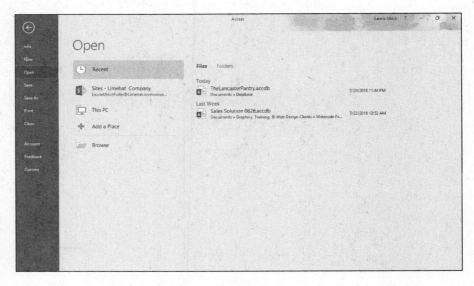

FIGURE 1-8:
Pick your recently used database from the Recent list on the right.

When the database opens, you can open and view its various parts just by double-clicking them in that leftmost panel; whatever you open appears in the main, central part of the window. Figure 1-9 shows an example: a table, ready for editing.

After you open a table, you can begin entering or editing records. You can read more about how that's done in Chapter 6, which demonstrates the different ways to edit your data and tweak your tables' setups. If you want to tinker with any existing queries, you can open these, too, just by clicking them in the list on the left side of the workspace. (For more information on queries, check out Chapters 12 and 13. You can do simple sorting and look for particular records with the skills you pick up in Chapters 10 and 12.)

Starting a new database from scratch

So you don't have a database to open, eh? Well, don't let that stop you. To start a new one, all you have to do is open Access, using any of the techniques listed earlier in this chapter (except the one that starts Access by opening an existing database file, which you don't have yet).

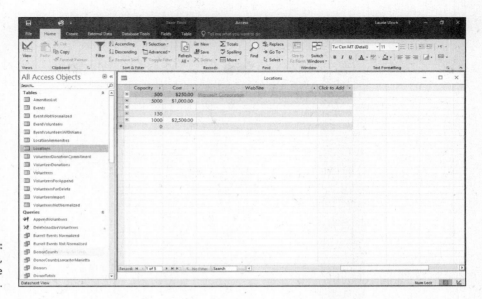

FIGURE 1-9:
An existing table, ready for more records.

REMEMBER

A database file holds *all* your database components. Everything associated with the data is part of the database, including:

>> All the tables that house your data

>> Queries that help you search and use the data

>> Reports that show what your data is and what it means

>> Forms that allow people to view, enter, and edit data

After Access is open, click the New command in the File tab (if that's not already the active command). From the resulting display, you can click the Blank Desktop Database button (shown in Figure 1-10) to get started.

Next, give your database a name (see the dialog box that appears in Figure 1-11), and click the Create button.

TECHNICAL STUFF

The *X* in Figure 1-11's caption represents a number — Access assigns consecutive numbers to the default names. Figure 1-11 shows a 1 added to the filename.

If this is your absolute first database in a fresh installation of Access, the filename offered in this panel will be Database1. Note that you don't need to type a file extension here; Access will add the correct one for you.

Click the Blank database button

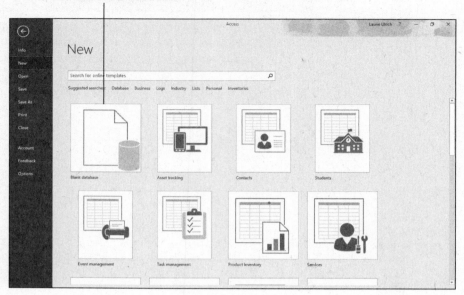

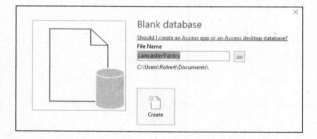

Blank database

Should I create an Access app or an Access desktop database?

File Name

LancasterPantry

C:\Users\Robert\Documents\

Create

TIP

What is that little yellow folder in the dialog box where you named your new database? It allows you to choose a folder (other than the default Documents folder in Windows 8/8.1) into which you can save your database. Click the folder icon after typing a name for your database, and then use the resulting File New Database dialog box to choose a location — an existing subfolder within Documents, the desktop, a network drive (if you're on a network, say at your office), or your Office 365 OneDrive. The dialog box looks very familiar to anyone who's used any Windows application, so this won't be new territory for you.

At this point, with your new database open, you can begin entering records into your first table or begin naming your fields and setting them up. The field names go in the topmost row (the ID field is already created, by default in the new table), and the label Click to Add is atop the column with the active cell. If you choose to save your table now (right-click the Table1 tab and choose Save), you can name your table something more useful than Table1.

Starting with a template

Access provides *templates* (prepared files that work sort of like database cookie cutters) for your new database needs. You'll find a set of template icons in the same New panel where we just chose a Blank Desktop Database. As shown in Figure 1-12, you can choose a template category by clicking any of the words under the Search for Online Templates search box, and search online for templates in that category.

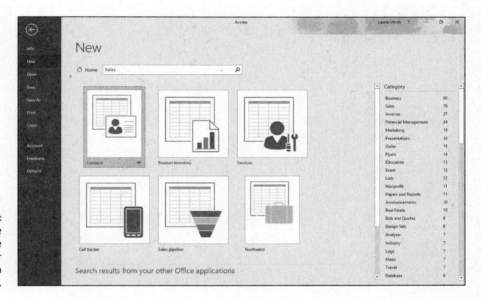

FIGURE 1-12: View the database templates for your chosen category.

Once the online search is complete (assuming you're online at the time), a series of big buttons, one for each template found that matches your search, appears. Note that a larger list of categories — to be used if you want to search again for another category of templates — appears on the right.

Now What?

So you've got a new database started. What do you do now? You can leaf on over to Chapter 2, where you can find out more about all the tools that Access offers — which tools are onscreen almost all the time and which ones are specific to the way you chose to dig in and start that database.

In Chapter 3, you actually begin building a database, setting up tables and the fields that give them structure. And you figure out which tables you need to set up, putting that great plan you built in this chapter to work!

Chapter **2**

Navigating the Access Workspace

I f you're upgrading to Access (or Office) 2019 from the 2013 or 2016 interface, you'll find it looks very familiar — and you'll find much of it to be the same as what you're accustomed to.

Of course, no matter how similar Access 2019 is to the 2010, 2013, and 2016 versions, we need to cover some of the key aspects of the interface — because we assume that if you're reading this book, you're looking for some help identifying and understanding key portions of the interface.

Let's start with the File tab, where a vertical list of commands creates context-sensitive changes to the main workspace — essentially everything to the right of that left-hand menu panel.

» To start a new database, click the word New in the File tab's vertical menu of options. Starter templates appear along with the Blank Desktop Database button. Most of the time, you'll be clicking the Blank Desktop Database button so you can create a completely customized database.

» If you've opened an existing database, click the Info command (as shown in Figure 2-1) to get important statistics related to the open database. Two big buttons and a link appear, from which you can Compact & Repair the database files, Encrypt the open database with a password, or see the Properties for the open database by clicking the View and Edit Database Properties link.

>> The Save, Save As, Print, and Options commands each lead to either more command choices or a dialog box. For example, choosing Save As produces two options — to save the open database with a new name (Save Database As) or to save a new version of the active database object (Save Object As), which allows you to save the table, form, query, or report you have open at the time with a new name.

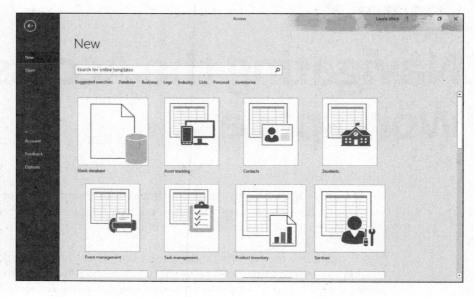

FIGURE 2-1:
When it comes to the interface, Access users will find a comforting similarity to earlier (post-2007) versions of Access.

I won't go into every possible combination of Access interface features in this chapter — you get to know a lot of them in subsequent chapters, in context, and that's the best way to learn about them.

For now, I'll show you the basic workspace in three states:

>> When Access first opens up

>> When a new database is being built, either from scratch or when you've started with one of Access's database templates

>> When you're working on an existing database

As you read through the following sections, you can refer solely to the accompanying figures or, if you want, try to work along with the procedures — you'll find doing what you see described here boosts your confidence when you're using Access later, on your own.

Diving Right In

So you're ready to dive in. Well done, you! It's easy to start Access. You can start the application in multiple ways, accommodating nearly any situation you're in. (Chapter 1 discusses most of them.) Whether you're starting Access to view and edit an existing Access database (which gives you what you see in Figure 2-2) or are about to create your own (which opens the application and displays the template icons, shown in Figure 2-3), you can get to the tools you need right away. Figure 2-2 shows an existing database open to one of its tables; its other components are listed on the left side of the workspace.

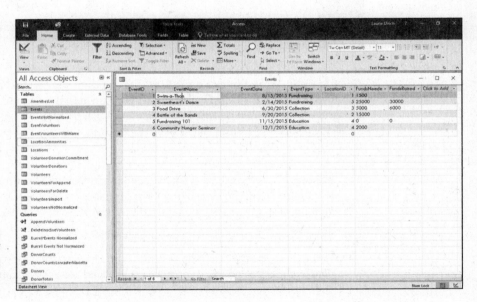

FIGURE 2-2: Open Access *and* your existing database in one fell swoop.

You can open an existing database by double-clicking it by name in the File Explorer window or from an icon on your desktop; you can start Access from the Start menu or the taskbar (if you pinned Access to it), and then pick which existing database you want to work with; you can start a new, blank database from scratch; or you can start out with one of the Access templates.

Figure 2-3 shows the various template icons displayed when you choose New from the left-hand panel.

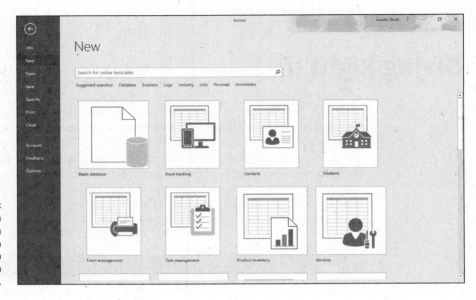

If you opened Access by using the Start menu or a desktop/taskbar icon and *now* you want to open an existing database, you can use the Open command in the panel on the left (see Figure 2-4). This allows you to open either a recently used database or browse for one you haven't opened in a while. The Open command's list of options includes:

>> **Recent:** Shows the list of recently used files and folders. When you use the Recent list, clicking any one of the Recent Databases listed opens that sucker right up, displaying its parts on the panel on the left side of the workspace.

>> **Sites:** Opens a chosen folder in your SharePoint server.

>> **This PC:** Provides a list of database files found in the last folder you used to save an Access database. If you have never saved an Access database in the open installation of Access, this takes you to the Documents folder, Windows' default location to save files generated in any application running on your computer.

>> **Add a Place:** Adds SharePoint and OneDrive locations.

>> **Browse:** Opens an Open dialog box through which you can navigate to the drive and/or folder containing the database you want to open.

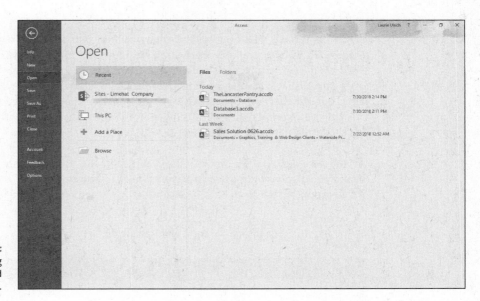

FIGURE 2-4:
Open an existing
or recently used
database.

So that's it, really — any way you want to get started is available either by opening the Access application from the Start menu, the desktop, or the taskbar — or File Explorer, if you want to open a database (.accdb) file and start both Access and your selected database at the same time.

After you get to working, however, it's time to use the onscreen tools that don't appear until you open a database. Read on for a whirlwind tour of the Access workspace, including views and explanations of all the major bells, whistles, and buttons.

Working with Onscreen Tools in Access

When you open a database — be it an existing one or one you're just starting from a blank database or a template — the workspace changes, offering the Ribbon and its tabs shown in Figure 2-5 (Home, Create, External Data, and Database Tools). These tabs are not to be confused with the context-sensitive tabs that appear when various database *objects* (the tables, forms, queries, or reports that make up your database) are created or edited.

FIGURE 2-5:
The main Ribbon
tabs appear
when you open
a database.

When the Ribbon tabs first appear, many of their buttons are dimmed — because they don't become available until you're doing something that warrants their use. For example, if you haven't opened any tables, forms, reports, or queries in your open database, the tools for editing or formatting your database will appear on the tabs, but they'll be dimmed, which indicates that they're unavailable. Tools for creating new components are available on the Create tab, but anything that works with existing data will be dimmed.

After you open a table, report, query, or form, the tools for that object become available. Displaying a form in Layout view, for example, adds the Form Layout Tools group of tabs to the main set of five tabs, as shown in Figure 2-6.

The Design, Arrange, and Format tabs

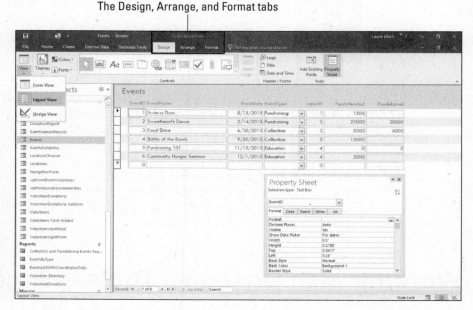

FIGURE 2-6:
The buttons relevant to what's open and active in your database are available when you need them.

Clicking tabs

To move from one tab on the Ribbon to another, simply click the tab's name. It's easy to see which tab is currently open — as shown in Figure 2-7, the Create tab stands out from all the other tabs, and you can see all its buttons. When you mouse over another tab, that tab brightens, too, but you don't see its buttons until or unless you click the tab.

FIGURE 2-7:
You can easily tell
the active tab
(Create) from the
inactive ones.

**TECHNICAL
STUFF**

After you've created an object — say a table, by clicking Table on the Create tab — the Home tab is displayed, and a new label (Table Tools) appears above the context-sensitive Fields and Table tabs. See? Access knows what you need based on whatever you've just done within the application.

Using buttons

Access buttons come in two varieties:

>> **Buttons that do something when they're clicked:** Either opening a dialog box or wizard or performing some change or task in your open table, report, query, or form.

>> **Buttons that represent lists or menus of choices:** This latter variety comes in two flavors of its own:

**TECHNICAL
STUFF**

- Drop-down list buttons are accompanied by a small, down-pointing triangle, appearing to the button's right. When you click the triangle, a list of options appears, as shown in Figure 2-8.

- Some buttons have a down-pointing triangle at the bottom of the button (as shown in Figure 2-9). Click the bottom half of the button (or on the triangle), and a menu appears.

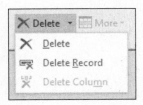

FIGURE 2-8:
Click the triangle
to the right of the
button and make
a choice.

The File tab and Quick Access tools

If you're fresh from using a pre-2007 version of Office (XP and previous), you'll be relieved to see a File tab. Office 2007 users lost that familiar word in that version's interface, replaced then by an Office button, with no comforting word *File* on it. The word *File* came back in 2010, however, displaying Backstage view, for opening files, saving files, starting new files, printing, and customizing Access through the Options command. The File tab remains in Access 2019, and is shown in Figure 2-10.

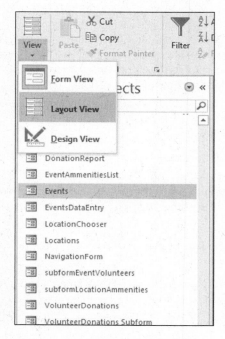

FIGURE 2-9:
Menu buttons
display a —
surprise! — menu
when clicked.

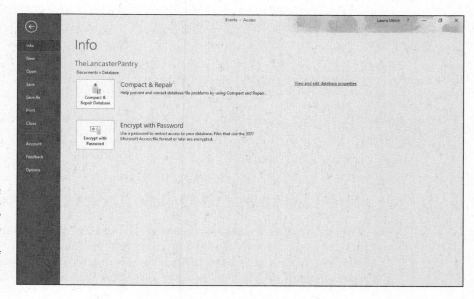

FIGURE 2-10:
Craving the File
menu's tools?
Click the File tab
to choose from a
series of
commands on
the left.

When you're in a database and click the File tab, you're taken to the Info display, showing information about the open database.

TIP

Where's the Quick Access Toolbar? It appears while you're in a database, but it disappears when you go to the File tab. No problem; to see it again, just click the Back button in the File panel, and you're back to your database, with the Quick Access Toolbar in the uppermost left of the workspace. If you want to customize the Quick Access Toolbar, click the triangle at the right end of the toolbar. It offers a pop-up menu with several choices, from a list of commands you can add to the toolbar (such as New, Open, Email, or Quick Print — the ones already in use have a check mark next to them) to commands that allow you to Customize Quick Access Toolbar and Show Below the Ribbon.

Accessing panes, panels, and context-sensitive tools

Depending on what's going on within the workspace — that is, what you've just done as you edit your table, report, query, or form, or which button you've clicked on one of the Ribbon tabs — Access offers relevant onscreen tools and panels. As an example of this context-sensitive feature, if you open a table and click the Report button on the Create tab (see the Reports section of the Create tab), not only does a report appear, but you also get new tabs — Design (shown in Figure 2-11), Arrange, Format, and Page Setup, under the heading "Report Layout Tools".

FIGURE 2-11:
Reporting-related tools appear precisely when they're needed.

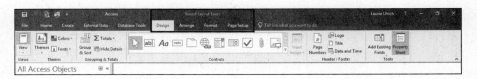

To find out more about reporting, including the capability to group, sort, and total your data, see Chapters 18 through 20.

As you work with Access, you'll get a feel for what's going to appear when you do certain things. Things appear and disappear as you work because Access offers you just what you need for the task you're performing or feature you're using.

Customizing the Access Workspace

Any good application provides some capability for the user to customize the workspace — from adding and rearranging buttons on the toolbar to dragging toolbars and panes around to optimize the layout.

Access is certainly a good software application, so it does what any good application does: It allows you to customize the workspace. You can move the Quick Access Toolbar, you can add buttons from the standard tabs to the Quick Access Toolbar, you can resize the Ribbon, you can tweak the status bar, and you can decide how (or if) your ScreenTips are displayed as you mouse over the tools.

There's no need to do any customization, really — the default settings for toolbar locations, button combinations, and onscreen help are designed with the average or most common user in mind, and they're pretty good. On the other hand, you may just want to tweak things to feel at home. (Think of the times you've fluffed the pillows on the couch before lying down — they may not have needed it, but you want to make your mark on your environment, right? Right.)

Repositioning the Quick Access Toolbar

For the position of the Quick Access Toolbar, you have two choices:

>> Above the Ribbon, which is the default location

>> Below the Ribbon

To move the Quick Access Toolbar, simply right-click it and choose Show Quick Access Toolbar Below the Ribbon. Figure 2-12 shows the pop-up menu with this command available. Note that if you click the down-pointing triangle at the right end of the Quick Access Toolbar, the command is Show Below the Ribbon.

FIGURE 2-12: Display your Quick Access Toolbar options to move it above or below the Ribbon.

When you place the Quick Access Toolbar below the Ribbon, should you for some reason decide to do so, you'll notice that the same command (viewed by right-clicking the toolbar in its new location) is now Show Quick Access Toolbar Above the Ribbon. So it toggles like that, switching from Above to Below, depending on its current location. Do I recommend moving it from its default location above the Ribbon? Nope. I think it's much easier to use when it's separate from the main workspace and Ribbon tabs. Leave it above the Ribbon, in other words!

TIP

You don't have to right-click specifically the Quick Access Toolbar in order to reposition it. The aforementioned command (Show . . .) is available in the pop-up menu that appears when you right-click the tabs, too.

Adding buttons to the Quick Access Toolbar

Speaking of the Quick Access Toolbar and all the ways you can access commands for customizing it, try this to add commands:

TIP

1. **With any database open (so that the Ribbon tabs are displayed), right-click any of the buttons on any of the tabs.**

   You can also right-click the Quick Access Toolbar or any Ribbon tab.

2. **Choose Customize Quick Access Toolbar (or More Commands, if you're already looking at the Quick Access Toolbar's menu from 2-12).**

   The Access Options dialog box opens (shown in Figure 2-13), with its Customization options displayed.

3. **Click the Choose Commands From drop-down list and choose a command category.**

   A list of Popular Commands appears by default.

4. **From any (or each) category, choose the commands you want to see at all times in the Quick Access Toolbar by clicking them one at a time and then clicking the Add button.**

   As you click the Add button, the command you choose is added to the list on the right. Note that you have up- and down-pointing triangles on the right side of the list of commands you've added — with one of the commands you've chosen to add selected, use them to reorder the list, which rearranges the left-to-right order in which they'll appear on the toolbar.

5. **Continue selecting categories and commands on the left and using the Add button to add them to the list on the right.**

   TIP

   Not all commands will be usable at all the times that the Quick Access Toolbar is displayed. For example, if you choose to place the Filter button from the Home tab on the Quick Access Toolbar, the button won't be available until and unless a table or set of query results is open.

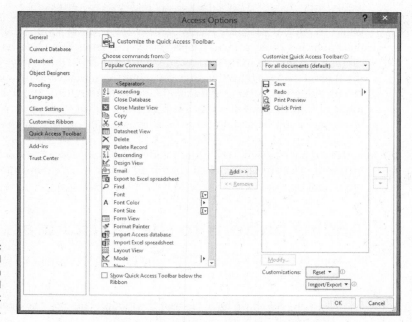

FIGURE 2-13:
Pick a command
category and a
command to add
to the Quick
Access Toolbar.

6. **When you've added all the commands you want to add, click OK to add them and close the dialog box.**

When you click OK, the changes to the Quick Access Toolbar are applied. The toolbar's space on the top of the workspace grows to accommodate all the new buttons, as shown in Figure 2-14.

FIGURE 2-14:
Add as many
buttons as you
want — the
toolbar will
expand
horizontally to
accommodate
them.

The toolbar expands horizontally as you add buttons

TIP

If you're in a hurry to add a specific button to the Quick Access Toolbar, and you're looking right at the button you want to add, just right-click the button and choose Add to Quick Access Toolbar from the menu that appears. The button you right-click instantly appears on the toolbar *and* remains in the tab where it was living when you right-clicked it.

Why, then, would you use the Access Options dialog box if a simple right-click takes care of business? Because it gives you the ability to select buttons from all the various tabs in one place — no need to go hunting on the tabs for the buttons you want to add. But when there's just one you want and you can see it at the time, the right-click method can't be beat.

Removing buttons from the Quick Access Toolbar

Want to remove a command from the Quick Access Toolbar? It's easy:

1. **Point to the unwanted button on the Quick Access Toolbar and right-click.**

2. **Choose Remove from Quick Access Toolbar from the pop-up menu (see Figure 2-15).**

   Voilà! It's gone.

FIGURE 2-15: Reconsidering that added button? No problem. Say bye-bye with a simple right-click.

Because the button remains on the tab where it originally lived, it's not lost — it's just not taking up space at the top of the Access workspace.

TIP

Be careful *not* to remove the default buttons — Save, Undo, and Redo. Why? Because they're used so often that it's silly to remove them from such a great location. If you do remove them by accident or in a moment of wildly bad decision-making, you'll have to use the Quick Access menu button and select them from that menu when you inevitably want to bring them back.

Minimizing the Ribbon

Need more elbow room? If you need to spread out and want more workspace, you can make the Ribbon smaller, reducing it to just a strip of the tab titles (whichever tabs are in place at the time you choose to minimize the Ribbon). When it's minimized, you can bring it back to full size with minimum fuss.

To minimize the Ribbon, follow these steps:

1. **Right-click anywhere on the Ribbon.**

A pop-up menu appears. Note that you can right-click a button, a Ribbon tab, or a group name (such as "Reports" on the Create tab, or "Text Formatting" on the Home tab) and the appropriate pop-up menu will appear.

2. **Choose Collapse the Ribbon.**

The Ribbon is reduced to a long bar with just the tab titles on it, as shown in Figure 2-16. You can, of course, use any of the tabs (displaying its buttons temporarily) by clicking the tab with your mouse.

FIGURE 2-16:
The Ribbon,
minimized.

3. **To bring the Ribbon back to its full glory, right-click the reduced Ribbon and then choose Collapse the Ribbon.**

Note that the command is now checked, indicating that the Ribbon is currently minimized. Performing this step — reselecting the command — toggles this setting off, and the Ribbon returns to full size.

Working with ScreenTips

ScreenTips are the little names and brief descriptions of onscreen tools that appear when you put your mouse pointer over buttons, commands, menus, and many of the other pieces of the Access workspace.

Not all onscreen features have ScreenTips, but for anything you can click to make something happen — as when a dialog box opens, Access performs some task for you, or something is created — these typically have associated ScreenTips that you can choose to view or not view. If you choose to view them, you can choose to see very brief or more elaborate tips.

To tinker with Access's ScreenTips settings, follow these steps:

1. **Click the File tab.**

The File menu (the red panel on the far left) and the Info view appear on the workspace, as shown in Figure 2-17.

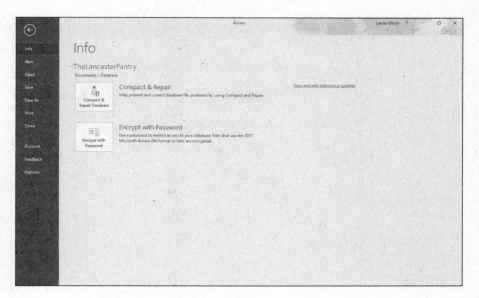

FIGURE 2-17:
The File tab's panel of commands gives you an Options command, which you can use to adjust how Access looks and works.

2. **Click the Options command, near the bottom of the menu.**

   The Access Options dialog box appears onscreen.

3. **From the list on the left side of the Access Options dialog box, select General.**

   The options in the dialog box change to show other options related to ScreenTips, file formats and folders, and how your name and initials are stored, as shown in Figure 2-18.

4. **In the first section of the dialog box, click the ScreenTip Style drop-down list.**

5. **Choose from the following options:**

   - *Show Feature Descriptions in ScreenTips:* This option displays ScreenTips with extra information, as shown in Figure 2-19. Here you see that in addition to the name of the button, a brief description of how it works (or its effect) is displayed for your benefit. It even points to more assistance and information — through the "Tell me more" link at the bottom of the ScreenTip.

   - *Don't Show Feature Descriptions in ScreenTips:* If you want just the facts, ma'am, this is for you. ScreenTips will show just the button name with no further explanation.

   - *Don't Show ScreenTips:* Want to go it alone? Turn off ScreenTips.

6. **Click OK to close the Access Options dialog box.**

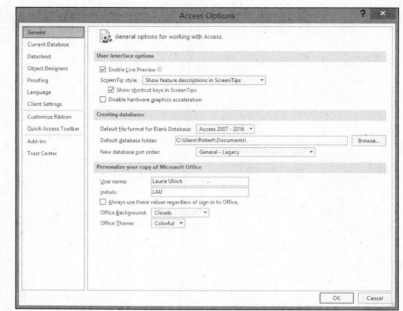

FIGURE 2-18:
The settings for just about everything you can see and use in Access are available through the Access Options dialog box.

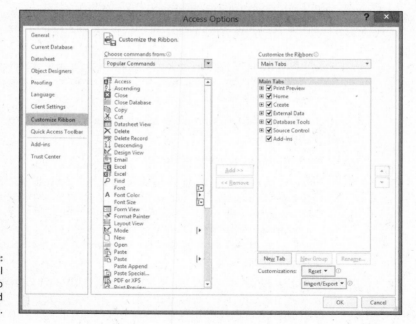

FIGURE 2-19:
View the helpful button and tab names and information.

TIP

Establishing the level of detail included in ScreenTips isn't the end of your options. You can also choose whether to include keyboard shortcuts in ScreenTips. This is on by default, and it's pretty useful.

Mousing Around

Access, like all Windows applications, is meant to be used with the mouse. The mouse is assumed to be your main way of communicating with the software — clicking Ribbon tabs, buttons, and drop-down lists, and making choices in dialog boxes to use things like the Report Wizard and the Access Options dialog box discussed in the previous sections of this chapter.

You can left-click to make standard choices from onscreen tools and right-click to access pop-up menus — also known as *context-sensitive* menus because the menu choices vary depending on what was right-clicked. If you right-click a Ribbon tab or button, you get choices for customizing its contents. If you right-click a database component tab (say, the Table tab while that table is open), you get choices related to the table.

TIP

Not a big fan of the mouse? Check out the online Cheat Sheet for this book, available at www.dummies.com/cheatsheet/access2019. It's full of powerful keyboard shortcuts.

Navigating Access with the Alt Key

If you like to use the keyboard as much as possible when you're working with software, Access makes it somewhat easy to do that. I say *somewhat* because you need to use a special key in order to make the rest of the keyboard work as a commander.

When you want to switch tabs and issue commands with the keyboard (rather than with the mouse), press the Alt key. As shown in Figure 2-20, pressing Alt causes numbers and letters to appear in small squares on the Quick Access Toolbar and the Ribbon's tabs. When the numbers and letters are visible, you can press one of those characters on your keyboard to issue a command (such as pressing 1 to Save) or to switch to a tab (such as pressing C to get to the Create tab).

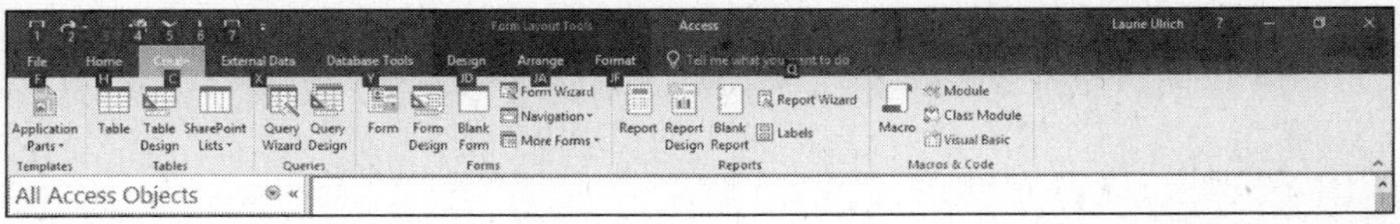

FIGURE 2-20:
Rather press a letter or number than click a tab or button with your mouse? The Alt key shows you how.

When you're on a tab (but only if you press its letter key to activate it), the individual buttons on that tab have their own keyboard shortcuts displayed. Instead of single numbers or letters, however, now you're looking at pressing key combinations, such as F+Z (displayed as FZ onscreen) to activate the Form Wizard. Figure 2-21 shows the keyboard shortcuts for the Create tab.

FIGURE 2-21:
Each button on a tab has its own keyboard shortcut.

REMEMBER

The goal is not to try to press the two keys at the exact same time. Instead, press the first one listed and then tap the second key. You are not holding the keys down at the same time!

» **Outstanding in your field(s)**

» **Deciding to go flat-file or relational with your database**

» **Getting a table started**

Chapter **3**

Database Basics

This may be the single most important chapter in this book. That might sound like a strong statement, but it's really true. When you want to figure out how to actually *do* something, it's essential to understand not just how it works, but *why* it works that way, and what's going on behind the scenes. So after you've read about why Access is the right tool for you (in Chapter 1) and how to get around in the Access interface (Chapter 2), it's time to really nail down how Access works and how to start building your database.

Database Lingo

Now, if the section heading ("Database Lingo") is making you panic because you think I want you to memorize a bunch of database jargon, don't worry. Just relax. Breathe normally. The next section, and many throughout this chapter, simply use some terms you need to know so you can figure out what Access is referring to in its various dialog boxes as well as on the various tabs it uses to give you access to commands in the Access workspace. Knowing these terms will, therefore, help you get around and get things done in Access.

Unfortunately, you simply must know technical terms — there are no two ways about it. I'm talking about only a handful of words, though — some of which you probably already know and maybe even use in reference to information in general — words like *record* and *database*. See? Nothing high tech, just some basic words and concepts you really need to absorb so you can move on and use Access effectively.

The terms in this section appear in size order, starting with the smallest piece of a database — the data — and advancing to the largest — the entire database itself. I've done it this way so you get the big picture, a little bit at a time, and see that the big picture is made up of smaller items. Seeing how they all fit together (and what to call each piece) is what this chapter's all about.

Data, no matter how you pronounce it

Data is the stuff that Access stores. Information you may store in your head one way will be stored in a different way in a database program like Access. For example, you may think of someone's name as *John Smith*, or you may only ever think of the guy as *John* — either because you don't know his last name or because you never use his last name. A database, however, stores his name as either *John Smith*, in a *field* called Name, or as two pieces — Last Name (Smith) and First Name (John). The latter approach is best because it gives you more freedom to use the data in more ways. You can sort the data by Last Name, for example, which is hard to do if you've just stored the entire name as one chunk.

Get the idea? As mentioned in Chapter 1 (where you plan out your database), it's a good idea to break down the data as much as possible. No matter how you pronounce it — "day-tah" or "dat-tuh" — it's your information, and you want to be able to get at it in the simplest, most logical way possible. As you read on in this chapter, and when you review Chapters 1 and 2, you'll see that Access gives you all the tools you need to do just that — it's just a matter of using the right tools at the right time!

Fields of dreams (or data)

Because people don't want their data to wander around homeless, the technical wizards created *fields* — places for your data to live. Each field holds one kind of data. For example, to track information about a baseball card collection, your fields might include Manufacturer, Player Name, Position, Year, Team, and Average (or ERA, for pitchers). If you have a name and address database, your fields might consist of Last Name, First Name, Middle Initial, Address1, Address2, City, State, Zip, Phone, Cell, and Email. When you think about it, it's pretty logical. What are all the things you can know about a baseball player? A client? A product? These *things* become *fields*.

As with the term *data*, other database programs (such as FoxPro and FileMaker) all agree on what a field is. In larger database packages, however (such as Oracle and Microsoft SQL Server), you find the term *column* replacing *field*. And to make things more exciting, Microsoft Excel stores your fields *in* columns when you use an Excel spreadsheet to store a list. The tabular structure of a database table is what leads Oracle and SQL to refer to columns rather than fields, but for heaven's sake — couldn't they have stuck to a term we all know?

Records

Having fields is a good start, but if you stop there, how do you know which last name works with which first name? Something needs to keep those unruly fields in order — something like a *record*. All the fields for one baseball card — or one client or one product — are collectively known as a *record*. If you have two baseball cards in your collection, you have two records in your database, one for each card. Fifty clients? Fifty records.

For a little more about records, check out the following:

>> Each record in a *table* contains the same fields but (usually) has different data in those fields. And not every record must have data in every field. If someone doesn't have a cell phone, you can't very well have any data in the Cell field for that person, right?

>> A single record contains all the information you need about a single item (accounting entry, recipe, or whatever) in your table. That's all there is to it.

Tables

A *table* is a collection of records that describes similar data. The key phrase to remember in that last sentence is *similar data.* All the records in a single table contain fields of similar data. The information about that baseball card collection may fit into a single table. So would the client or product data. However, a single table would *not* handle both baseball cards *and* clients because they're unrelated databases. You wouldn't put the records for your car's repairs in the folder where you keep your Christmas cookie recipes, right?

Why? Because if anyone else needs to know when you last had the tires rotated, they aren't going to know to look in the same place one finds the best recipe for Ginger Snaps. *You* might remember that they're stored in the same place, but it's just too confusing for anyone else. And too limiting. Access lets you write reports and queries based on your data, and if the data in your database isn't all related, it'll be chaos trying to write a report or generate a query that pulls data from that database. You could end up with a recipe that calls for motor oil or a maintenance schedule that tells you to preheat the car to 350 degrees. Such a report might be amusing, but it's hardly useful.

The database

An Access *database,* or *database file* (the terms are interchangeable), is a collection of everything relating to a particular set of information. The database contains all the tables, queries, reports, and forms that Access helps you create to manage and work with your stuff. Instead of storing all those items *individually* on the disk drive — where they can become lost, misplaced, or accidentally erased — Access groups them into a single collective file.

Here's an important point: All those parts — the tables, the reports, queries, and forms — cumulatively make a database. And that's before you even enter any records into the tables. The database, therefore, is more than the data; it's the tools that store, manipulate, and allow you to look at the data, too.

Field Types and Uses

A field, you remember, is where your data lives. Each field holds one piece of data, such as Last Name or Batting Average.

Because there are so many different kinds of information in the world, Access offers a variety of field types for storing it. In fact, Access puts the following field types at your disposal:

>> Short Text

>> Long Text

>> Number

>> Currency

>> AutoNumber (this data type is applied, by default, to the starting ID field in any new table)

>> Date/Time

>> Yes/No

>> Lookup & Relationship

>> Rich Text

>> Attachment

>> Hyperlink

>> OLE Object

>> Calculated

>> Lookup Wizard

The types just listed are those available for fields you create in addition to that first field — the ones that will contain your data.

For now, suffice it to say that the aforementioned AutoNumber field is a field that contains an automatically generated number so that each record is unique in that it has a unique AutoNumber, or *ID*. You get the word about the need for (and ways to create) unique fields later on, in Chapter 4.

As for the Lookup Wizard, we also get to that one much later in the book, in terms of its actual use. But you'll find out more about when and how this data type is used later on in this very chapter!

TIP

For now, don't worry about figuring out what each field type is or what it does based on its name — I go over each one shortly. As you can see, though, the list covers just about any type of data you can imagine. And remember, each one can be customized extensively, resulting in fields that meet your needs exactly. If you absolutely cannot wait to find out about modifying all the specs for your fields, Chapter 4 should be your next stop.

The upcoming bulleted list introduces the available field types and how they're used. You'll also find out a little bit about how you can tweak them to meet your specific needs:

>> **Short Text:** Stores up to 255 characters of text — letters, numbers, punctuation, and any combination thereof.

>> **Long Text:** This replaces the Memo field type found in versions 2010 and previous. A Long Text field holds up to 64,000 characters of information — that's almost 18 pages of text. This is a *really big* text field. It's great for general notes, detailed descriptions, and anything else that requires a lot of space.

REMEMBER

Numbers in a text field aren't numbers to calculate with; they're just a bunch of digits hanging out together in a field. Be careful of this fact when you design the tables in your database — you don't want to enter, say, a value that you intend to use in a Calculated field or to extract some other kind of information from a report and have that value stored as text, rendering it inoperable as a number. If the data is numeric, store it that way.

Text fields have one setting you need to know about: size. When you create a text field, Access wants to know how many characters the field holds. That's the field *size*. If you create a field called First Name and make its size 6, *Joseph* fits into the field, but not *Jennifer*. This restriction can be a problem. A good general rule is to make the field a little larger than you think you need. It's easy to make the field even larger at some later point if you need to, but it's potentially dangerous to make it smaller. Surgery on fields is covered in Chapter 4.

>> **Number:** Holds real, for-sure numbers. You can add, subtract, and calculate your way to fame and fortune with number fields. But if you're working with dollars and cents (or pounds and pence), use a Currency field instead.

>> **Currency:** Tracks money, prices, invoice amounts, and so on. In an Access database, the buck stops here. For that matter, so do the lira, the mark, and the yen. If you're in the mood for some *other* kind of number, check out the Number field.

>> **Date/Time:** Stores time, date, or a combination of the two, depending on which format you use. Use a Date/Time field to track the whens of life. Pretty versatile, eh?

>> **Yes/No:** Holds Yes/No, True/False, and On/Off, depending on the format you choose. When you need a simple yes or no, this is the field to use.

>> **Lookup & Relationship:** If you want a field within one table to actually display content from a field in another table, choose this as the field type. A simple Lookup Wizard opens as soon as this field type is chosen, through which you select the table and field to look up through this new field in your table.

>> **Rich Text:** Need the content of a particular field to be formatted just so? Choose this field type, and the formatting applied to the data in the field (using the Text Formatting tools on the Home tab) will be how it appears onscreen and in reports.

>> **OLE Object:** You can use the OLE Object data type to link or embed an object — such as an Excel worksheet or Word document — to an Access table.

>> **Attachment:** Use this field type to attach files — Word documents, Excel worksheets, PowerPoint presentations, or any other kind of file, including graphics (a photo of the volunteer, product, or location, perhaps?) — to the record.

>> **Hyperlink:** Thanks to this field type, Access understands and stores the special link language that makes the Internet such a powerful place. If you use Access on your company's network or use the Internet extensively, this field type is for you. You'll find out more about hyperlinks and other neat ways Access and the Internet play well together in Chapter 11.

>> **Calculated:** Use this field type when you want to fill the field in question with the result of a formula that uses one or more other fields in the same table. For example, in a table that contains a list of your products, other fields might include Price and Discount. If you want to also have a field that calculates the new price (the Price, less the Discount), you'd make that a Calculated field. When you choose this as the field type, you use a submenu to choose what kind of data will house the result, and then an Expression Builder dialog box appears, through which you set up the formula.

To help you start thinking about your database and your data and to begin imagining the fields you could use for some common types of data, Table 3-1 presents a breakdown of field types and ways you might use them.

TABLE 3-1   **Common Fields for Everyday Tables**

Name	Type	Size	Contents
Title	Short Text	4	Mr., Ms., Mrs., Mme., Sir, and so on.
First Name	Short Text	15	Person's first name.
Middle Initial	Short Text	4	Person's middle initial; allows for two initials and punctuation.
Last Name	Short Text	20	Person's last name.
Suffix	Short Text	10	Jr., Sr., II, Ph.D., and so on.
Job	Short Text	25	Job title or position.
Company	Short Text	25	Company name.
Address 1, Address 2	Short Text	30	Include two fields for the address because some corporate locations are pretty complicated these days.
City	Short Text	20	City name.
State, Province	Short Text	4	State or province; apply the name appropriately for the data you're storing.
Zip Code, Postal Code	Short Text	10	Zip or postal code; note that it's stored as text characters, not as a number.
Country	Short Text	15	Not needed if you work within a single country.
Office Phone	Short Text	12	Voice telephone number; increase the size to 17 for an extension.
Fax Number	Short Text	12	Fax number.
Home Phone	Short Text	12	Home telephone number.
Cellular Phone	Short Text	12	Cell phone (or "mobile phone" for you cosmopolitans).
Email Address	Short Text	30	Internet email address. If the person whose record you're building has multiple email addresses, make this one Email1, and number the alternatives — Email2, Email3, and so on.
Website	Hyperlink		Web page address; Access automatically sets the field size.
SSN	Short Text	11	U.S. Social Security number, including dashes.
Comments	Long Text		A freeform space for notes; Access automatically chooses a field size.

All the field types listed as samples in Table 3-1 are really *text* fields, even the ones for phone numbers. This is because Access sees their content as text rather than as a number that could be used in a calculation. (Check out Table 3-2 for field-naming no-nos.)

Of course, another field type (listed in the Type column) is neither a Short Text nor Long Text field — you also see the Hyperlink field. This data type is also considered text, but the Hyperlink data type stores URLs, as URLs — not just as a string of text and punctuation.

If all this text versus numbers stuff is confusing you, remember that computers think there's a difference between a *number* (that you'd use in a calculation) and a *string of digits,* such as the digits that make up a phone number. When it comes to different kinds of text fields, it's a matter of how much text will be stored in the field, and if it needs any special formatting in order to work properly in the database.

FUN WITH FIELD NAMES

Of all the Windows database programs out there, I think Access has the simplest field-naming rules. Just remember these guidelines to make your field names perfect every time:

- **It's a good idea to start with a letter or a number.** Although Access won't stop you from using certain characters at the beginning of or within your field name, it's not a good idea. It can make things confusing for other people who might use your database, and symbols are hard to read if the type is very small. They also have only limited logical use in identifying the content of the field — what would "^Address" tell you that "Address" wouldn't? Of course, after the first character, you might find logical uses for symbols such as plus signs and underscores. You can include spaces in field names, too. Oh — and which symbols are no-nos? See Table 3-2.

- **Make the field name short and easy to understand.** You have up to 64 characters for a field name, but don't even think about using all that space. On the other hand, don't get stingy and create names like N1 or AZ773 unless they mean something particular to your company or organization.

- **Use letters, numbers, and an occasional space in your field names.** Although Access lets you include all kinds of crazy punctuation marks in field names, don't do it. Keep it simple so that the solution you develop with Access doesn't turn into a problem on its own.

TABLE 3-2

Prohibited Symbols

Symbol	Name
/	Forward slash
?	Question mark
*	Asterisk
-	Dash
;	Semicolon
"	Double quotes
:	Colon
'	Single quote
!	Exclamation point
$	Dollar sign
#	Pound sign
%	Percent
&	Ampersand

Choosing Between Flat and Relational Databases

Unlike ice cream, databases come in just two flavors: flat-file and relational. Also unlike ice cream, it's not really a matter of preference as to which one you choose. Some databases require a relational approach; others would be overwhelmed by it. Read on to figure out how to tell the difference.

Isolationist tables

In a *flat* system (also known as a *flat-file system*), all the data is lumped into a single table. A phone directory is a good example of a flat-file database: Names, addresses, and phone numbers (the data) are crammed into a single place (the database). Some duplication occurs — if one person has three phone lines at home, his or her name and address are listed three times in the directory — but that's not a big problem. Overall, the database works just fine.

Tables that mix and mingle

The *relational* system (or *relational database*) uses as little storage space as possible by cutting down on the duplicated (also known as *redundant*) data in the database. To accomplish this, a relational database splits your data into several tables, with each table holding some portion of the total data.

Borrowing the preceding phone book example, note that one table in a relational database can contain the customer name and address information, whereas another can hold the phone numbers. Thanks to this approach, the mythical person with three phone lines has only one entry in the "customer" table (after all, it's still just one customer) but has three distinct entries in the "phone number" table (one for each phone line).

The key to relational databases

The *key field* (or *linking field*) is the key to this advanced technology. All related tables in a relational database system contain this special field. The key field's data identifies matching records from different tables.

The key field works just like the claim stub you receive when you drop off your dry cleaning. To pick up your dry cleaning when it's finished, you present the claim check, complete with its little claim number. That number identifies (or *links*) you and your cleaning so the clerk can find it.

Likewise, in the phone book example, each customer can have a unique customer ID. The "phone number" table stores the customer ID with each phone number. To find out who owns a phone number, you look up the customer ID in the "customer name" table. Granted, it takes more steps to find someone's phone number than it does in the plain flat-file system, but the relational system saves storage space (no more duplicate names) and reduces the chance of errors at the same time.

If this process seems complicated, don't feel bad. Relational databases *are* complicated! But that's mostly behind the scenes, where Access is doing the stuff it does when you make a selection in a tab or ask it to run a wizard for you. A good deal of the complexity is invisible to you; all you see is the power it gives you. When you're ready to find out more about all that behind-the-scenes stuff, check out Chapter 4.

But do your tables need to relate?

Now you at least have an idea of the difference between flat-file and relational databases. But do you care? Yes, you do. Each approach has its unique pluses and minuses for your database:

>> **Flat-file systems are easy to build and maintain.** A Microsoft Excel spreadsheet is a good example of a flat-file database. A list of records is stored, one record per row, and you have as many records as can fit on the worksheet. Simple, easy, and in many cases, the way to go — if your database is simple and easy, too.

>> **Relational systems shine in big business applications such as invoicing, accounting, or inventory.** They're also a big help if you have a small business — your customer data, for example, could require several tables to store customer names and addresses, purchase history, and credit information. Storing everything you need to store about customers could be too big a job for a single, flat-file database.

WARNING

I don't recommend that you set off to build a relational database system all by yourself after reading just some (or even all) of this book. It's a big job; you'll likely just end up discouraged if you dive in too quickly. If you're sure that you need a relational database, enlist some help in the form of a friend or colleague who's had some experience building databases. He or she can walk you through it the first time, and then, with this book (and Access help files) at your side, you can try it on your own later.

TIP

Although Access is a relational database program, it does flat-file systems quite nicely because even though it lets you set up several tables and set up relationships between them, it's also quite happy to set up a single flat-file table if you want one. Whether you choose flat-file or relational for your database project, Access is the right program.

Building a Database

So you've read a few chapters here at the beginning of the book, maybe you've leafed ahead where I've referred to other chapters, and now you feel ready. You want to dive in and start building a database. Keeping in mind my previous advice to take it slowly, you can take a whack at it here.

In the following procedure, you set up a new database and then use the Table Wizard to build the first table in the database. Ready? Here we go . . .

1. **If Access is not already running, take a moment to start it.**

Chapter 1 shows you how to do this.

In the Access workspace, a series of large template icons appears, below a Search for Online Templates box, accompanied by links to likely searches for templates that store Assets, Events, Tasks, Contacts, Students, Inventory, and so on.

2. **Click the Blank Desktop Database icon.**

   A Blank Desktop Database dialog box appears, as shown in Figure 3-1.

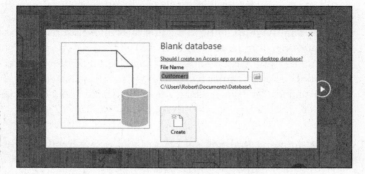

FIGURE 3-1:
New blank
databases need
names. Give
yours one here.

3. **Type a name to replace the generic Database*X* (where *X* is the number assigned chronologically to the database).**

   You don't need to type a file extension (.accdb); Windows 8/8.1 displays your extensions automatically, and Windows 10 hides it by default. If you have your Windows 10 extensions showing or you're using Windows 8/8.1 and you accidentally delete the file extension while changing the filename, don't worry — Access adds it to the filename you type.

4. **If you don't like the folder that Access picked out for you, click the little folder icon and choose where to store the new database.**

   As shown in Figure 3-2, when you click that little folder icon, the File New Database dialog box opens. From here, you can navigate to anywhere on your local system or on a network to which you're connected and select the drive and folder on which to store your new database. When you've finished selecting a spot for your new database, click OK to return to the workspace.

5. **Click the Create button.**

   A blank table, called Table1, appears in the central section of the workspace, and on the left, a panel lists the parts of your database (there's just one part so far). Figure 3-3 shows your new table and the left-hand panel.

WARNING

   When you click Create, if a dialog box pops up and asks whether you want to replace an existing file, Access is saying that a database with the name you entered is already on the disk.

   - If this is news to you, click No and then come up with a different name for your new database.

   - If you *intended* to replace that old database with a new one, click Yes and proceed.

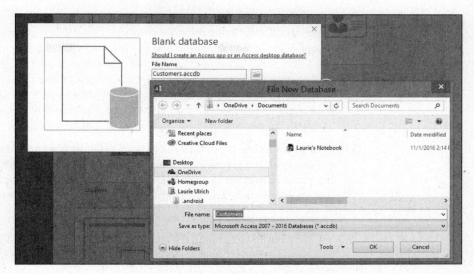

FIGURE 3-2:
Select a home
for your new
database.

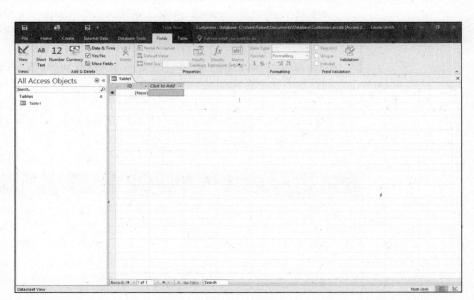

FIGURE 3-3:
New table,
new database.

6. **Create and name your fields in the table by clicking where it says Click to Add at the top of the second column in the table.**

7. **Click the arrow to the right of the words Click to Add and choose the type of field you want to add.**

   The many choices are discussed earlier in this chapter. For most fields, Short Text will be the type — and that's why it's the default data type for new fields — but your data and its nature (and your desired uses for it) will dictate what's best to choose here.

TIP

What's that ID field in the first column? It's there by default and will contain a unique number for each record you create (when you start entering records, later). This provides the unique field that each table requires, especially if you're going to relate your tables. You can change its name by double-clicking the name "ID" and adding the table name — to differentiate this ID field from the ID fields in your future tables in this same database. This would mean adding Customer before ID, for "CustomerID" with no spaces.

8. **Click to select the generic Field*X* (where *X* is a number added to differentiate between the placeholder Field name applied to new fields until you manually name them). Type a new field name (to replace the highlighted placeholder name), and press Enter to save the new field name.**

As soon as you press Enter, a new field appears in the next column, with a blank at the top, awaiting a name.

Repeat Steps 7 and 8 until you have all the fields you think you'll need in this table. You can always rename them later (by double-clicking the current names), so don't worry about perfection at this point. Just start setting up fields so you can start entering data. Figure 3-4 shows a new field name in place and a new one awaiting the Enter key to confirm it.

9. **To save your new table and the entire database, press Ctrl+S or click the Save button on the Quick Access Toolbar.**

It's a good idea to save each time you've done something important — building a table, updating some fields, adding records, and so on — essentially after anything you'd hate to have to do over again.

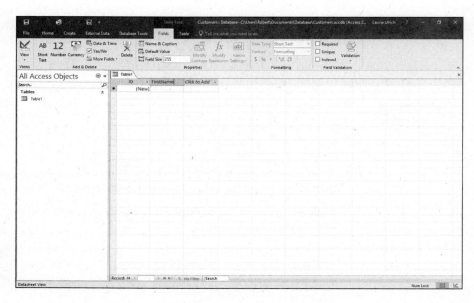

FIGURE 3-4:
Create new fields by pressing Enter after naming each one.

TIP

Rarely is "Table1" a really useful name for a table. Before or after saving your database, renaming a table is easy. Just follow these steps:

1. **Right-click the Table tab.**

2. **Choose Save from the pop-up menu that appears.**

3. **Type a name for the table in the resulting Save As dialog box.**

4. **Click OK to keep the name.**

5. **Resave your database to include this change.**

Adding and Removing Tables

Nobody's expecting perfection at this stage of the game. Certainly not in your first foray into database creation, and not even on your second or third attempt. Even seasoned experts forget things now and then, realizing after they've built a table that they didn't need it, or after they've started setting up reports and queries that they've forgotten a table that they needed. It can happen to anyone.

What to do? Use Access's simple interface to add the tables you want and delete the tables you don't.

One more, please

If, after you start building your database, you decide that your database warrants more than one table — in other words, if you realize you need a *relational* database — then you need to add another table. If you already knew that your database was going to need multiple tables, then — after building the first one — the only thing to do is build the rest, one by one.

To add new tables to an existing database, repeat the following steps for each new table:

1. **Click the Create tab on the Ribbon.**

   The Create tab's buttons appear, as shown in Figure 3-5.

2. **Click the Table button on the Ribbon.**

   A new table, blank and awaiting the name for the first field, appears, as shown in Figure 3-6.

FIGURE 3-5:
The Create tab is
the logical place
to go when you
want to create a
new table.

FIGURE 3-6:
Looks familiar,
doesn't it? A new
table awaits fields
and field names,
not to mention
records.

3. **Build and name the fields for this new table as shown in the previous procedure.**

TIP

Save your database periodically as you work.

4. **Continue adding tables, using Steps 1 through 3 for as many tables as you need in the database.**

REMEMBER

You don't have to do this perfectly from the start — you can always go back to rename fields and add or remove tables (more on how to do that in a second). The goal here is to just *do it* — just get started and get the database going so you can see what you have and start working with it.

TIP

Naming tables is important — because you're going to need to know, at a glance at that left-hand panel, what's in Table1 or Table2 or Table3, right? Better to name them Customers, Orders, Products, and so on, so you don't have to remember each one by a generic number. To name a table, you can do so when you first close it and are prompted to save it. As shown in Figure 3-7, the Save As dialog box gives you a Table Name box. Type the name and press Enter. If you decide you don't like the name later on, simply right-click the name it currently has, as displayed in the left-hand panel, and the current name is highlighted. Type the new name, and press Enter to confirm it. You can also choose Rename from the menu that appears if you right-click the table's name in the left-hand panel that lists your database components. This also gives you the opportunity to type a replacement name.

FIGURE 3-7:
When you close
the table, you will
be prompted to
save the table.

Oops, I didn't mean to do that

So you have a table you didn't want. Maybe you realize after building Table C that you really only need Tables A and B — or that Table D, which you've also created, really makes Table C unnecessary. Whatever the reason, tables, even ones with records in them, are easy to get rid of.

WARNING

Let me state that again: Tables are easy to get rid of. Perhaps too easy. Before you delete a table, check and recheck your database to make sure you aren't deleting information that you need to keep. When a table is deleted, *all connections to it* — including all relationships and references in queries and reports — are deleted, too. A prompt appears when you choose to delete a table, reminding you of this.

Still committed to ditching the table? Here's how it's done:

1. **With your database open, look at the panel on the left side of the workspace.**

You should see a list of your tables in that panel, as shown in Figure 3-8.

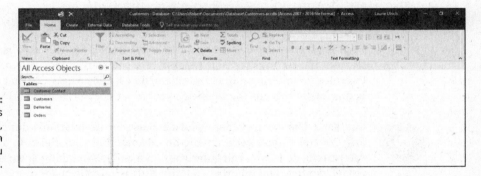

FIGURE 3-8:
Each table has its own button, emblazoned with the name you gave the table.

2. **Right-click the table name in the panel on the left side of the workspace, and choose Delete from the pop-up menu, as shown in Figure 3-9.**

3. **Click Yes in response to the resulting prompt if, in fact, you do want to delete the table.**

All gone!

Now, you probably think it's time to start entering records, but no, I don't advise doing that yet. Before you start populating your tables with data, it's a better idea to set up your table relationships, establish the key fields that will connect your relational tables, and define the specs for each of your fields — taking advantage of those field options I mention earlier in this chapter.

FIGURE 3-9:
Choose Delete
to get rid of the
unwanted table.

Even if your database will be a (relatively simple) flat-file database, you need to iron out the settings for your fields before you start entering data — establishing the rules for entering names, numbers, dates, and so on — so that what you enter is graciously accepted by the fields you've set up.

Chapter 4 helps you prepare your database for its relational duties. In Chapter 5 and Chapter 6, you get a handle on customizing your fields to suit your needs. After that's done, you can enter your data and begin taking advantage of Access's forms, queries, and reports — all the stuff covered in the *rest* of the book!

TIP

2

Getting It All on the Table

Contents at a Glance

Chapter **4**

Sounds Like a Plan

A s a professional Access database developer, I've seen a lot of things over the years. And one of the most common is poor table design. Planning a database is like building a house; if you don't get the foundation right, you'll start to see cracks or worse! Same thing with an Access database. Access tables are like the foundation of your house. Design them right and all will go well. Design them wrong, and you'll start to see those cracks as you get further into the project.

REMEMBER

Back in Chapter 1, we discussed planning out your database. In this chapter, we'll dig deeper into how to turn that plan into the best possible table design.

Planning Your Database Tables

As you know, tables are made up of fields — the bits of information you want to store in your database. Hopefully, you put your list of fields together back in Chapter 1 and you broke them into logical groups. You did do that, didn't you? You see, I keep harping on it because table design is the most important part to building a database but, oftentimes, not given the attention it deserves. So, time to do the work, or if you already did, pull your field list out so we can get started!

Reviewing fields

Take a look at your field list and think about how you'll use that data. For example, you might have Volunteer Name as one of your fields. Now, should that be one field or two? Well, if you'll always refer to your volunteers by full name, like Ken Cook, then one field is fine. However, that seems unlikely. Suppose your database produces emails to volunteers. It's unlikely you'll want the email to begin with "Hi Ken Cook". It would say "Hi Ken". So, now you know that you need two fields, one for first and one for last name.

Address is another example. Do you want to group your volunteers by city on a report? If the answer is yes, you can't lump the entire address in one field. You'll need fields for street, city, state, and zip code. This gives you the most flexibility.

Take a good look at your field list and make sure you have each piece of information at the most granular level. You'll thank yourself for taking time now to think this through. Once you have your volunteer field on two forms and five reports and it's time to build that email functionality, if you have two fields (first name and last name), you'll smile! If you have one field, you'll frown because you have to split the name into two fields and change all the forms and reports that use that field to incorporate the two fields.

Determining data types

After you have a good field list, it's time to think about the type of data each field will store. Will it store a date, a number, text, or perhaps just the choices of true or false? Setting data types correctly affects overall database size and performance. Next to each field, write down the type of data the field will store and the maximum size of that data.

Text data

Suppose a state field stores the two-letter state abbreviation for a volunteer's state of residence. Access has a Long Text and Short Text data type. Long Text stores up to 64,000 characters. Short Text stores up to 255 characters, and you can specify the exact number of characters using the Field Size property. I'm sure you've figured out which data type to choose but might want to know the reasons why.

If you choose Long Text for your state field, you'll be reserving the capacity to store 64,000 characters in that field even though you'll never store more than two. What a waste! This inflates the size of your database and over time degrades its performance. The larger the amount of data in a database, the slower it may perform over time. So, choose Short Text with a Field Size of 2 and you'll be all set!

Now, the flipside of that is being too conservative. Back to your volunteer first and last name. If you specify 10 characters and a Short Text data type for the `LastName` field, you're fine unless the volunteer has a last name that's 11 characters long. Now, you've got a problem. Access won't allow you to type an 11-character name in that field. You'll have to edit the Field Size property for that field and increase the number to accommodate the longest possible name. So, choose wisely when setting data types.

Number data

The rules that apply to text apply to numbers, too. Pick the number field size that fits closest to the size of the number you'll store in the field without going under. Table 4-1 shows the number field sizes and the maximum number and number of decimal places that the data type can hold.

TABLE 4-1 **Number Field Sizes**

Field Size	Numbers It Can Store	Significant Digits
Byte	0-255	3
Integer	−32,768 to 32,767	5
Long Integer	−2,147,483,648–2,147,483,647	10
Single	−3.4 x 1038 to +3.4 x 1038	7
Double	−1.797 x 10308 to +1.797 x 10308	15
Decimal	−9.999. . . x 1027 to +9.999. . . x 1027	29

TECHNICAL STUFF

A significant digit is a non-zero number either to the left or right of the decimal place. So, 0.123 has three significant digits, 22.00013 has four significant digits, and 42 has two significant digits. A Single field size will accept 0.1234567 but not 12.1234567 because the first number has seven significant digits and the second nine. The second number will appear in a field sized as single as 12.12346 (the 5 is rounded to a 6 and the 6 and 7 are dropped).

If the number is not a number that you'll perform calculations with, use one of the text data types. A zip code is the classic example. Many zip codes begin with a zero. If you choose a number data type for your zip code field and type 08888 in your zip code field, you'll get a nice surprise. Access removes the leading zero when you tab out of the field and 08888 becomes 8888. Thank you Access! Easy to fix. Just choose Small Text with a Field Size of 9 and you're leading zero will stick around like it should.

TIP

Assigning data type and size is not an exact science. If you're not sure what to choose, bigger is better than smaller. Choose a type and size that will accommodate what you think is the largest possible entry for that field. If you choose 50 as the Field Size for your LastName field and the longest last name is only 40 characters, no big deal. But if you choose 10 and the longest last name is 40 characters, then you've got to go back and edit the field properties in the table, which, depending on where you are with the project, can be a big deal.

The new normal

I've seen lots of databases over the years from teaching Access and finishing or updating Access databases started by someone else. The most common flaw I see in databases from the new Access developer is a spreadsheet-like table. Yes, that right. One table with everything in it. This is why many people move to Access — to get away from updating the same data in three different places in their spreadsheet. A one-table database doesn't harness the power of a relational database such as Access. What to do? Get normal.

Understanding normal forms

The process of building tables so you don't repeat data or repeat fields is called *normalization*. There are five guidelines, called *forms*, you should follow to arrange your data into tables that don't repeat information. The first two are the most important for the new database developer. The last three are for the database nerd. Because you're reading this book, I'll assume you aren't a nerd and focus on just the first two forms.

>> **No duplicate columns:** It's easy to understand that a table shouldn't contain two fields with slightly different names like Zip and ZipCode that hold the same information. That is a no-no. However, suppose you have a City, State, and Zip field and a field called CityStateZip because you use those three together all the time on reports. Might seem okay but it's not efficient. If one of your volunteers moves to a new city, you not only have to update the City, State, and Zip fields, but also CityStateZip. This is duplicate data entry and would be a violation of the first normal form. So, the CityStateZip field is out!

>> **Put duplicate data in a child table:** The second normal form follows all guidelines for the first normal form and instructs you to put duplicate information in a new child table. Suppose you collect up to three phone numbers for your volunteers (work, home, and cell) and you have three fields in your Volunteers table, Phone1, Phone2, and Phone3. This may seem okay, but how will you know which phone is which? Do you add a PhoneType1,

PhoneType2, and PhoneType3? The answer is no, and for two good reasons: What if a year from now you decide to keep an emergency contact number for each volunteer? Where would you put it? Add yet another phone field? Also, how would you query all the phone numbers in the 303 area code? Query three fields? What happens to that query when you add a fourth phone number field? It must be rewritten. Sorry, Q&A time is over. The phone data to follow the second normal form must go in a new table, a child of the Volunteers table called perhaps VolunteerPhone. In it, you'd have fields like PhoneID, PhoneType, and PhoneNumber. It will be easier to add more phone numbers for the same volunteer and find phone numbers by querying a single field rather than multiple phone number fields.

TECHNICAL STUFF

Want to become a database nerd? Just search the internet for *database normalization forms* and you'll find lots of gripping articles and white papers on the third through fifth normal forms.

Normalizing your tables

At this point, you've done some great work specifying each field and the data type and size for each field. You've also learned about the first two normal forms and the importance of table normalization. Now it's time to organize your fields into tables. This may seem easy. Just one table for everything, right? If you said yes, you clearly didn't read the previous section and should read it! If you answered a resounding no, then here are some plain-English guiding principles to follow when grouping fields into tables.

>> **Make sure the data is related.** The data should share a common theme like volunteer contact information, events, or locations.

>> **Make sure the data does not repeat.** If you find yourself entering the same volunteer into the Volunteers table two times because they have two addresses, you need a new table.

>> **Make sure related choices do not become field names.** If you have three volunteer fields in your events table called Volunteer1, Volunteer2, and Volunteer3, then you've got a problem. Querying data like this is difficult. If you need to specify multiple volunteers for the same event, then you need a new table.

Take your list of fields and group them by subject. Then check for duplicates per points two and three in the previous list. When you're done, you might have something like Figure 4-1.

	A	B	C	D	E	F	G	H	I
1	**Table**	**Field**	**Data Type**	**Size**		**Table**	**Field**	**Data Type**	**Size**
2	Volunteers					Events			
3		FirstName	Short Text	50			EventName	Short Text	50
4		LastName	Short Text	50			LastName	Short Text	50
5		Email	Short Text	50			EventDate	Date/Time	
6		CellPhone	Short Text	15			EventType	Short Text	25
7		Street	Short Text	50			LocationName	Short Text	75
8		City	Short Text	50					
9		State	Short Text	2					
10		Zip	Short Text	10					
11		FullName	Short Text	100					
12	Locations					EventVolunteers			
13		LocationName	Short Text	75			EventName	Short Text	50
14		Street	Short Text	50			Volunteer	Short Text	100
15		City	Short Text	50					
16		State	Short Text	2					
17		Zip	Short Text	10					
18		LocationType	Short Text	25					
19		Cost	Currency						
20									
21									
22									
23									

Sheet1 | Sheet2 | Sheet3 | ⊕

FIGURE 4-1: Tables, fields, data types, and sizes.

Figure 4-2 shows a table that is not normalized. Can you figure out why?

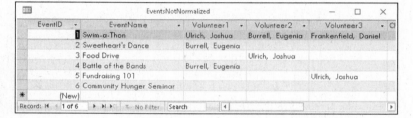

FIGURE 4-2: The sadly abnormal Events table.

Didn't figure it out? Okay, I'll give you a hint. Suppose the Swim-a-thon requires a fourth volunteer? What would you do? Add a new field? That would fix the problem for now, but what happens if a fifth volunteer is needed? You can't keep adding fields. The answer is to remove the volunteer series of fields and create a new table called EventVolunteers. This new table allows you to add as many volunteers as you need to each event.

If you know you could have two addresses per volunteer or ten volunteers per event, then you need a new table for addresses and another for event volunteers. This step is crucial to proper table design.

TIP

If the figures in this section make no sense, not to worry. Queries are covered in Part 4. I need to show you this so you understand how good table design saves time and effort!

Why? Because it becomes very difficult to get a list of events that Burrell volunteered for if you have ten volunteer fields. Figure 4-3 shows the query in Design view with the abnormal events table.

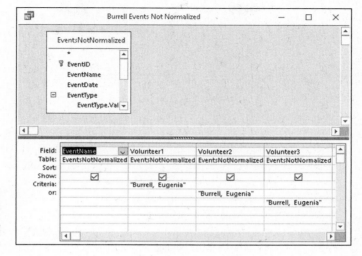

FIGURE 4-3:
Getting Burrell's events with *abnormal* table design.

Just imagine if there were ten volunteer fields! You'd have to type Burrell's name ten times on ten different rows (see Figure 4-4). Also, notice how Burrell's name shows in multiple columns along with names of other volunteers that you're not interested in at the moment. If you had ten volunteer fields, you'd see a lot of names of other volunteers.

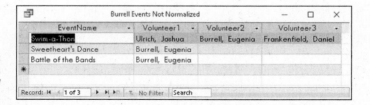

FIGURE 4-4:
Burrell's events with *abnormal* table design.

Now look at the same query with normalized tables, as shown in Figures 4-5 and 4-6.

If you compare Figure 4-4 to 4-6, you'll see that Figure 4-6 returns the results you want without the extra names you don't want. If you compare Figures 4-3 and 4-5, I think you'll agree that Figure 4-5 is the easier query to write. Both queries return the same number of events, but the second one is easier to build and has cleaner results! This is why it's so important that the table design is right the first time around. I can tell you from personal experience, getting design right the first time will save you a lot of aggravation!

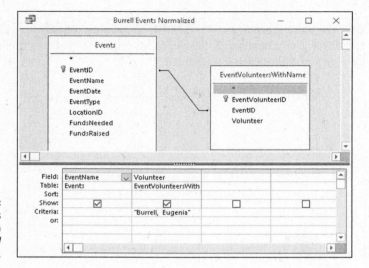

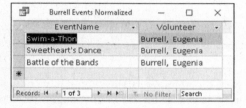

Building Tables in Design View

Now that you've organized, you can build your tables. Here's how to start:

1. **Click the Create tab on the Ribbon.**

2. **Click the Table Design button in the Tables group.**

A new table appears in Design view ready for your new fields (see Figure 4-7). The Property Sheet and Field Properties appear as well. If you don't see the Property Sheet, press F4 to open it.

Creating fields

You can't save a table unless it has at least one field. Because you've done the legwork of organizing your data into fields and tables up front (if you didn't do this, see the section "Planning Your Database Tables" earlier in this chapter), this part should be easy. These steps assume you have a table open in Design view.

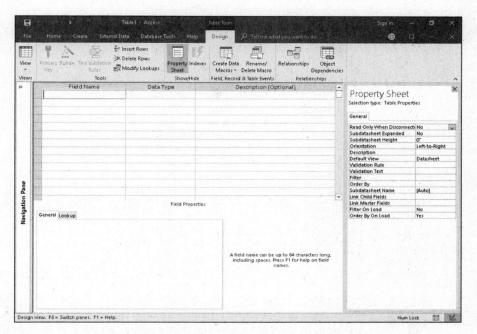

FIGURE 4-7:
The birth of a
new table.

1. **Click in the first blank row in the Field Name column.**

2. **Type your field name.**

   A field name can be a maximum of 64 characters.

TIP

Keep your field names short and descriptive of what they'll store. You'll
sometimes need to type field names out when referring to them in queries or
on forms and reports. Long field names mean more typing! Avoid using spaces
in field names. Field names with spaces must be surrounded by square
brackets ([]) that you'll have to type. If your field name does not have a space
and you need to type it out, Access will enter the square brackets for you. That
Access is one awesome helper, don't you think?

3. **In each subsequent blank row, type each field name that belongs with
   your new table.**

   This is shown in Figure 4-8.

4. **Choose File ➪ Save (or press Ctrl+S) to save your new table.**

   Care to guess the maximum size of a table name? If you said 64, you're a
   winner!

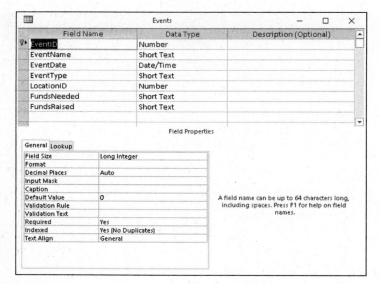

FIGURE 4-8:
Fields entered
in Table
Design view.

TIP

Keep table names short and avoid using spaces in them for the same reasons I mention in the field name tip. Avoid special characters in field and table names; many of them aren't allowed. Stick to letters, numbers, and underscores (_) and you won't have any problems. Use underscores rather than spaces if you need to differentiate words in your names. Don't like underscores? Capitalize the first letter of each word in your table name to differentiate the words.

Setting data types

After you have your field names entered, tell Access what data they will hold by choosing a data type. If you don't know what a data type is or what to choose, see the sections "Field Types and Uses" in Chapter 3 and "Determining data types" earlier in this chapter. Here are the data type steps:

1. **Click in the Data Type column next to the new field, as shown in Figure 4-9.**

A drop-down list appears with data type choices.

2. **Select a data type from the list.**

3. **Enter a field size on the Field Size property row in the Field Properties section of Table design view.**

Not every data type needs a field size, but most do.

4. **Repeat Steps 2 and 3 for each field in the table.**

5. **Save the table.**

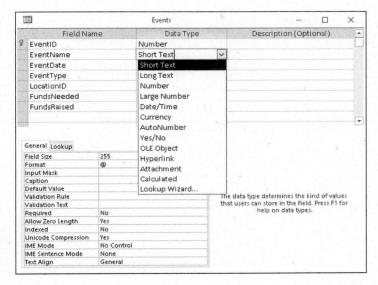

FIGURE 4-9:
Choosing a
data type and
field size.

Take your time to build tables. Get it right the first time and you'll save yourself a lot of aggravation down the road.

Chapter **5**

Table Tune Ups

Life in today's world is all about doing things faster and more efficiently to increase productivity. Isn't that what your life is about? Oh, you have a life outside the office, too? (What a concept.) Maybe you have a relationship? This chapter is about making your databases faster and about building good relationships (the database kind, not the human kind!).

As with any good relationship, the end result is often harmony and happiness. Making your Access tables work well together will make things so much easier in so many ways as you move on to build your queries, forms, and reports. The good news is that building relationships in Access takes a lot less time than building human relationships.

How can you make Access work faster and more efficiently? With key fields and indexes, that's how! Each table should have that one special field assigned as a *primary key*. A primary key prevents duplicate records from being entered into a table — hence more efficient data entry. (I love the word *hence!*) To retrieve your data faster, you need to create the proper balance of indexes for each table. Not enough indexes, and querying 100,000 records will take forever; too many, and the same could be true. So assigning indexes to the correct fields is an art form. You find out all about the art of indexes in this chapter.

The Primary Key to Success

A table's primary key is a special field in your table. You use this field to uniquely identify each record in the table.

TECHNICAL STUFF

Usually the primary key is a single field. In *very* special circumstances, *two or more* fields can share the job. The technical term for this type of key is a *multifield key.*

The lowdown on primary keys

Before we discuss how to create a primary key, you'll need to know some rules and guidelines for using one. This section contains the when, where, and why of the primary key.

Uses

Almost every table you create needs a primary key. Here's why:

TIP

>> **A primary key organizes your data by *uniquely* identifying each record.**

That's one reason why a primary key makes your database work a little faster. For an explanation of indexes and their creation, see the section "Indexing for Faster Queries," later in this chapter.

For example, a Volunteer table typically contains a `VolunteerNumber` field. This field is the primary key. If your Volunteer table contains a dozen Jane Smiths, you need a way to tell them apart. The `VolunteerNumber` field for each record *uniquely* identifies each Jane Smith — and every other volunteer, too.

>> **Tables, by default, are sorted by primary key.** A primary key helps Access find a particular record much faster due to this sorting.

>> **Your database could freak out if you don't have a primary key.** Without a primary key, finding the requested records can be difficult for Access. Think of the Jane Smith example just used. How does Access know which Jane Smith you want if multiple Jane Smith volunteers are in your database? Well, by the primary key, that's how! It is unique for each volunteer and therefore can be used to uniquely identify each Jane Smith. Problem solved!

Rules

Before you create a primary key, you need to know a few guidelines. Here's a handy listing:

TIP

>> **Location:** Access doesn't care where the primary key field appears in the table design. The key can be the first field, the last field, or buried in the middle.

Even if Access doesn't care where you put things, I always recommend that you make the primary key field the first field in your table. It makes relationships easier to build (as you see later in this chapter).

>> **Defaults:** Access tries to save you time and trouble with the default actions it gives to the primary key:

- Access really, really wants you to have a primary key in your table.

- If you create a new table in table design mode without a primary key, Access suggests adding a primary key field when you save the table.

TECHNICAL STUFF

  Access gives this automatic primary key field a wildly creative name — ID — with an AutoNumber data type.

- If the first field you add in a table is an AutoNumber type, Access automatically makes that AutoNumber field the primary key.

- Access indexes the primary key field automatically.

TIP

>> **Restrictions:** You can't just create primary keys willy-nilly. Access imposes these limits:

- A table can have only one primary key.

- You can't use the Calculated, Attachment, and OLE Object data types or a multivalued field for a primary key.

WARNING

  Don't use the Yes/No field type in a primary key. You can have only two records in such a table: Yes and No.

- All primary key indexes must have a name (just as all fields must have a name).

- Access automatically names all primary key indexes PrimaryKey.

Creating a primary key

To create a primary key, follow these steps:

1. **Open the table in Design view.**

TIP

If you just asked yourself "how do I do that?" then it might not be time for you to create a primary key. Chapter 3 shows you the table basics you need before you can create a primary key.

2. **Click the field name for the primary key.**

TIP

Don't know which field to select for your primary key? See the sidebar, "The key to table happiness." The preceding section, "Rules," relates the guidelines for selecting a primary key.

3. **On the Ribbon, click the Primary Key button (shown in Figure 5-1).**

A key symbol appears on the button next to the field name you selected.

Primary Key button

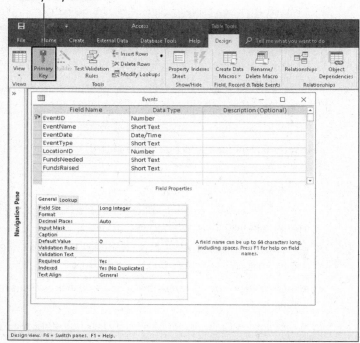

FIGURE 5-1:
The completed
primary key.

The primary key is set!

WARNING

Avoid using confidential information such as Social Security or driver's license numbers as primary keys. Only collect this type of information if necessary, and never use it as a primary key for privacy reasons.

THE KEY TO TABLE HAPPINESS

What makes a good key field? How do you find the right one? Good questions! In fact, they're the two most important questions to ask about a primary key.

Primary key values must be unique for each record. Leaving a primary key field blank is not an option. So start by looking at some sample data that will go into your table. Is there something like a phone number or customer number that will be unique for each record? If so, you've just found your primary key field. If not, then an AutoNumber field is the way to go. When you designate a field's data type as AutoNumber, Access assigns sequential numbers to each record entered into the table. (Isn't our good pal Access the best?)

AutoNumber fields always create a unique identifier for each record. When you delete a record with an AutoNumber field, Access even keeps track of those numbers and will not use them again. (Access, you are quite a pal indeed!)

Making Tables Get Along

Relational databases split data among two or more tables. Access uses a linking field, called a *foreign key*, to tie related tables together. For example, one table may contain volunteer names and addresses, whereas another table tracks the volunteer event participation history. The event participation information is tied to the volunteer information with a linking field, which (in this example) is probably a `Volunteer ID`.

Why is this important? Well, suppose you need to print an events schedule for volunteer Anita Cash. By placing the `Volunteer ID` in the Events table and relating the Events table to the Volunteer table via the `Volunteer ID`, you can pull Anita Cash's name and address information for the schedule without having to put that information in the Events table.

Rules of relationships

Keep these rules in mind when relating tables:

>> **Tables you want to relate must have at least one field in common.**
Although the field name need not be identical, its data type must be the same in each table. For example, you can't relate a text field to a number field.

Keep key field names consistent between your tables. If you don't, that ball of confusion will roll your way at some point down the road.

>> **Usually, the linking field is one table's primary key but rarely the primary key in the other table.** The Volunteer table, for example, is probably arranged by Volunteer ID, whereas event data is likely organized by Event ID.

>> **After the two tables have been created and share a common field, you're not done.** You still have to build that relationship. (You'll find out how to actually do that in the later section, "Building Table Relationships.")

Relationship types

There is more than one type of table relationship in Access. When you relate two tables, you can choose one of three possible relationship types.

Unless you want to be an Access expert, you only need to understand the one-to-many table relationship. It's the most common one.

One-to-many

One-to-many relationships connect one record in the first table to *many* records in the second table. This is the default relationship type.

Typical example: One volunteer may participate in many events, so one volunteer record is linked to many event records in the Events table.

One-to-one

One-to-one relationships link one record in the first table to *exactly* one record in the second table.

One-to-one relationships aren't common. Instead of creating a one-to-one relationship between two tables, it is usually easier to combine them into a single table.

Many-to-many

Many-to-many relationships link *many* records in one table to *many* records in another table.

Here's a common example of a many-to-many relationship:

>> A customer-order database contains separate tables for:

- Customers

- Individual products

>> Every individual product needs to be available to every customer.

In other words, *many* customers need to be able to order *many* of the same products. The database needs to satisfy queries that look for *both* of these:

- Every customer who ordered the same product

- Every product that one customer ordered

In Access 2019, you can link *many* customers to *many* of the same products two ways: *multivalued fields* and *junction tables.*

MULTIVALUED FIELDS

Access 2019 allows the creation of many-to-many relationships between two tables via *multivalued* fields.

Multivalued fields were a new capability in Access 2007. Prior to Access 2007, many-to-many relationships between two tables were bad — so bad that Access didn't allow them. Older versions of Access required creating a third table called a junction table (more on junction tables in a minute) to accomplish a many-to-many relationship.

A multivalued field can store many similar data items. Adding a multivalued field ends the need for creating multiple records to record multiple products ordered on one customer order. For example, you can add a multivalued field called ProductID to the Order Detail table. All products ordered can be stored in one field, so only one record per order is required.

Multivalued fields are not all peaches and cream. Use a junction table if you need to sort the data stored in the multivalued field or you think you'll upsize down the road to SQL Server. Sorting these fields is quite cumbersome and multivalued fields don't upsize to other platforms such as SQL Server. If you think you'll upsize to a more robust database platform at some point, avoid multivalued fields.

Microsoft created multivalued fields as an easy alternative to junction tables — and to make Access more compatible with SharePoint. Unless you're certain you'll never need to sort the field or upsize your database, avoid multivalued fields.

JUNCTION TABLES

A *junction table* is a special table that keeps track of related records in two other tables:

>> The junction table has a *one-to-many* relationship with both tables.

>> The result works like a direct *many-to-many* relationship between both tables.

For example, a junction table called Orders can connect the customers to the order details for a particular order. The junction table has a one-to-many relationship with *both* the Customer and Order Details tables.

Building Table Relationships

If you can drag-and-drop, you can build a table relationship.

REMEMBER

Keep these three limitations in mind:

>> You can only relate tables that are in the same database.

>> You can relate queries to tables, but that's unusual.

>> You need to tell Access specifically how your tables are related.

When you're ready to play the matchmaker between your loving tables, here's how to do it.

The Relationships window

To build a table relationship, first open the Relationships window. Follow these steps:

1. **Click the Database Tools tab on the Ribbon.**

   The Relationships group appears on the Ribbon. (See Figure 5-2.)

2. **From the Relationships group, click the Relationships button.**

   The Relationships window appears. The first time you set a relationship, the Show Table dialog box appears as well. More on that in the next section.

WARNING

If some tables are already listed in the window, someone (or some wizard) has already defined relationships for this database. If you're not sure how they got there and if more than one person is working on your database, stop and consult all database developers before changing the relationships. What might work for you could be disastrous for your colleagues.

Relationships button

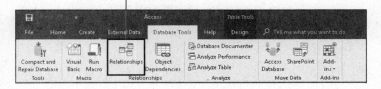

FIGURE 5-2:
The Relationships button on the Database Tools tab.

When the Relationships window is open, you can select and relate tables.

Table relationships

For each pair of tables you relate, you must select the tables and then join their common fields. The following sections show you how.

Selecting tables

To select tables to relate, open the Relationships window (as described in the preceding section) and follow these steps:

1. **Choose Show Table from the Ribbon's Relationships group. (If you don't see the Relationships group, select the Database Tools tab on the Ribbon.)**

   The Show Table dialog box appears, listing the tables in the current database file.

2. **For each pair of tables you want in the relationship, follow these steps:**

   a. *Click the table.*

   b. *Click Add.*

   In the large Relationships workspace, a little window lists the fields in the selected table. As you add tables to the layout, a separate window appears for each table. You can see these windows below the Show Table dialog box in Figure 5-3.

   Repeat Step 2 for each pair of tables you want to relate. If one of the tables in the pair is already present (because of an existing relationship it has with another table), you don't have to add it again.

3. **After you finish adding tables, click the Close button.**

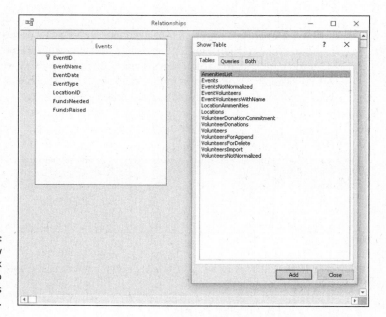

FIGURE 5-3:
Use the Show
Table dialog box
to add tables to
the Relationships
diagram.

When you have all the tables present, you're ready for these tables to get to know each other. The following sections show how to relate the tables.

Managing relationships

This section contains all the information you'll need to create, edit, and delete your table relationships.

CREATING RELATIONSHIPS

After you select the tables (as shown in the preceding instructions), follow these steps to create a relationship between two tables:

1. **Decide which two tables you want to relate.**

   Because the one-to-many relationship is the most common, these instructions pertain to it. The two tables in a one-to-many relationship are designated as fulfilling one of two roles:

   - *Parent:* In the parent table, the related field is the primary key. Each record in the parent table is uniquely identified by this related field.

   - *Child:* In the child table, the related field contains the same information as the field in the parent table. Typically, it has the same name as the corresponding field in the parent table — although this is not a requirement.

TIP

To make relating tables easier, put related fields near the beginning of the field list. In Access, you must see the related fields on the screen before you can make a relationship. If the related fields are not at the beginning of the field list, you have to do a lot of scrolling to find them. To move a field, open the problem table in DesignView, point to the button that's left of the field name, then press and drag on the button to move the field up.

2. **Follow these steps to select the parent field from the list:**

   a. *Put the mouse pointer on the field you want to relate in the parent table.*

      Usually the field you want to relate in the parent table is the primary key.

   b. *Hold down the left mouse button.*

3. **While holding down the left mouse button, follow these steps to join the parent field to the child field:**

   a. *Drag the mouse pointer from the parent field to the child table.*

      A plus sign appears at the base of the mouse pointer.

   b. *Point to the related field in the child table.*

   c. *Release the mouse button.*

      The Edit Relationships dialog box appears, detailing the soon-to-be relationship, as shown in Figure 5-4.

WARNING

Be very careful before releasing the mouse button. Put the tip of the mouse pointer *directly* on the child field before you let go.

- If you drag between the two fields correctly, the Edit Relationships dialog box displays the parent and child fields side by side, as shown in Figure 5-4.

- If you miss, click Cancel in the Edit Relationships dialog box and try Step 3 again.

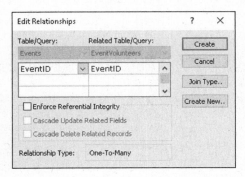

FIGURE 5-4:
The Edit Relationships dialog box details how Access connects two tables.

4. In the Edit Relationships dialog box, select the Enforce Referential Integrity option.

5. Double-check that your field names are the correct ones and then click Create.

Access illustrates the new relationship in the Relationships window:

- A line between the related fields shows you that the tables are related.

- If you checked the Enforce Referential Integrity option in the preceding step, Access places a 1 next to the parent in the relationship and an infinity symbol next to the child, as shown in the relationship in Figure 5-5.

To relate another pair of selected tables, repeat Steps 1 through 5.

TIP

Access also provides tools for modifying and removing relationships. The following section shows how to use them.

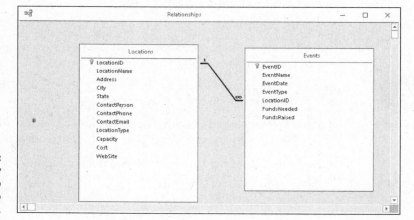

FIGURE 5-5:
A one-to-many relationship between two tables.

CHILD TABLES' "PROTECTIVE SERVICES"?

Enforce Referential Integrity sounds harsh, doesn't it? It simply means that Access makes sure that a record is present in the parent table before you can add one to its child table. (Shouldn't every child have a parent watching?) For example, with Referential Integrity enforced, Access won't let you assign a location to an event in the Events table that is not present in the Locations table.

MODIFYING RELATIONSHIPS

After you relate tables, you can see, organize, and remove the relationships.

TIP

If you create a relationship you don't want, open the Relationships window and follow these steps to delete the relationship:

1. **Click the Relationship line connecting the two tables.**

   If you are successful, the line will thicken. That means the line is selected.

2. **Tap the Delete key on your keyboard and then Yes in the resulting message box.**

   Voilà! The relationship is gone.

If you're relating many tables together, the Relationships window may look a little messy because Relationship lines will cross each other. This makes it difficult to determine which tables are related to each other. To rectify this situation, click and drag the title bar of a table window to another part of the screen. It's good practice — although not always possible — to show parents either *above* or to the *left* of their children. Try to arrange the parent and child tables so the lines between the parent and child tables don't cross over any lines that illustrate other table relationships.

TIP

Having trouble understanding your relationships? (Who isn't?) Are you scrolling all over the place in the Relationships window to see everything? If so, the Relationship Report is just for you. To preview this report, click the Relationship Report button in the Tools group on the Ribbon's Design tab. All the related tables in your database will display in an easy-to-read report. (Okay, *easier* to read!)

Indexing for Faster Queries

You may find yourself sitting for a minute or two waiting for a query or report to run. (I've sat longer than that for some reports during the development stage.) So what can be done to speed up your queries? Add *indexes* to your tables, that's what.

REMEMBER

A table index in Access works just like the index in a book. It helps Access find a record in a table just as a book index helps you find a topic in a book.

Indexes dramatically speed up queries and sorts. When you sort or query a table on an indexed field, the index has already done most of the work.

HOW AN INDEX WORKS

An index is essentially a copy of the table that's already sorted on the indexed field.

When a table is indexed properly, queries run faster because the indexes help Access locate the data faster.

Here's an example. Suppose you need to produce a list of all your Pennsylvania volunteers, and you often query your volunteer table by state:

- If you index the State field in your Volunteers table, all the Pennsylvania volunteers will be in one place. When Access reaches the Pennsylvania volunteers, it can stop there and return them to you in your query. It doesn't have to continue to the end of the table through the rest of the states.

- Without the index, Access must scan every record in the table to return the desired results.

The benefit of an index depends on the number of records in the table:

>> If you have 100 volunteers, an index won't improve performance much.

>> If you have tens of thousands of volunteers, an index will improve performance significantly.

Creating your own index

Here's the lowdown on indexes:

>> Each field in a table can be indexed if it isn't a *Calculated, Attachment, OLE object data type,* or *Multivalued* field.

>> As with the primary key, an index may have a unique name that's different from the field name. It can also have the same name as the field name. Access won't balk either way.

>> You don't have to name your index; Access does that for you.

>> Indexes either *allow* or *prevent* duplicate entries in your table.

TO DUPLICATE OR NOT TO DUPLICATE

When you create an index, you have two options for handling duplicate values:

- If records can have the same value in this field, click Yes (Duplicates OK).

  Yes (Duplicates OK) is the most common choice.

- If every record needs a unique value in this field (such as volunteer IDs in your Volunteer table), click Yes (No Duplicates), as shown in the figure included here.

  The No Duplicates setting tells Access to make sure that no two records have the same value in the indexed field.

  Access indexes primary key fields automatically as No Duplicates when you designate the primary key.

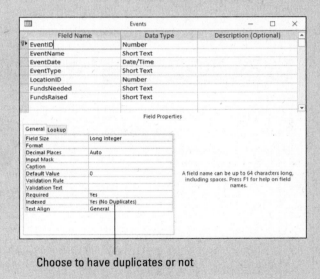

Choose to have duplicates or not

Here are some guidelines to help you decide which fields to index, presented in their recommended order:

1. Start by querying the table whose query performance you'd like to improve (for more on queries, see Chapter 13).

Make note of the time it took to run the query.

2. Next, index each field that you know you'll query frequently.

For example, in a Volunteer table, you might query by `Volunteer ID`, `Volunteer Last Name`, and `Volunteer State`.

3. Finally, query the newly indexed table.

If the query time improves, your indexes are correct. If your query time worsens, try removing one index at a time, starting with the field you think you'll query the least. Rerun your query and note performance.

When you've optimized performance, your indexing is complete.

4. Apply an index type.

The sidebar "To duplicate or not to duplicate" shows which index type to apply.

To list a table's indexes, follow these steps:

1. Open the table in Design view.

2. On the Design tab, click the Indexes button in the Ribbon's Show/Hide group. (See Figure 5-6.)

Indexes button

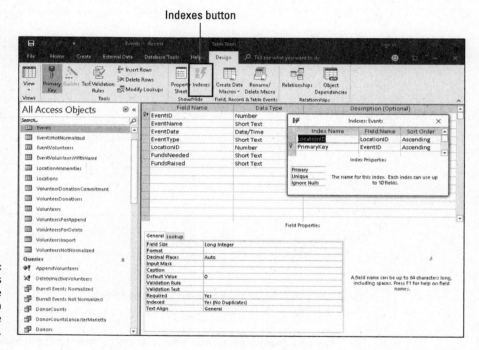

FIGURE 5-6:
The Indexes window with the Indexes button above it on the Ribbon.

WARNING

Building too many indexes in a table slows down some tasks. Adding records to a table with several indexes takes a little longer than adding records to a non-indexed table. Access spends extra time updating all those indexes behind the scenes. The trick is to get the right number of indexes assigned to the right fields.

Sometimes it comes down to trial and error when you're optimizing query performance via indexes.

Adding and removing indexes

After you decide on the correct fields to index (as outlined previously), creating an index is a snap.

TIP

In the following instructions, Step 4 can *delete* an existing field index. You may decide to delete a field index if it's hindering data input more than it's enhancing query performance.

To add or remove field indexes, open the table in Design view and follow these steps:

1. **Click the name of the field you want to index.**

The blinking cursor lands in the field name.

2. **In the General tab of the Field Properties section, click the Indexed box.**

Now the cursor moves into the Indexed box, and a down arrow appears on the right end of the box.

WARNING

If the Indexed property is unavailable, this field type doesn't work with indexes. You can't index Calculated, Attachment, OLE Object, or Multivalued fields.

3. **Click the down arrow at the end of the Indexed box.**

A list of index options appears:

- *Yes (Duplicates OK)*
- *Yes (No Duplicates)*
- *No*

TIP

Don't know what index setting to choose? The previous sidebar "To duplicate or not to duplicate" shows how to determine the correct index setting.

4. **Select the index type you want from the list.**

To *remove* an existing index from the selected field, click *No.*

5. **To make the change permanent, click the Save button on the Quick Access Toolbar.**

If your table contains thousands of records, Access may take a few moments to create the index.

» Adding new records to your table

» Changing an existing record

» Renaming fields and tables

» Deleting unwanted records

» Turning back time — to before you made your mistake

Chapter **6**

Remodeling Your Data

rom remembering to change your car's oil every 3,000 miles to cleaning out your rain gutters in the autumn, everything in your surroundings needs a little maintenance now and then. Most of that maintenance involves tidying up, getting rid of old or unwanted things, or making improvements. Sometimes *all* these things are part of the maintenance process.

Well, it's no different for your database — an Access database needs a tune-up now and then, just to keep things running right. This can be as simple as checking for blank fields where you need to plug in missing data, as common as purging old or inaccurate records, or a practical matter such as changing the names of tables and fields so your database makes more sense to the people who use it.

Unlike getting your car serviced or cleaning out your gutters, however, maintaining your database isn't expensive or difficult. Of course, *not* keeping your database in good working order *can* get expensive — it can cost you in terms of your time, the potential impact of inaccurate records on your organization, more time (and paper) wasted printing reports that include obsolete data, and the confusion that plagues those who use a database that has incorrect (or vague) field and table names.

Don't worry, though — for all those doomsday potentialities, the solution is as simple as a few clicks, a couple of double-clicks, and a little bit of typing, and it's free!

Opening a Table for Editing

When you open Access 2019 (as we discuss in Chapters 1 and 2), the workspace offers you a list of recently opened databases, along with templates you can use to start a new database, as shown in Figure 6-1.

To open a database from the Recent Databases list, just point to it and click once.

If you remember where your database is stored, but it isn't in the Recent list, use either of the following options to use the Open view:

1. **Click the File tab to the left of the Home tab, and choose Open from the list of commands (shown in Figure 6-1).**

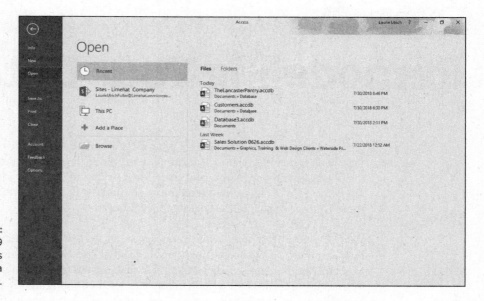

FIGURE 6-1:
The Access 2019 workspace makes opening a database easy.

Either way, the Open view appears onscreen, as shown in Figure 6-2.

By default, the Open view displays your most recently used databases — as well as the folders and file locations you've saved to recently.

2. **If the database isn't displayed, click This PC in the series of Open commands.**

This displays the view shown in Figure 6-3.

3. **When you find the database, open it by clicking its name.**

The database file opens immediately, as shown in Figure 6-4.

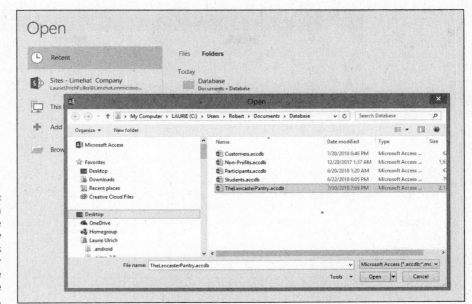

FIGURE 6-2:
Use the Open view to choose from recently used databases or pursue other routes to the database you're looking for.

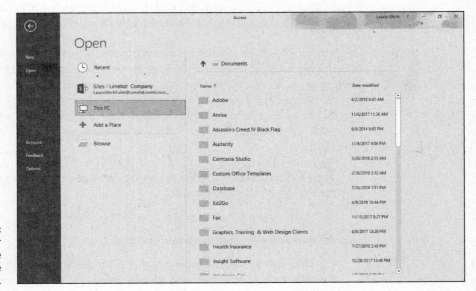

FIGURE 6-3:
Open your database through the This PC option.

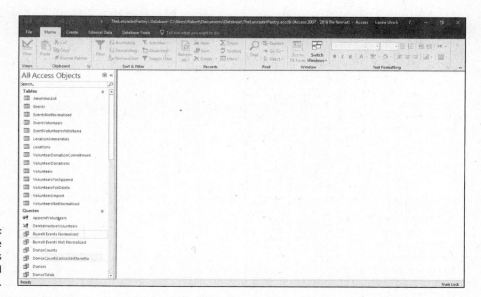

FIGURE 6-4:
The database file
opens, and its
objects are listed
on the left.

If you don't see your database listed on the right-hand side of the workspace (after clicking This PC), click the Browse button instead. This opens a dialog box through which you can navigate to the folder that contains your database.

TIP

An introductory screen known as a *switchboard* (or perhaps — utilizing a feature introduced in Access 2010 — a *Navigation form*) may appear rather than the Open dialog box. Access is telling you that your database either contains some custom programming or was created by the Database Wizard. You probably have some special forms that help you interact with the information in your database. If you want to find out how to create your own navigation form, check out Chapter 8.

1. **Within the All Access Objects list on the left side of the workspace, look for the table you want to open.**

Each table has its own listing, accompanied by a table icon.

2. **Double-click the table you want to edit.**

The table opens in Datasheet view, and you can begin your maintenance of the data. You can add or remove fields or change the names of your fields — topics discussed later in this information-packed chapter.

Inserting Records and Fields

Ever gone on vacation and forgotten your toothpaste? Sure, you can probably just pick up a tube at a drugstore in the place you're visiting, but it's still a pain. The same "Darn!" feeling overcomes you when you realize you've left something out of your database suitcase. (Okay, you might use a different four-letter word in that case, but this is a family publication.)

Luckily, adding a forgotten record or field to your table is about as easy as making a quick trip to the drugstore for that forgotten toothpaste — so easy that you may forget to say "Darn!" (or any other word expressing regret) when you discover a missing field. Instead, you'll calmly launch into the following steps — one set for inserting a missing record and one set for inserting a missing field.

Adding a record

To add a record, follow these steps:

1. **In the Datasheet view of the table that's missing a record, click inside the first empty cell at the bottom of the table — below the last displayed record in the table.**

   Your cursor blinks in the first field in that record, as shown in Figure 6-5.

2. **Type your information for the first field.**

   If the first field is an AutoNumber type, then you're automatically placed in the second field when you click the row. In the second field, you can begin typing the data for that field. As soon as you start typing, the AutoNumber field generates a new number and displays it in the field.

   TIP

   Don't panic if the AutoNumber field seems to skip a number when it creates an entry for your new record. When an AutoNumber field skips a number, it means you probably entered (or at least started to enter) a record at some point during this (or a previous) data-entry session and then deleted it.

3. **Press Tab to move through the fields and enter all the data for this new record.**

4. **When you finish entering data into the last field for the new record, you're finished!**

   Because Access saves the new record automatically while you're typing it, you have nothing more to do. Pretty neat, eh?

   If you want to add another record, press Tab and type away, filling in yet another new record.

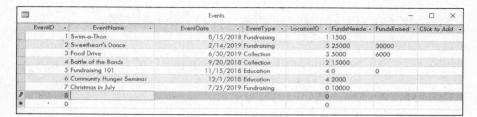

FIGURE 6-5:
A new record
awaits its data.

If you change your mind and want to kill the new addition, you have a couple of options:

>> While the new record is in progress, press Ctrl+Z to undo whatever work you've done thus far on the new record.

>> Right-click anywhere in the undesired record's row — on any field in the record. From the resulting pop-up menu, choose Delete Record. Click Yes when asked whether you're sure about the deletion.

Inserting a field

With the field-challenged table open, follow these steps to add the field you're missing:

1. **In Datasheet view, find the field heading aptly called Click to Add (see Figure 6-6).**

The column is typically placed at the end of your existing fields — so be prepared to scroll all the way to the end to see it.

Click to add a field

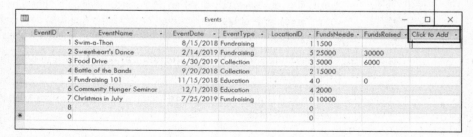

FIGURE 6-6:
Right there in the
table is a new
field, awaiting
creation.

2. **Click the instructional Click to Add heading you found in Step 1.**

A pop-up menu appears, from which you can choose the type of field this new field will be, as shown in Figure 6-7.

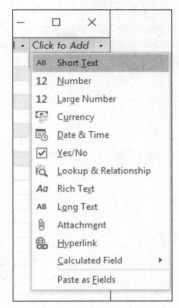

FIGURE 6-7:
Not sure what
field type to
choose? Short
Text is a good
choice, because it
was the default
for new fields
when you built
the table
originally.

3. **Choose a field type from the list.**

   The new field appears, entitled `Field1`, and the Click to Add column moves
   over one column. `Field1` is highlighted and awaiting your new name for it, as
   shown in Figure 6-8.

4. **Type the name of your new field and press Enter.**

   Your new field is created.

Type a field name here

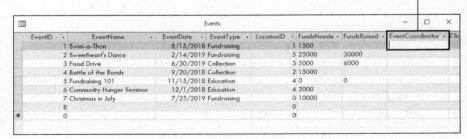

FIGURE 6-8:
Name that new
field, and make it
feel at home in
your table.

5. **To rearrange your fields so the new field is where you want it to be among the existing fields, click the heading of the field column you just created — and then click again.**

On the first click, the entire column is highlighted, and the black down-pointing arrow changes to a left-pointing white arrow. On the second click, the arrow acquires a small box just below it, indicating that you're ready to move the column.

6. **Drag to the left or right depending on where you want to drop your new field.**

A thick vertical line follows you, indicating where the field will appear as soon as you release the mouse button, as shown in Figure 6-9.

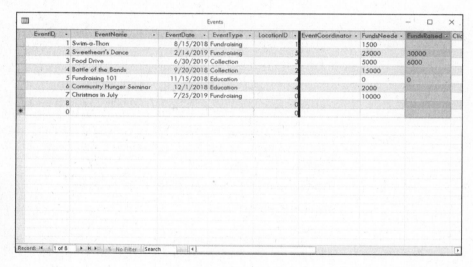

FIGURE 6-9:
Drag-and-drop
your field to
reposition it
among the other
fields in the table.

7. **When you're happy with the intended location of the field, release the mouse button.**

Your field is relocated.

TIP

By default, all fields created in Datasheet view are Short Text fields. If this isn't the type of field you want, you can change the data type (as well as other settings) for the new field by doing the following:

1. **With the field selected, click the Ribbon's Fields tab from the Table Tools group.**

2. **In the Formatting group within the Fields tab, click the Data Type drop-down arrow, as shown in Figure 6-10.**

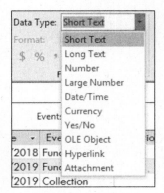

FIGURE 6-10:
The Data Type
drop-down menu
gives you
formatting
options.

3. **Choose a format — Short Text, Date/Time, Currency, Hyperlink, whatever — from the resulting list (also shown in Figure 6-10).**

You can also tinker with settings that go with the data type you choose — for example, if you choose a Number format, you can use the buttons in the Formatting section to determine how many decimal places will appear onscreen.

WARNING

If you've already entered records into the table you're currently editing, making a change to the data type will result in a warning prompt if you attempt to save the table after making the change. The warning indicates that existing data may not match the new settings, and you're given the chance to not continue if this worries you.

Deleting a field

Getting rid of a field is no big deal — in fact, it might be too easy. Access does, at least, give you a little nudge (in the form of a dialog box) to make sure you're *positive* you want to get rid of the field in question.

To get rid of an existing field that you no longer need, follow these steps:

1. **Right-click the heading for that field column.**

2. **From the resulting pop-up menu, shown in Figure 6-11, choose Delete Field.**

3. **When prompted, click Yes to confirm your desire to complete the deletion.**

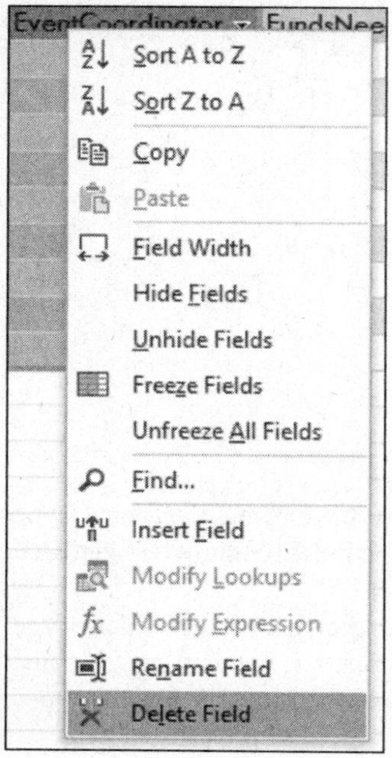
EventCoordinator
FundsNee
Sort A to Z
Sort Z to A
Copy
Paste
Field Width
Hide Fields
Unhide Fields
Freeze Fields
Unfreeze All Fields
Find...
Insert Field
Modify Lookups
Modify Expression
Rename Field
Delete Field

FIGURE 6-11: Bid your field a fond adieu with just two clicks of the mouse.

Modifying Field Content

Although your stuff is safely tucked away inside a table, you can reach in and make changes easily. In fact, editing your data is so easy that it's hard to tell whether this is a good feature or a bad one.

WARNING

Whenever you're browsing through a table, please be careful! Access doesn't warn you before saving changes to a record — even if the changes are accidental. (If I were that kind of preachy author, I'd probably make a big, guilt-laden point about how this "feature" of Access makes regular backups all the more important, but that's not my style.)

To change something inside a record, follow these steps:

1. **Scroll through the table until you find the record that needs some adjusting.**
2. **Click the field (the individual cell in the table) that you want to change.**

   The blinking line cursor pops into the field.

TIP

   If your mouse has a wheel button, use the wheel to take a quick spin through the table. (For such a small innovation, that wheel is a big timesaver!)

3. **Change the field.**

What you change and how you change it is up to you:

- *Replace the entire field:* Press F2 to highlight the data and then type the new information. The new entry replaces the old one.

- *Repair a portion of the data in a field:* Click the field and then use the right and left arrow keys to position the cursor exactly where you want to make the change. You can also double-click to select a word you want to change within any field, or click and drag with your mouse to select multiple words or numbers in the active record.

- *Remove or add characters:* Press Backspace to remove characters to the left of the cursor; press Delete to remove characters to the right. Insert new characters by typing.

TIP

If you're in a Date/Time field and want to insert the current date, press Ctrl+; (semicolon). To insert the current time, press Ctrl+Shift+; (semicolon).

If you change your mind and want to restore the original data, press Esc or Ctrl+Z to cancel your edits.

4. **When you're finished with the record, press Enter.**

Name-Calling

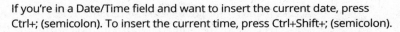

You've built your table, and maybe you've done a stellar job from the get-go — you didn't forget any fields, you put the fields in the right order, and you set up the fields to house the right kind of data. Well done, you!

Okay, back to reality. (Of course nothing in life is that simple, is it?) It's not uncommon to realize, after building your table (and accepting my previous "Well done, you!") that you need to make a few changes. You may need to change the table's name or you might need to change one or more of the field names in the table. Or both! If this happens, it doesn't mean you messed up or anything, it just means you're a human being who, with even the most scrupulous planning and preparation, can make a mistake or change your mind — or perhaps the terminology has changed since the table was first created, and now it needs updating. Luckily, regardless of the reason you need to do it, Access makes it easy to make either kind of change.

Renaming fields

Uh-oh. The field name you used when you first built the table has been the source of some confusion. People don't know what "Status" means — does it mean the members have paid their dues or does it refer to whether they're active in the organization? It's clear enough to you, but it's important that other folks who use the data feel confident that they understand what's in it.

This sort of field-naming dilemma is common when you're setting up a table for the first time, and can even crop up later on, when you're working with a table that's been around and in use for a while. The need to edit field names can arise for any reason, at any time; it's never too early or too late to edit them.

So, for whatever reason, you find you have to edit a field name. What to do?

TIP

Access makes it incredibly easy to rename a field — to keep it simple, do it first in Datasheet view. The simplicity doesn't end with how the actual renaming takes place, either — as soon as you rename a field, Access updates a whole slew of things automatically:

>> All connections from that field to other tables (if you've already set up your table relationships, as discussed in Chapter 5)

>> All queries, reports, and other goodies that already use the field

What could be easier than that?

Working in Datasheet view

So when you're ready, follow these steps:

1. **Double-click the field name, as shown in Figure 6-12.**

The current name is highlighted in place, atop the column.

Edit Field Name

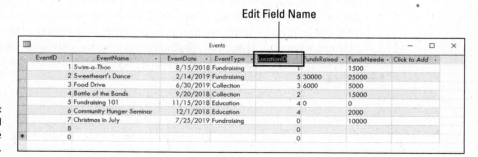

FIGURE 6-12:
A selected field name is ripe for editing.

2. **Edit the name as needed:**

- *To replace the current name entirely,* type the new name while the current name is still highlighted.

  While the field name is highlighted, the very next thing you type will replace the current name — so don't start typing at that point unless you want to replace the entire field name.

- *To edit the name (leaving some of the current name in place),* click inside the existing, selected name and then insert or remove characters as needed.

REMEMBER

3. **When you like the name you see, click in any cell in the table.**

The new name appears at the top of the column, and you're ready to do whatever you need:

- Enter new records.

- Edit another field.

- Save the table (for design changes) and close it (if you've finished working).

Using the Fields tab

To rename a field in the Fields tab in Datasheet view, follow these steps:

1. **Click the field name that you want to edit.**

   You can also click in any cell in that column — just give Access some way of knowing which field you want to rename.

2. **Click the Fields tab, in the Table Tools section of the Ribbon.**

3. **In the Properties section, click Name & Caption.**

   A dialog box opens (as shown in Figure 6-13) in which you can rename the field.

4. **Type the new name in the Name field in the dialog box.**

5. **Press Enter or click OK to change the name.**

   This tells Access to accept your change, and you return to the table, with your field's new name in place.

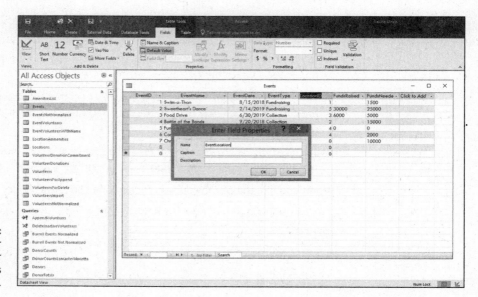

FIGURE 6-13: Rename your field in the Enter Field Properties dialog box.

TIP

If you prefer the quick-and-easy way to change a field name (and have no other changes you need to make, such as editing the Field Size, via the Fields tab in the Table Tools section of the Ribbon), you can double-click the existing field name, and when it highlights, type the new name. Press Enter to confirm your change.

Renaming a table

Renaming an entire table is not as common as needing to rename a field, but it can happen. Maybe you misspelled the name. Maybe the name you gave it is too long, too short, or is misleading to people who have to guess which table to open when they're looking for something in particular.

To edit the name of a table, follow these steps:

1. **Open the database that contains the table you want to rename.**

   With the chosen database listed on the left side of your Access workspace, look for the table you want to rename.

WARNING

   Don't open the table itself. It can't be open during the renaming process if you want these steps to work.

2. **Right-click the table name.**

3. **Choose Rename from the menu that appears, as shown in Figure 6-14.**

   The name is highlighted.

FIGURE 6-14:
To rename a table, you have to be able to see its name listed in the All Tables panel on the left.

4. **Change the table name.**

   You can make the change in either of two ways:

   - Type the new name.

   - Modify the current name (use your arrow keys to move within the name and your Backspace and/or Delete keys to edit).

   After changing the name, press Enter to commit to the new name.

TIP

After you've renamed your table, all the items that link to or use it within your database will be updated to use the same table with the new name. You don't need to re-create any of your queries, reports, forms, or relationships.

Turn Uh-Oh! into Yee-Hah!

It happens to everyone. You add, move, or change the name of a field and regret it later — or you rename your table and wish you hadn't. What can you do? Call upon Access' techniques for avoiding the panic that ensues when a mistake is made and you think you're stuck with the results.

Now, none of the following three methods for cleaning up after a regrettable change are magical or really high-tech, but they are helpful. Here goes:

>> **You can recover from one addition or edit with the Undo command.** Unfortunately, you cannot undo the deletion of a record. Access will warn you, though, if you attempt to delete one or more records; you can choose not to proceed if you're not absolutely sure.

>> **Double-check any change you make before saving it.** This sounds painfully obvious, but really — just do it. And if the change is important, triple-check it. When you're sure it's correct, press Enter and commit the change to the table. Until you're sure about the change you're making, don't click outside of the field.

>> **Keep a good backup so you can quickly recover missing data and get on with your work.** Good backups have no substitute. If you make good backups — which is as easy as using the File tab's Save As command and then choosing Save Database As (I like to name the backup "*Database*Backup-*xx-xx-xxxx*", where the *x* characters represent the date of the backup, and the word *Database* is exchanged for the name of the database you're backing up) — the chance of losing data is greatly reduced, your boss promotes you, your significant other unswervingly devotes his or her life to you, and you may even win the lottery. At the very least, you'll sleep better, knowing that your data is safe.

TIP

You should close your backup copy of the database when you've finished saving it. This prevents you from editing or adding records in the backup copy and leaving the live, working copy without the new or changed data.

Chapter **7**

Types, Masks, and Triggers

I f you have a sound table structure but poor data collection, your database won't report anything of interest to its intended audience. You know the old saying, "garbage in, garbage out"? This chapter helps you limit the garbage that is put into your tables by detailing five tools Access puts at your disposal. (Access doesn't call them tools; it calls them *properties*.)

REMEMBER

You don't want the task of going back and cleaning up your data after it has all been typed. Better to type it correctly the first time. This chapter shows you how to use formatting, input masks, required fields, and validation to keep your data nice and tidy.

Access Table Settings

This chapter shows how to use the following five properties to help keep incorrect data out of your database:

>> **Format:** Control how your data appears without changing the way it is stored.

>> **Input mask:** Force data entry to follow the correct structure, such as typing phone numbers in the (###) ###-#### format.

>> **Required:** Force the entry of data in the field before the record can be saved.

>> **Validation Rule:** Require that data be typed in a field following a specific set of rules, such as a number between 0 and 100.

>> **Default Value:** Auto-enter data when a new record is inserted.

All five properties are in the same place: In Table Design view on the General tab in the Field Properties section. Use the following steps to access and modify the five properties:

1. **Open the database file that contains the data you want to keep clean. From the Navigation pane, right-click the table you want to modify.**

The shortcut menu appears.

2. **Choose Design View from the menu, as shown in Figure 7-1.**

The table flips to Design view, showing its fields and field properties.

TIP

If the table you want is already on the screen in Datasheet view, just click the View button from the Home tab of the Ribbon. This toggles between Design and Datasheet views.

3. **Repeat these steps for each field whose properties you want to alter:**

a. Click the name of the field.

The General tab in the Field Properties section (the bottom half of the window) displays the details of the current field, as shown in Figure 7-2. You're ready to do your thing!

b. In the Field Properties section, click in the Format, Input Mask, Default Value, Validation Rule, or Required boxes, and type your changes.

In the remainder of this chapter, I delve into these properties in more detail to show you what they do and how to modify them to suit your needs.

TIP

The Format, Required, Validation Rule, and Default Value properties can be modified in Datasheet view. Just click the Fields tab on the Ribbon and check out the Formatting, Properties, and Field Validation groups.

Validation Text has a box, too. It goes with the Validation Rule box (kind of like coffee and cream). The "Making your data toe the line with validation" section, later in this chapter, explains how these two properties work together to prevent the entry of unwanted data.

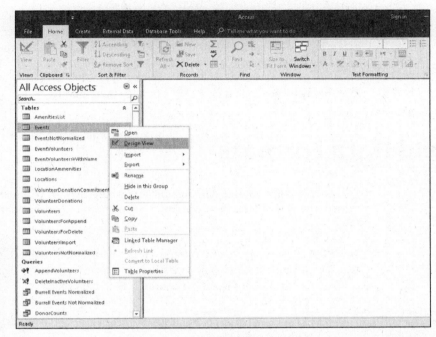

FIGURE 7-1:
You can see and edit a table's structure, including its field properties, in Design view.

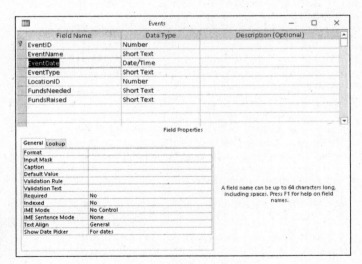

FIGURE 7-2:
Working on the EventDate field.

4. **When you've made all necessary property changes, click the Save button on the Quick Access Toolbar to keep your changes.**

TIP

To *reject* your changes, close the table (click the x in its upper right corner) and click No in the resulting dialog box. Your table will revert to its settings from the last time it was saved.

Using formats, masks, required fields, validations, and default values involves many more details, but use the preceding steps to get started. These steps are the same regardless of which property you apply.

The following sections tackle each property individually.

Field Data Formats

Formatting helps you see data in a recognizable, clear arrangement. Formats only change the way you *see* your data on the screen, not how your data is *stored* in the table.

Some field data types require different formatting codes than others. For example, text formatting uses different codes than numeric formatting. The following sections cover formats for the most common field data types.

TIP

APPLY FORMATTING, MINIMIZE DATA-ENTRY ERRORS

Although formatting won't stop inaccurate data entry, it can make data-entry errors more recognizable. Here's how formatting can cut down on errors:

- **Make errors more visible.**

  For example, suppose you need to type the number *one million* into a numeric field. Without formatting, you see this: 1000000. (Uh, how many zeros are in that?) With standard formatting, you see this: 1,000,000.

- **Cut down on typing during data entry.**

  For example, phone numbers are often seen as (111) 222-3333. With text formatting applied to a phone number field, simply type **1112223333**. Access displays the phone number with the parentheses and the dash. (Can you say "fewer keystrokes"?)

TIP

If your format command doesn't work the first time, follow these steps to troubleshoot it:

1. **Double-check the data type.**

   For example, if you see left-aligned numbers without a standard number of decimal places, you may have selected the Text data type for a numeric field. Just change the data type to Number or Currency and like magic, you have beautiful numbers!

2. **Review the format commands and make any necessary changes.**

   For example, if you see percent signs and your intention is dollar signs, just flip the format from Percent to Currency by using the Format Property drop-down list.

Text fields

Text fields can be formatted using four characters that affect *capitalization*, *spacing*, and *punctuation*.

Access does not have predesigned formats for text fields, but you can make your own. Just string together some special characters to construct a formatting string that Access can use to display the text in a standardized way.

Table 7-1 lists the special characters that you can use to build your text formats.

TABLE 7-1

Formatting Codes for Text Fields

Character	Display Option
>	Show whole field as uppercase (capital letters).
<	Show whole field as lowercase.
@	Show a space in this position if there isn't a data character.
&	Display a character if there is one; otherwise, don't do anything.

Here's what you need to know about the formatting codes in Table 7-1.

Capitalization

By default, Access displays text fields with the actual capitalization of the stored data. However, Access can automatically display a field in all *uppercase* (capital) or *lowercase* letters, regardless of how the data is stored.

Set the Format property of a short text or long text field to the greater-than or less-than symbol to affect the capitalization of the whole field.

UPPERCASE

The *greater-than* symbol (>) makes all the text in that field appear in uppercase (capital) letters, regardless of how the text was typed. To use this option, type a single greater-than symbol in the Format box.

TIP

This format is great for abbreviating the names of U.S. states, whose abbreviations are normally seen as uppercase. However, it doesn't change the way the text is stored. This means you need to format the text with the greater-than symbol each time the field appears on a form or report.

LOWERCASE

The *less-than* symbol (<) makes all the text in that field appear in lowercase, regardless of how the text was typed. To use this option, type a single less-than symbol in the Format text box.

Spacing and punctuation

Access allows you to format the spacing and punctuation of typed text. Through formatting, you can add extra spaces or special characters like dashes.

REMEMBER

When using the @ or & character in a format, always include one @ or & to represent *each typed character* in the field. For example, use @@ for two spaces and @@@ for three.

SHOW FILLER SPACES

The *at sign* (@) forces Access to display either a character or a space in the field. If the typed field data is shorter than the formatting code, Access adds extra spaces to fill the format.

For example, if a field uses @@@@@@ as its format, but the field's data is only three characters long (such as *Tim* or *now*), Access displays three spaces and *then* the data. If the field data is four characters long, the format pads the beginning of the entry with two spaces.

DON'T SHOW FILLER SPACES

The *ampersand* (&) means "display a character if there's one to display; otherwise, don't do anything."

MAKE ACCESS SEE RED SO YOU DON'T

Here's a great tip for highlighting missing text data in a record: When you're typing data, sometimes you need to skip a text field because you don't have that particular information at hand. Wouldn't it be great if Access automatically marked the field as blank to remind you to fill in the info later?

Access can create such a custom text format. For example, the following character string displays the word *Unknown* in red if the field doesn't contain a value. Type the following command in the field's Format text box exactly like this (there are no spaces between the characters in the string and punctuation):

@;"Unknown"[Red]

It's easy to customize the preceding formatting example to suit your needs:

- **Text:** Between the quotes, substitute any display text you want instead of Unknown.

- **Color:** Between the square brackets, substitute any display color you want instead of Red.

You can use the ampersand to create special formats. For example, a Social Security number can use this format: &&&-&&-&&&&.

If someone types **123456789** in that field, Access applies the format and displays 123-45-6789, adding the dashes in the middle of the numbers by itself.

TIP

Formatting changes only the appearance of data, not the data itself. Therefore, if you intend to export the data to another program (such as Excel), the formatting won't necessarily go with it. So if you type **pa** in a State field and apply the > formatting code to that field, the data will appear as PA in Access but will export to Excel as pa.

Number and currency fields

Microsoft makes it easy for you to apply numeric formats to your numeric fields. It built the seven most common formats into a drop-down menu in the Format property row.

To set a Number or Currency field format, follow these steps:

1. **With your table in Design view, click the Format text box for the field you'd like to format.**

TIP

2. **Click the down arrow that appears at the right side of the box and select a format for your field.**

Figure 7-3 shows the drop-down menu, which is divided vertically:

- The left side shows each format's given name.

- The right side shows a sample of how each format looks.

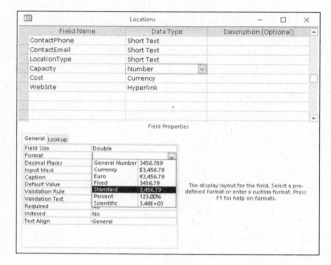

FIGURE 7-3:
The number format list.

REMEMBER

Numeric formats change only the appearance of the number, not the number as it is stored. So if you select the Single Field Size and choose Standard to format a field that contains the number 1.235678, you see 1.24 on the screen — but Access *stores* 1.235678 in the field. Any calculations done with the numbers in that field will use the actual typed-in number, not the formatted number seen onscreen.

The following sections describe the numeric formats built into Access.

General Number format

The General Number format is the Access default. It merely displays whatever you put in the field without making any adjustments to it. This includes decimal places. If you format the number 1.23456 to General, two decimal places, it will display as 1.23456. I know, it doesn't make sense, but it is what it is!

Currency format

The currency format makes a plain number field look like a currency field.

REMEMBER

Some numeric fields store decimal characters, and others do not — it all depends on the field size you select. So decimal formatting is irrelevant if you select a field size that doesn't store decimal places (the Long Integer size, for example). Chapter 3 covers number fields and field sizes in more detail.

These two formats show the data with two decimal places (the "cents" part of a dollar amount), substituting zeros if decimals aren't already present:

WARNING

>> **Currency:** Shows the local currency sign and punctuation (based on the Region & Language Settings in Windows Settings).

Don't assume that the Currency formats automatically perform an exchange-rate conversion for the selected currency. They don't. They merely display the selected currency symbol in front of the value typed in the field.

>> **Euro:** Uses the Euro symbol (ε) regardless of the Region & Language Settings.

Scientific, Percent, and Decimal formats

The remaining built-in formats are used for a variety of purposes, from displaying a large number in scientific notation to showing decimals as a percent:

>> **Fixed:** Shows the decimal value without a comma as a thousands separator.

>> **Standard:** Shows the decimal value with a thousands separator.

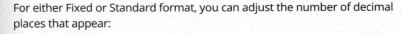

For either Fixed or Standard format, you can adjust the number of decimal places that appear:

TIP

• By default, Fixed and Standard round the display to two decimal places via the Auto setting, which is the default.

• To specify a different number of decimal places, type a number between 0 and 15 in the Decimal Places setting right below the Format setting.

>> **Percent:** This format adds a percent sign after the number.

There's no need to convert percentages to decimals for data entry. To enter 97%, type **97** in the field.

REMEMBER

If your percentages are displayed only as 0.00% or 100.00%, the sidebar "What happened to my percentages?" has a solution.

>> **Scientific:** Displays numbers in *scientific notation* (the first *significant digits* plus the number of places where the digits belong on the left or right side of the decimal point).

WHAT HAPPENED TO MY PERCENTAGES?

When you create a field with the Number data type, Access assigns the Long Integer field size by default. Because integers are by definition whole numbers, Access rounds any decimal number entered in such a field. So if you enter **25** in a field with the Percent format and Access displays your entry as 0.00%, your entry:

- Automatically rounds to the nearest whole number (in my example, 0)

- Always displays zeros in the decimal places

The solution? Change the Field Size setting (pictured in the following figure) from Long Integer to Single. This setting tells Access to remember the decimal part of the number.

General	Lookup	
Field Size	Single	⌄
Format	Byte	
Decimal Places	Integer	
Input Mask	Long Integer	
Caption	Single	
Default Value	Double	
Validation Rule	Replication ID	
Validation Text	Decimal	
Required	No	
Indexed	No	
Text Align	General	

Scientific notation is mostly for very *big* numbers (like the distance light travels in a year) and very *small* numbers (like the distance light travels in a trillionth of a second) that are hard to measure precisely or read at a glance. Unless you are a scientist, avoid this format.

Date/time fields

Microsoft provides you with a drop-down menu full of ready-to-use date and time formats. Here's how to apply a date/time format to a field:

1. **With your table in Design view, click the Format text box for the field you'd like to format.**

2. **Click the down arrow that appears on the right side of the text box.**

The menu shown in Figure 7-4 drops down to serve you.

3. **Select the format you want to use.**

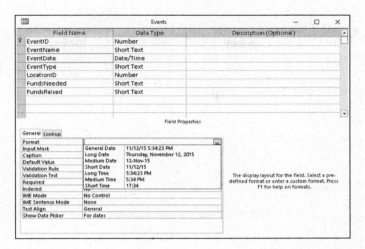

FIGURE 7-4:
The ever-popular date/time format list.

Keep these tips in mind when you apply a date/time format:

>> When you use one of the longer formats, such as General Date or Long Date, make sure that the datasheet column is wide enough to display all the information. Otherwise, Access will fill the field with number symbols (#), making the date unreadable.

>> If more than one person uses the database, choose a format that provides *more* information, not *less* information.

TIP

My clients often ask me to provide a date in the *m/d/yy* format with a two-digit year (such as 10/1/19 rather than 10/1/2019). To display a date with a two-digit year, type the following in the format box: **m/d/yy**.

Yes/No fields

You can say only so much about a field with three options. Oddly, Yes/No fields are set to the Yes/No formatting by default.

TIP

If you want the ability to type Yes/No, True/False, or On/Off in the field, make sure that Display Control in the Lookup tab (next to the General tab) is set to Combo Box. Otherwise, you'll have check boxes in your field (because Check Box is the default display for a Yes/No field).

Allowable Yes/No field entries

Here's what you can type in a Yes/No field (see Figure 7-5):

» Yes and No (this is the default)

» On and Off

» True and False

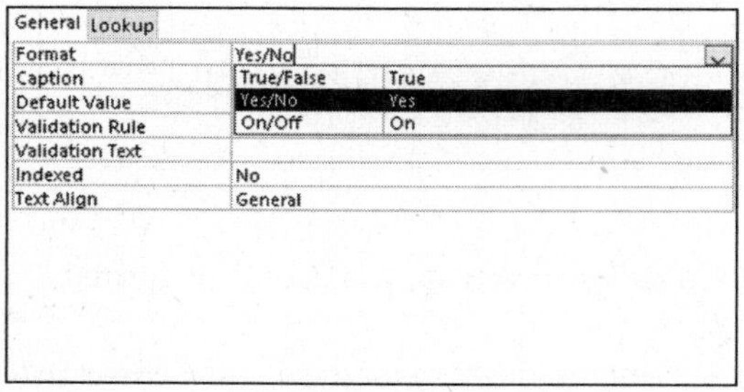

FIGURE 7-5:
Not much to talk
about with Yes/
No formatting.

Yes and No is the default, but you can change how a Yes/No field formats its content. Here's how:

1. **With your table in Design view, click the Format text box for the field you'd like to format.**

2. **Click the down arrow that appears on the text box's right side.**

   The menu of three Yes/No formats drops down for your selection.

3. **Select the format you want to use.**

Create your own Yes/No format

To display your *own* choices instead of a boring *Yes* and *No*, type a customized entry in the Format box. An example looks something like this:

```
"REORDER"[Red]; "In stock"[Green]
```

The No and Yes parts of the format are separated by a semicolon (;).

» The part on the left appears if the field is equal to No.

» The part on the right appears if the field is equal to Yes.

With the preceding example, type **Yes** in the field, and the text *In stock* appears in green. Type **No** in the field, and *REORDER* screams a warning in bright red.

REMEMBER

A custom Yes/No format simply changes the way the typed data appears. A Yes/No field will still accept only the entries as outlined in the previous section "Allowable Yes/No field entries," regardless of the custom format applied to it.

You can type any words between the quotes and any Access-allowed color names between the square brackets. Who knew that formatting could be so much fun!

Gaining Control of Data Entry

The remaining sections in this chapter explore Access field properties that allow you to control what data is entered in a field. The more you control the data that goes into your tables, the less you'll need to clean it up after it's been entered.

You really need to put a mask on those fields

An *input mask* is a series of characters that tells Access what data to expect in a particular field — and actually prevents users from typing data that does not fit the mask. If you want a field to contain all numbers and no letters, an input mask can do the job. It can also do the reverse (all letters and no numbers) and almost any combination in between. Short Text, Number, Date/Time, and Currency field data types accept input masks.

TECHNICAL STUFF

Formatting (shown previously in this chapter) can make some data entry errors *visible*, but formatting doesn't *block* errors. Input masks, on the other hand, keep that bad data out.

Input masks are stored in the Input Mask property box of the field's General tab. (The beginning of this chapter shows the steps to follow to access the General tab.)

Add these masks to fields that contain dates, times, phone numbers, Social Security numbers, passwords, and zip codes, among other things. You'll be so glad you did. If you don't, expect to see plenty of phone numbers like 111–123 and zip codes like 0854.

TIP

Input masks work best with *short, consistent* data. Numbers and number-and-letter combinations that follow a consistent pattern are excellent candidates. Phone numbers, dates, and zip codes are common examples of data items that follow a consistent pattern.

You create an input mask in one of two ways:

>> **Ask the Input Mask Wizard for help.**

The Input Mask Wizard can't possibly contain every mask for every situation. It only knows about text and date fields, and offers just a few options.

Always start with the wizard. If it doesn't have your solution, then you need to manually build the mask.

>> **Type the mask manually.**

Create the mask manually if your data follows a consistent pattern (such as a six-digit part number) that isn't a choice offered by the Input Mask Wizard.

Using the Input Mask Wizard

The Input Mask Wizard gladly helps if you're making a mask for text fields (such as those containing phone numbers, Social Security numbers, and United States zip codes) or simple date and time fields.

TIP

If your data doesn't fit one of the masks that the wizard provides yet follows a consistent pattern, check the next section. It shows you how to create a mask manually.

To ask for the wizard's help, follow these steps:

1. **Open the database file that contains the data you want to mask. From the Navigation pane, right-click the table you want to modify and choose Design View.**

   The table flips into Design view.

REMEMBER

2. **Click the name of the field that will receive the input mask.**

   You can use the wizard only with text and date/time fields.

   The General tab in the Field Properties section (the bottom half of the window) displays the details of the current field.

3. **Click the Input Mask box.**

   The cursor monotonously blinks away in the Input Mask box. To the right of the box, a small button with three dots appears. That's the Builder button, which comes into play in the next step.

4. **Click the Builder button.**

   The wizard appears, offering a choice of input masks, as shown in Figure 7-6.

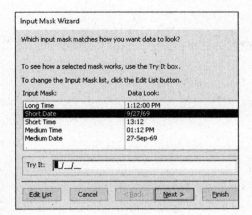

FIGURE 7-6:
The Input Mask
Wizard for a
Date/Time field.

5. **Scroll through the list of input masks to find what you want.**

6. **Click the input mask you want.**

   To play with the mask a bit and see how it works, click the Try It area at the bottom of the dialog box and then type a sample entry.

7. **Click Finish to close the wizard and use the mask with your field.**

TECHNICAL
STUFF

If you click Next instead of Finish, the wizard gives you more options, but I recommend avoiding them. (The sidebar "The rest of the Input Mask Wizard" has the details.)

The chosen mask appears in the Input Mask text box in the table's Field Properties section, as shown in Figure 7-7.

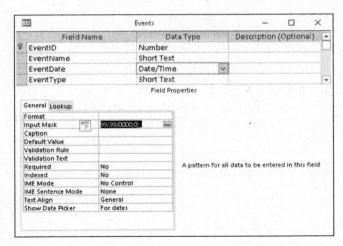

FIGURE 7-7:
The Input Mask
Wizard completes
its maskterpiece!

THE REST OF THE INPUT MASK WIZARD

This sidebar shows our recommendations for the last two steps of the Input Mask Wizard. If you click Next instead of Finish at the end of my steps, the Input Mask Wizard continues asking you about changing some obscure settings that are best left at the defaults:

- **The placeholder character for the input mask**

  The *placeholder* character in the mask represents the user's actual typed character. The default is a dash. You can change from the default to a #, @, !, $, %, or *.

- **Storing the data with the symbols included within the input mask**

  For example, a Social Security number could be stored with or without the dashes.

  The default is Without the Symbols in the Mask (for *don't store the symbols*). I recommend you keep it that way. The mask takes care of the data display. Why store extra characters in your database?

Making a mask by hand

It's not uncommon to need a mask that the Input Mask Wizard doesn't provide. If your fingers can string together a seemingly nonsensical string of characters on the keyboard, then you can make your own input mask. The trick is making sense out of all the nonsensical characters.

Table 7-2 shows the codes you can use in an input mask; each code has an explanation of the character(s) that it represents:

>> **Required Code:** Users must type that type of character (whether they actually want to or not).

>> **Optional Code:** Users can type or not type the kind of character mentioned in the first column. For example, if your input mask is 99/99/0000;0;_, you can type 1/1/2019 or 01/01/2019 but you can't type 1/1/19 or 01/01/19.

You must use the input mask codes to design an input mask.

TABLE 7-2

Codes for Input Masks

Kind of Characters	Required Code	Optional Code
Digits (0 to 9) only.	0 (zero)	9
Digits and + and -.	(not available)	# (U.S. pound sign)
Letters (A to Z) only.	L	? (question mark)
Letters or digits only.	A	a (must be lowercase)
Any character or space.	& (ampersand)	C
Any character typed into the mask is filled in from right to left instead of the usual left to right.	!	None
Any literal character.	\ (for example, * displays as just *)	None
All characters typed into the mask are forced to lowercase.	<	None
All characters typed into the mask are forced to uppercase.	>	None

DESIGNING AN INPUT MASK

Before you can create a mask, you must determine what mask codes you'll need to build the mask. Here's how:

TIP

1. **On a piece of paper, write several examples of the data that the mask should allow into the table.**

   If the information you're storing has subtle variations (such as part numbers that end in either a letter/number or letter/letter combination), include examples of the various possibilities so that your input mask accepts them all. You can't build a mask if you don't know your data.

2. **Write a simple description of the data, including which elements are required and which are optional.**

   For example, if your sample is a part number that looks like 728816ABC7, write *six numbers, three letters, one number; all parts are required.*

   Remember to allow for the variations, if you have any. The difference between *one number* and *one letter or number* can be crucial.

If you need to include a special character in your mask, like a dash or parentheses or a combination of static characters, use this list for guidance:

- **Dash, slash, or parenthesis characters:** Put a backslash (\) in front of it, such as \– for a dash.

- **Multiple characters:** Put quotation marks around them.

  For example, an area code may be separated from the rest of the number by *both* a parenthesis and a space, like this:

  (567) 555-2345

  The corresponding mask has quotes around the parenthesis and the space, like this: ! \(999") "999\–9999.

The phone-number mask also begins with an exclamation point. The exclamation point forces the typed data to fill the mask from right to left rather than left to right (the default). What's the big deal about that? Some phone numbers don't require an area code; others do. Suppose you have to type a seven-digit phone number. If not for the right-to-left entry, you'd have to move the cursor past the area code (___) placeholder part of the mask to get to the beginning of the seven-digit part.

If your field includes letters and you want them to be stored as all-uppercase, add a greater-than symbol (>) to the beginning of your mask. To store the letters as all-lowercase, use a less-than symbol (<) instead.

3. **Write the mask codes that represent the elements you've written in Step 2.**

   If (for example), you wrote "*six numbers, three letters, one number; all parts are required*" in Step 2, then you need the mask codes 000000LLL0. Refer to Table 7-2.

PUTTING ON YOUR INPUT MASK

Now that you have your mask written on paper, it's time to enter it in Access. Here's how:

1. **With the database file open, right-click the table you want to work with and then choose Design View from the shortcut menu.**

   The table flips to Design view.

2. **Click the name of the field you want to adjust.**

3. **Click the Input Mask box.**

   The cursor blinks in the Input Mask box.

4. **Carefully type your finished mask into the Input Mask area of the Field Properties section (as shown in Figure 7-8).**

   If you don't know what to type here, see the preceding section.

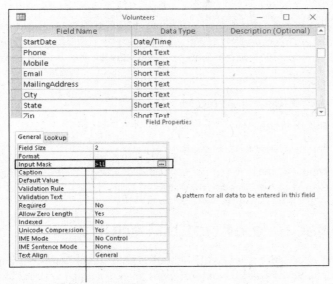

FIGURE 7-8:
Manually adding
a capitalization
mask.

Capitalization Input Mask

TIP

5. **Click the View button on the Ribbon to switch to Datasheet view and place the cursor in the masked field to check out your new mask.**

   When prompted to Save, click Yes so you don't lose your work.

   When you've entered the mask and have saved the table, try these tests:

   a. *Type something unacceptable into the masked field.*

      The input mask should prevent you from typing an incorrect value (see Figure 7-9).

   b. *Try an acceptable entry.*

      The mask should accept your entry.

   c. *Try all the variations you identified in the mask-planning process.*

      All should be accepted by the mask. If they are not, switch back to Design view and tweak your mask until all possible variations of your entry are acceptable to the mask.

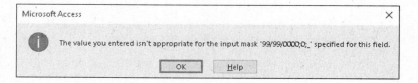

FIGURE 7-9:
I have violated
the input mask.

WARNING

If you're adding a mask to an existing table with data, Access doesn't report to you on existing records that fail the mask; it gives that data a free pass to exist as typed. To enforce the mask on existing records, you'll need to repeat these steps for each record:

1. **Click the field in the record.**

2. **Edit the data.**

   You can delete the last character and then retype it.

   When you move the cursor out of the field, you'll see the warning if the data doesn't comply with the mask.

To require or not to require

On many occasions, you will not want a record typed until all the facts are in. For example, you certainly wouldn't want an order typed without an order date, customer, and product information. The Required property prevents records that are missing essential data from being saved to a table.

The Required property has two settings:

» **Yes:** The user cannot save the record without putting something in the field.

» **No:** Anything goes. (This is the default.)

To require data entry in a field, follow these simple steps:

1. **While in a table's Design view, click the field in which you want to require data entry.**

2. **Click in the Required box on the General tab in the Field Properties section.**

   An arrow appears at the end of the box. By default, the box reads No.

3. **Click the arrow and select Yes from the list that appears, as shown in Figure 7-10.**

   Watch out, the field is now required!

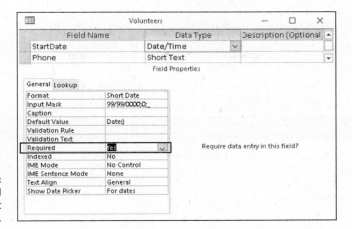

FIGURE 7-10:
The Required property is set to Yes.

4. **Click the View button on the Ribbon to switch to Datasheet view and then test your work.**

   Type a new record, omitting data entry in the required field. You should see a message box gently reminding you for forgetting the required data.

WARNING

Don't get overzealous with the Required property and set it to Yes for nonessential fields. For example, a volunteer without an email address is usually better than no volunteer at all.

Making your data toe the line with validation

With a *validation*, Access tests the incoming data to make sure that it's what you want in the table. If the data isn't right, the validation displays an error message (you get to choose what it says) and makes the user try the entry again.

Like the other options in this chapter, validations are stored in the General tab of the Field Properties area. Two options relate to validations:

>> **Validation Rule:** This rule is the validation itself.

>> **Validation Text:** The text is the error message you want Access to display when some data that violates the validation rule is typed.

TIP

Validations work best with number, currency, and date fields. Creating a validation for a text field is possible, but the validations tend to get very complicated very fast.

Tables 7-3 and 7-4 contain some ready-to-use validations that cover the most common needs. These are ready for you to type into the General tab of the Field Properties area.

TABLE 7-3

Common Number-Field Validations

Validation Rule	What It Means
> 0	Must be greater than zero
<> 0	Cannot be zero
> 0 AND < 100	Must be between 0 and 100 (noninclusive)
>= 0 AND <= 100	Must be between 0 and 100 (inclusive)
<= 0 OR >= 100	Must be less than 0 or greater than 100 (inclusive)

TABLE 7-4

Common Date-Field Validations

Validation Rule	What It Means
>= Date ()	Must be today's date or later
>= Date () OR Is Null	Must be today's date, later, or blank
< Date ()	Must be earlier than today's date
>= #1/1/2018# AND <= Date ()	Must be between January 1, 2018 and today (inclusive)

Here's how to enter a validation rule:

1. **With the database file open, right-click the table you want to work with and choose Design View from the shortcut menu.**

   The table flips to Design view.

2. **Click the name of the field you want to adjust.**

3. **Click the Validation Rule box.**

   The cursor blinks in the Validation Rule box.

4. **Type the validation rule that matches your data.**

   For example, if you want to allow only numbers between 0 and 1,000 in the field, type >0 AND <1000.

5. **Click in the Validation Text field.**

   The cursor blinks in the Validation Text box.

6. **Type the message you'd like the user to see if he or she breaks the validation rule.**

   Keep it short and simple. For my example in Step 4, you might type **Please enter a number greater than 0 and less than 1,000.**

When you apply a validation rule to a field, watch out for these gotchas:

>> When using AND, both sides of the validation rule must be true before the rule is met.

>> With OR, only one side of the rule needs to be true for the entire rule to be true.

>> Be careful when combining >= and <=. Accidentally coming up with one that can't be true (such as <= 0 AND >= 100) is too easy!

TIP

TIP

You can test your new validation rules against existing table data by clicking the Test Validation Rules button in the Tools group of the Ribbon's Design tab. Just follow the prompts in the resulting message boxes (to save your table, for example), and you'll know if your data likes the new rules!

Give Your Fingers a Mini Vacation by Default

Wouldn't it be a dream come true if every time you entered a new volunteer, you didn't have to type the current date in the Start Date field? Well, guess what? Access is all about making your dreams come true! (Your data-entry dreams, anyway.) It accomplishes this feat through the Default Value property. The Default Value property places the data that you specify for a field into that field every time a new record is inserted into the field's table. Yes, it sounds too good to be true — but I assure you it is not!

Here's how to enter a default value:

1. **With the database file open, right-click the table you want to work with, and choose Design View from the shortcut menu.**

   The table flips into Design view.

2. **Click the name of the field you want to adjust.**

3. **Click the Default Value box.**

The cursor blinks in the Default Value box. The Builder button appears.

4. **Type the data that you'd like to appear for that field when a new record is inserted.**

For example, if you want the current date to appear in a Start Date field for each new record, type **Date()** in the Default Value text box. (See Figure 7-11.)

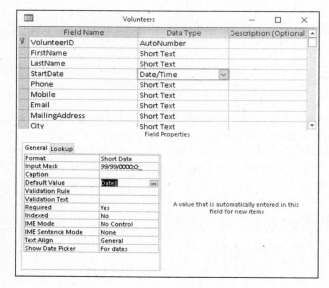

FIGURE 7-11:
The Default Value property set to return the current date with the Date() function.

5. **Click the View button on the Ribbon to switch to Datasheet view and then test your work.**

Here's a quick test: Add a new record, then scroll to the field that contains the default value you just set. Note the contents of the field.

3
Data Management Mania

Contents at a Glance

Chapter **8**

A Form for All Reasons

Access forms are similar to paper forms in their function — they're used in part to collect data — but Access forms go beyond paper forms by having a direct connection to the database tables that store the collected information. Electronic databases such as Access simultaneously place the data typed into an electronic form in the table connected to that form.

Like reports and queries, forms are named and stored in the database file. Forms are full-fledged Access objects, so you can customize them easily to meet the needs of your business.

This chapter shows what forms can do for you, shows you how to make forms, and provides tips for customizing forms so they're exactly what you need.

Generating Forms

Depending on your needs, you can create forms in three ways:

» The Form tools make attractive forms with a click of the mouse.

» The Form Wizard asks some questions and then creates an attractive form based on your answers.

» The Form Design and Blank Form buttons let you start with a blank form and build from the ground up.

TECHNICAL STUFF

WHY USE FORMS?

Access forms have all kinds of advantages when typing data directly into a table — and they'll spoil you if you're used to wandering through your data in Datasheet view (where the data appears in a spreadsheet format).

Here are the most important reasons for using Access forms to manage your data:

- **Say goodbye to Datasheet view:** Maintaining your data in Datasheet view isn't much fun. The constant scrolling back and forth and up and down can drive you crazy. With a form, you focus on one record at a time with all of its data laid out on a single screen. Maintaining your data becomes a snap, and you can watch those datasheet-induced headaches disappear.

- **Modify at will:** When your needs change, update the form in Design view. When you need to collect a new piece of data, just add a field to the appropriate table and to the form associated with that table.

- **See your data any way you want:** Access lets you take one set of data and maintain it with as many different forms as you want. Create a special form for the data-entry department, another for your manager, and a third for yourself. Each form can display just the fields that those people need to see. Well-designed forms give the right information to the right people without revealing unnecessary data.

- **View the entries in a table or the results of a query:** Forms pull information from tables or queries with equal ease.

- **Combine data from multiple tables:** One form can display data from several related tables. Forms automatically use the relationships built into your database. So you can (for example) see a list of volunteers and their corresponding event participation all on one form.

TECHNICAL STUFF

The Form tools and the Form Wizard make it easy to create a form. I focus on using these two methods to build forms. Building forms from scratch in Design or Layout view is beyond the scope of this book.

The Form Wizard and Form tools are a time-saving gift from your friends at Microsoft. Use them to create your forms. They do the hard stuff so all you have to do is provide the finishing touches.

TIP

Use these criteria to determine which form-building tool to use:

» Use the Form tools if:

- You want all fields in the selected table or query to appear on the form.
- You don't want control over the type of style that is applied to the form.

» Use the Form Wizard (covered later in this chapter) if:

- You want to select specific fields for your form.
- You want to select fields from more than one table or query.
- You want to choose from a list of layouts for your form.

Keeping it simple: Form tools

I have good and bad news about these tools:

» **Good news:** They're fast, and they don't ask any questions or talk back!

» **Bad news:** They're extremely inflexible.

  You want a larger font and a different background color? Keep it to yourself. The Form tools decide what font, colors, and layout you get.

TIP

After you create a form with a Form tool, you can *modify* the form. In this chapter, the "Customizing Form Parts" section gives you the straight scoop.

To create a form using one of the Forms tools, open your database and follow these steps:

1. **From the Navigation pane, select the table or query that contains the data your new form should display.**

2. **Click the Create tab on the Ribbon.**

  Several button groups appear on the Ribbon, including the Forms group. (See Figure 8-1.)

Forms group

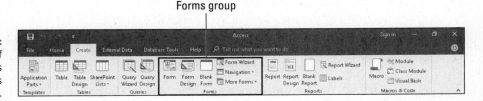

FIGURE 8-1:
The Create tab of the Ribbon holds the Forms buttons.

MEET THE FORM TOOLS

There are three kinds of Form tools:

- **A simple form** displays one record at a time.

  Suppose you have a Locations table and an Events table related by a Location ID field (see Chapter 5 for an explanation of table relationships). If you select the Locations table before you click the Simple Form tool, you get a form that displays not only locations data but also events data for that location.

- **Split forms** display one record on the top half of the form and all records on the bottom half — think a single volunteer record on the top half and the remaining volunteers on the bottom half. Click a volunteer on the bottom half, and you'll see that entire volunteer's record on the top half.

  Use a split form if you want to browse and edit multiple records in a user-friendly fashion. The split-screen format lets you easily browse records in the datasheet portion (bottom half) of the form and see and edit each record's detail in the currently selected record portion (top half) of the form.

- **Multiple Items** shows all records from the data source in a beautiful datasheet-like format.

  Create a Multiple Items form if you want to see all records at a glance. This usually works best with tables that contain only a small number of fields; each field translates into a column on your screen.

3. **Click the form button of your choice from the Forms buttons.**

The Simple Form button is labeled Form. The Multiple Items and Split Form buttons are on the More Forms drop-down list.

TIP

Don't know which Form tool to choose? The sidebar "Meet the Form tools" shows the best Form tool for your data.

A beautiful form appears before your eyes (and in Figure 8-2)!

4. **To finish your form, follow these steps:**

a. *Click the Save button on the Quick Access Toolbar.*

   The Save As dialog box appears.

b. *Type a name for the form in the dialog box, and click OK.*

Your form name appears on the Navigation pane.

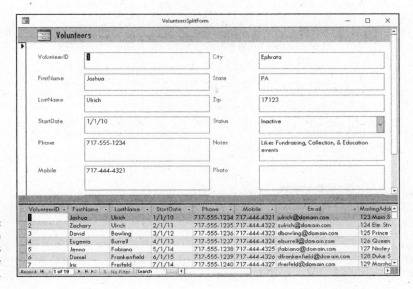

FIGURE 8-2:
Form based on the Volunteers table using the Split Form button.

Granting most wishes: The Form Wizard

When you want to control field selection and the style of form design, use the Form Wizard.

As with all Access wizards, the Form Wizard steps you through the creation process. To use the Form Wizard, follow these steps:

1. **Open your database file.**

2. **Click the Create tab on the Ribbon.**

Several button groups appear on the Ribbon, including the Forms group.

3. **Click the Form Wizard button. (Refer to Figure 8-1.)**

The Form Wizard springs into action, as shown in Figure 8-3.

4. **Using the Tables/Queries drop-down menu, select the source of the form's fields:**

a. Click the down arrow to list the database's tables and queries.

b. Select the table or query that contains the fields you want to view with this form.

The Form Wizard lists the available fields.

5. **Select the fields you want.**

- To select *individual* fields, double-click each field you want in the Available Fields list. (Again, see Figure 8-3.)

- If you want to add *all* the fields from your table or query to your form, click the >> button in the middle of the screen.

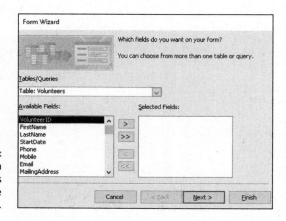

FIGURE 8-3:
Select the data
source and fields
you want to see
on the form.

TIP

Feel free to select fields from different tables, provided the tables are related properly. The wizard will not let you select fields from unrelated tables. For more on relating tables, see Chapter 5, Table Tune Ups.

TIP

To remove a field that you accidentally choose, double-click its name in the Selected Fields list. The field jumps back to the Available Fields side of the dialog box.

6. **After you've selected all the fields you want to include on your form, click Next.**

TECHNICAL
STUFF

If you selected fields from more than one table, the Form Wizard takes a moment to ask how you want to organize the data in your form. If you choose to organize your data by the parent table (Chapter 5 shows how), you'll be asked to show the child table data as either

- *Subform:* Shows data from both tables on one form.

- *Linked form:* Creates a button that, when clicked, will take you to a new form that displays the child table data.

7. **When the wizard asks about the form layout, choose one of the following layouts and then click Next:**

- *Columnar:* Records are shown one at a time.

- *Tabular:* Multiple records are shown at the same time with an attractive style applied to the form.

- *Datasheet:* Multiple records are shown at the same time in a rather unattractive spreadsheet-like way.

TIP

TIP

- *Justified:* Arranges the fields on the form in a tidy block of rows that have pronounced left and right margins.

Don't know which layout is best? Check out the "Giving forms the right look" sidebar.

8. Enter a descriptive title in the What Title Do You Want for Your Form? box at the top of the Form Wizard screen.

There are good reasons to give your form a descriptive title rather than the default name (which is the name of the data source):

- Tables and forms that share the same name can become confusing.

- The name you type is used to save your form. Letters and numbers are allowed in form names. It's a great opportunity to understand form usage through its name.

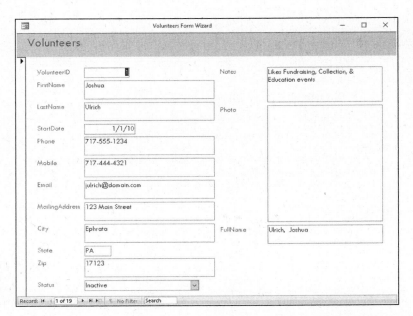

TIP

Before finishing off the Form Wizard, design your new form by clicking the Modify the form's design radio button. If you'd prefer to view it first, leave the default choice (Open the form to view or enter information) that opens the form in Form view.

9. Click Finish to open the form in Form view.

Your new form appears onscreen, as shown in Figure 8-4.

The Form Wizard automatically saves the form as part of the creation process. You don't need to manually save and name it. All saved forms appear in the Forms section of the Navigation pane.

FIGURE 8-4:
Lookin' good. A form created by the Form Wizard.

The rest of this chapter shows how to customize forms you've created with the Form Wizard and Form tools.

GIVING FORMS THE RIGHT LOOK

Depending on the data you select for your form (for example, whether you use more than one table), you have different options for displaying your data:

- **Columnar:** A classic, one-record-per-page form.

  Most data-entry forms are Columnar.

- **Tabular:** A multiple-records-per-page form.

  This layout is best for tables with few fields, like the form based on the AmenitiesList table (shown in the figure to the right). For tables with a larger number of fields, be prepared to scroll back and forth if you select Tabular.

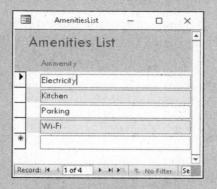

- **Datasheet:** A spreadsheet-like grid.

  Essentially, this is an Access Datasheet view embedded in a form. It's appropriate when an Excel-style presentation suits your needs.

- **Justified:** One record of data is laid out across the whole form over multiple rows (shown in the following figure).

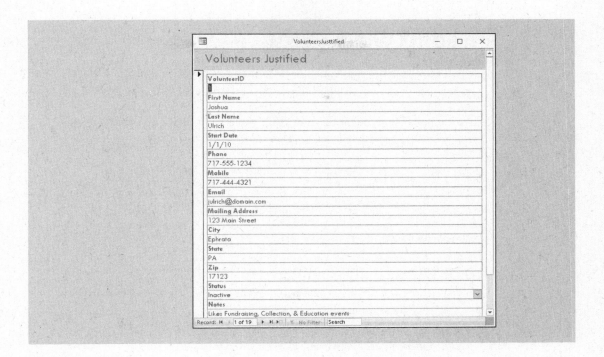

Customizing Form Parts

The Access 2019 Form tools and Form Wizard do a great job building forms. In fact, for the typical user, they do just about everything — but they don't always do it all. So you may need to do some form-tweaking.

If you know some form-design basics, you can clean up most of the problems left behind by the Form tools and Form Wizard.

This section shows how to change the overall look of the form. In particular, you get a handle on moving, sizing, labeling, and formatting *controls* on your forms. (A *control* is any design element on a form — say, a line, label, or data-entry box — that affects the appearance of the form. More about that later in the chapter.)

Taking the Layout view

You can make form-design changes in either Design or Layout view. The sidebar "A form with a view" explains these views.

A FORM WITH A VIEW

Access forms have multiple personalities, all useful: They can be displayed in several ways, called views. Each view serves a purpose in using or maintaining the form.

Use the view buttons on the right side of the status bar to switch between these views. (The following figure shows the Form View tools on the status bar.)

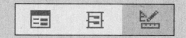

Here are the views:

- **Design:** Sound familiar? Every Access object has its Design view.

  In this view, you can modify the layout and appearance of the objects (called *controls*) on the form.

- **Layout:** Use this view to see data on the form and edit its layout and appearance simultaneously. Now if that isn't fun, I don't know what is!

  This view is very helpful for stuff like sizing controls properly and choosing fonts.

- **Form:** Yes, a form has a Form view. Bizarre but true.

  This view displays the data connected to the form, but unlike Layout view, the design of the form cannot be altered. End users of the database typically see and use all forms in Form view.

These instructions concentrate on Layout view because it's easier to use.

To enter Layout view, follow these steps:

1. **On the Navigation pane, right-click the form you'd like to modify.**

The shortcut menu appears.

2. **Select Layout View from the shortcut menu.**

TIP

How can you tell whether you're in Layout view or Form view? Look at the status bar in the lower left corner of your screen. It tells you the current view for an open form.

The theme's the thing

After building your new form with the Form Wizard or Form tools, you may not like the appearance that the tools have chosen for your form. Fear not! It's easy to change the look of the form by using the Theme group of buttons. Here's how:

1. **From the Navigation pane, right-click the form that needs a new look and choose Layout View from the menu that appears.**

   The form opens in Layout view.

2. **Click the Design tab on the Ribbon.**

   Several button groups appear on the Ribbon, including the Themes group. (See Figure 8-5.)

3. **Click the Themes button.**

   An illustrated list (called a Gallery) of themes opens.

4. **Roll the mouse pointer slowly over each theme.**

   The form in the background changes to match the highlighted theme.

5. **When you've found the theme you like, click it to select it from the drop-down list and apply it to the form.**

Themes group

FIGURE 8-5: The Themes group on the Ribbon.

TIP

Choose a theme with fonts and colors that are easy on the eyes, such as soft colors and simple fonts. Form users will thank you for it!

Managing form controls

A *control* is any design element (such as a line, label, or data-entry text box) that appears on a form. The Form Wizard and Form tools do a fine job of constructing forms but often don't place or size them just right. This section discusses how to take charge of your controls.

Control types

The two most common control types display data pulled from an underlying table or query (as with a text box) or supply a design element to keep the data organized on the form (as with a line).

Here are the most common form controls:

>> **Text box:** The box where you type your data.

Text boxes are either *bound* (a way of saying *linked*) to a table field or *unbound* (containing a calculation derived from other fields in a table, for example).

>> **Label:** The descriptive text next to the control, or the title of the form.

>> **Combo box:** A drop-down list of choices.

>> **List box:** A box that contains a list of choices, from which the user can choose more than one item.

>> **Check box:** A square box attached to a field that can store only true/false, on/off, or yes/no answers. For example, a personnel table may have a field called Married. Either you are or you aren't.

>> **Option Group:** A box that contains related choices where only one choice is allowed. For example, suppose a marital status field contains Married, Single, and Divorced choices. The option group control bound to that field would allow only one of those three choices.

>> **Subform:** A form inside another form.

Subforms usually display the "many" records of the "one" record when tables are in a one-to-many relationship. (For details on table relationships, see Chapter 5.)

TIP

If your form is *columnar* (most are) and you've created it with the Form Wizard or Form tools, all text boxes and labels on the form are *anchored*. Anchored controls behave as a group when you size them. Additionally, you can move anchored controls as long as they're among the other controls in a group; you can't move them if they're outside the group.

Creating controls

Most controls have a Control Wizard associated with them. Once you create the control, the wizard appears and guides you through the process. Here are the general steps to create a control:

1. **From the Navigation pane, right-click the form that's to get the new control and choose Design View.**

2. **Click the Design tab on the Ribbon if necessary.**

The Controls group appears (see Figure 8-6).

3. **From the Controls group, click the appropriate button for the new control (such as combo box) and roll the mouse onto the form.**

The mouse pointer changes to a plus sign and icon of the control selected.

4. **Position the mouse at the location on the form where you'd like the new control to appear, then press and drag diagonally to draw the control.**

The control wizard appears if applicable.

5. **If you've selected a control that has a Control Wizard, follow the steps in the Control Wizard and then click Finish.**

The control appears on the form.

Controls group

FIGURE 8-6:
The Controls
group on the
Ribbon.

TIP

Don't see a Control Wizard after creating a new control? Control Wizards are turned on by default. If, for some reason, yours are not on, choose Use Control Wizards toward the bottom of the Controls group. *Note:* Click the More button (dash with down arrowhead button) located at the lower right of the Controls group to see the Use Control Wizards option (see Figure 8-7).

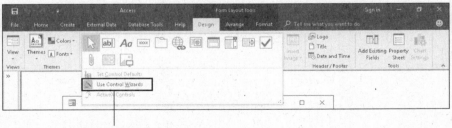

FIGURE 8-7:
If the wizards
aren't coming out
to play, turn
them on!

Control Wizards turned on

Moving controls

To move a control, enter Layout view (as shown previously in this chapter) and then follow these steps:

1. **Put the mouse pointer anywhere on the control that you want to move.**

The mouse pointer changes to a four-headed arrow.

2. **Hold down the left mouse button.**

The control is *selected*, so a thick border appears around it. See Figure 8-8 for an example of a selected control.

To select additional controls such as a label corresponding to a text box, press and hold the Ctrl key while clicking the additional control. A thick border will appear around all selected controls.

3. **Drag the control to its new location.**

A line follows the mouse pointer as you drag up, down, left, or right.

4. **When the control is in position, release the mouse button.**

The control drops smoothly into place.

If you don't like an adjustment you've made, press Ctrl+Z to undo the change and start over from scratch. Access has multiple undo levels, so play to your heart's content; you can always undo any mistakes.

Selected control

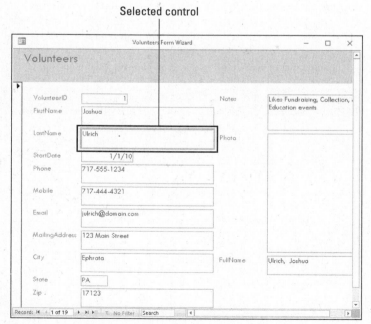

FIGURE 8-8:
A selected control on the Customers form.

Sizing controls

Sometimes the Form Wizard and Form tools fall a bit short (literally) when they're sizing your text boxes and labels. A common problem is that the last part of the information displayed in a label or text box is cut off.

To size a control, enter Layout view (as shown previously in this chapter) and then follow these steps:

1. Put the mouse pointer on the control that you want to size.

The mouse pointer changes to a four-headed arrow. If the controls are anchored, it doesn't matter which control you roll the mouse pointer over.

2. Click to select the control.

A thick border appears around the control to indicate that the control is selected.

3. Move the mouse pointer to the edge of the selected control.

A double-arrow pointer shape appears.

4. Click and drag to resize the control.

TECHNICAL
STUFF

Anchored controls size together horizontally within the same column and vertically within the same row. So when you change the width of one control in a column, all are changed to that same width. When you change the height of one control in a row, all in that row are changed to the same height.

Editing labels

The Form Wizard and Form tools use field names or captions as control labels when they build your forms. If you abbreviated a field name (say, FName for First Name) or caption when creating a table, that abbreviation will become the label for the control created by the Form Wizard and Form tools. So, if a label doesn't quite say what it should, you'll need to know how to edit the text in it.

To edit a label, enter Layout view (as shown previously in this chapter) and try this:

1. Put the mouse pointer anywhere on the label that you want to edit.

The mouse pointer changes to a four-headed arrow.

2. Click to select the label control.

A thick border indicates that the control is selected.

3. Click the word you'd like to edit.

A blinking cursor appears on the word.

4. **Edit the word.**

5. **Click outside of the label control.**

   The label is deselected and the edit is preserved.

Deleting controls

Sometimes an Access form contains an unneeded or unwanted control:

» Maybe you selected an unwanted field while using the Form Wizard.

» Maybe you added a control (such as a line) and in retrospect decided it wasn't needed.

» Maybe you're just tired of looking at that control.

Here's how you remove the control:

1. **In Layout view, put the mouse pointer anywhere on the control that you want to delete.**

   The arrow mouse pointer changes to a four-headed arrow.

2. **Click to select the control.**

   A thick border appears around the control, indicating that it is selected.

3. **Tap the Delete key on your keyboard.**

   The unwanted control disappears into digital oblivion.

TECHNICAL
STUFF

When you delete a text box, its corresponding label will also be deleted. When you delete a label, however, its corresponding text box (if there is one) won't be deleted. Go figure!

Managing Data in Form View

You're done with form design and ready to take it for a drive. This section explains how to move between records, start a new record, and more.

Navigating and finding records

How do you move between records on the form? The Navigation buttons at the lower left of the form (see Figure 8-9) make it easy to

>> **Move between records:** Click the right arrowhead (>) to move forward, the left arrowhead (<) to move backward, the right arrowhead with line (>|) to move to the last record, and the left arrowhead with line (<|) to move to the first record.

>> **Go to a new record:** Click the right arrowhead with asterisk (>*) button to go to a new record.

>> **Search for data:** Type a search word in the Search box and Access will find the first record that contains your search word. For example, type "Prince" in the Search box and Access will dutifully move to the first record that contains the word *Prince*.

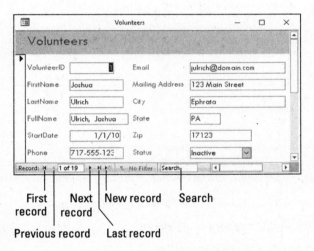

FIGURE 8-9:
Navigation 101.

First record   Next record   New record   Search

Previous record   Last record

Saving, clearing, and deleting

Saving is very confusing to those from the Word and Excel world entering the Access world. In most other programs, you enter something new in a document and click Save to save your work. Access is different. The second you move to a new record or close a form, your good friend Access saves the record for you. So, it's very hard to lose data in Access! Clearing field data and deleting records is not quite so automatic, but that's a good thing.

TIP

If you're the overly cautious type, you can save a record before moving off of it or closing the form by clicking the Save button in the Records group of the Home Ribbon (see Figure 8-10). You can also press Ctrl+S on your keyboard.

Records group

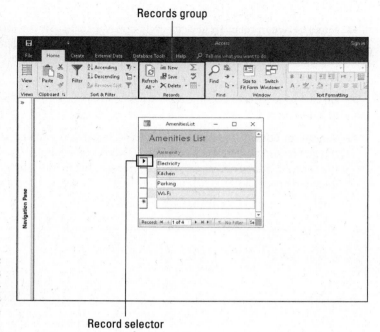

Records group

FIGURE 8-10:
Record selectors
and the ever-
popular Records
group on the
Home Ribbon.

Record selector

To clear the contents of a field, follow these steps:

1. **While in Form view, tab to the field that contains the unwanted data.**

The contents of the field are selected.

2. **Tap the Delete key on your keyboard.**

The contents of the field are deleted.

Here's how to delete an entire record:

1. **While in Form view, navigate to the poor record that will meet its demise.**

2. **Click the Record Selector button located on the left edge of the form (refer to Figure 8-10).**

3. **Click Delete Record in the Records group on the Home tab of the Ribbon.**

Access asks you if you want to delete the record and related records if appropriate.

4. **Click Yes in the confirmation dialog box to delete the record.**

Adios record!

Deleted records can't be undone. Confirm you're on the correct record before you delete, and back up your database file often should you need to restore a deleted record!

WARNING

Chapter **9**

Importing and Exporting Data

I t would be nice if all computer software spoke the same language, but unfortunately this is not the case. Software applications have proprietary languages called *file formats.* Just as a person who speaks only English can't easily communicate with one who speaks only Spanish, software of one file format cannot directly communicate with software of another file format.

If you're a typical business user, you'll come across a situation in which you need some data in your Access database, but it happens to be in another file format. Or you'll get the question, "Can you put that data in a spreadsheet for me so I can play around with it?"

Do you get ready for tedious hours of data reentry? Not with Access! Access provides tools that speak the languages of other software applications. This chapter looks at these *import* and *export* capabilities of Access. If you work with Access and almost any other program, you need this chapter — because sometime soon, you *will* need to move data to and from Access.

TIP

If you'd like to try the import and export techniques described in this chapter, download the sample files used in the chapter at www.dummies.com/go/ access2019. There you'll find the Access database used for the screenshots in the book and a sample spreadsheet to import.

If you're using databases of your own for testing, make copies of your databases *before* trying the techniques in this chapter.

Retrieving Data from Other Sources

Access includes two ways of grabbing data from other applications:

>> **Importing:** This capability translates the data from a foreign format into the Access database file format — and then adds the translated data to an Access table. You can import in one of two ways:

- *Create a new table in an Access database for the data.* You might do this if you're creating a new database and some of your data is already in spreadsheets.

- *Append the data as new records at the end of an existing table.* Perhaps you need to import monthly expense data into your expense reporting database from your credit card company and that data can be provided only in spreadsheet format.

>> **Linking:** Build a temporary bridge between the external data and Access. The data remains at its original source — yet Access can manipulate it just as though it were residing in the source (usually an Access database). When a link is established, it remains until the link is deleted or the source file is moved or deleted.

When you link tables between two Access databases, you can't edit the source table's structure in the destination database (the database that contains the links). You must open the source database to edit the structure of a table linked to a destination database.

Translating data formats

Regardless of whether you import or link the data, Access understands only certain data formats.

Always back up your data before importing, exporting, or mowing the lawn — er, trying anything that could do serious damage to the data. The "I should have backed up" lesson is one of the most painful to learn — and one of the most common. Make a copy of your database *before* trying the techniques in this chapter.

Tables 9-1 (files), 9-2 (databases), 9-3 (online services), and 9-4 (other sources) list the data formats that Access can understand. These tables cover the vast majority of data formats used all over the world.

TABLE 9-1   ## Files

Program	File Extension	Versions	Comments
Excel	.XLS, .XLSX, .XLSB, .XLSM	9.0/2000, 10.0/2002, 2003, 2007, 2010, 2013, 2016, 2019	Although Excel is a spreadsheet program, many people use it as a simple flat-file database manager. See Chapter 3 for more on flat-file databases.
HTML	.HTM, .HTML	All	The descriptive codes that make a web page a web page.
XML	.XML	All	XML (eXtensible Markup Language) stores and describes data.
Text	.TXT	n/a	Plain text, the "if all else fails" format; Access understands both delimited and fixed-width text files.

TABLE 9-2   ## Compatible Database File Formats

Program	File Extension	Versions	Comments
Access	.MDB, .ADP, .MDA, .MDE., .ADE, .ACCDB, .ACCDA, .ACCDE	9.0/2000, 10.0/2002, 2003, 2007, 2010, 2013, 2016, 2019	Although they share the same name, these versions use different file formats.
Azure	n/a	n/a	Microsoft's cloud (web hosted) database.
Outlook/ Exchange	n/a	n/a	Link your Outlook or Exchange folder straight to an Access database.
dBASE	.DBF	All versions	Many programs use the dBASE format.

TABLE 9-3   ## Online Services

Program	File Extension	Versions	Comments
Dynamics 365	n/a	n/a	Web-based planning and contact management application
SharePoint list	n/a	n/a	Collaborative software using web-based data
Salesforce	n/a	n/a	Web-based customer relationship management application

TABLE 9-4 **Other Sources**

Program	File Extension	Versions	Comments
ODBC	n/a	n/a	Use ODBC (Open Database Connectivity) to connect to other databases, such as Oracle and SQL Server.
Outlook/ Exchange	n/a	n/a	Link your Outlook or Exchange folder straight to an Access database.

Here is some additional information on how to prepare the most common import file formats so that your import will go smoothly. I don't mention prepping other database formats because, typically, no preparation is needed. I'll get to the step-by-step instructions on importing (see "Importing and linking") and exporting (see "Hit the Road, Data") later in this chapter.

Spreadsheets

When you import a spreadsheet file, each spreadsheet *column* becomes an Access table *field:*

>> **The first row in the spreadsheet (the *column headings*) becomes the field *names*.**

TECHNICAL STUFF

If you want to use the first row for field names, you must check the First Row Contains Column Headings check box during the import process.

An ideal spreadsheet for import will have field names in Row 1.

>> **Each following row becomes a *record* in the Access table.**

An ideal spreadsheet for import will have data starting in Row 2.

WARNING

When you import data from spreadsheets, watch for these quirks:

>> **Double-check spreadsheet data to be sure that it's *consistent* and *complete*.**

>> **Make sure that all entries in each spreadsheet column (field) are the same *data type* (numbers, text, or whatever).**

>> **Remove *titles* and *blank rows* from the top of the spreadsheet.**

>> **Make your spreadsheet column headings *short* and *unique*.**

Shorten your spreadsheet column headings to the field names you'd like Access to use so you don't get scolded during import about field name issues.

>> **If you're adding data to an *existing Access table*, make sure the spreadsheet columns are of the same number and in the same order as the Access table fields.**

Your spreadsheet columns and table fields must line up exactly.

Text files

If you have difficulty importing a format (such as an Excel spreadsheet) into Access, you may be able to import the data as text. Text is the most widely recognized form of data known to man (or computer). Try these steps to import the data as text:

1. **Open the file with the existing software product (like Excel).**

2. **Use the existing product's exporting tools or Save As command to export your data into a text file.**

TECHNICAL STUFF

A *delimited* text file is preferred if the existing product supports this type of text file. A delimited file contains a marker character (such as a comma) to separate each field from the next so Access can easily understand where one field ends and another begins.

3. **Import the text file into Access (as shown later in this chapter).**

Importing and linking

Because Access offers two ways to get existing data in — linking and importing — a logical question comes up: Which method should you use? The method depends on the situation:

>> **Link:** If the data in the other program must remain in that program, link to the source.

If the data is in a SQL Server database that's a permanent business fixture, it's not going anywhere; link to the source.

>> **Import:** If you want the database in which you're placing the data to *replace* the source, then import. This is the option for you if you're creating an Access database to replace an old spreadsheet that no longer meets your needs. Also import if the source data is supplied by an outside vendor in a format other than an Access format. For example, suppose you receive historical trend data from an outside vendor monthly in spreadsheet format. Access is a great tool for reporting, so you can import the data into Access and use its reporting tools to generate your reports.

The following section shows how to link and import data from the file formats discussed in the previous sections of this chapter.

Steps for importing

Here are the steps for importing or linking data sources to your Access database:

1. **Open the Access database that will hold the imported data.**

2. **Click the External Data tab on the Ribbon.**

The Import & Link group of buttons appears on the Ribbon (see Figure 9-1).

Import & Link group

3. **Click the New Data Source button.**

A list of data source categories appears, such as From File and From Database.

4. **Select the category as described in the "Translating data formats" section previously in this chapter.**

A Get External Data dialog box specific to the selected file format appears onscreen. (See Figure 9-2.)

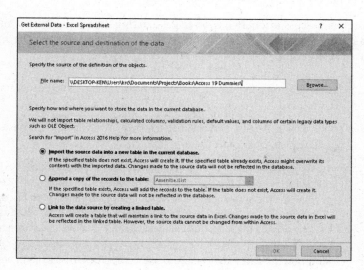

5. **Use the Browse button to select the data source that you want to import or link to Access.**

This could be a file, website, or an Outlook folder.

6. **Select the method of data storage.**

This is where you tell Access whether to *import* or *link* the data. You can link to most data formats except XML.

The sidebar "Storing data from external data sources" shows the common data storage options.

7. **Follow the remaining steps in the Get External Data dialog box.**

From this point forward, the steps depend on which data format you're importing. Follow the prompts carefully. The worst that can happen is that you get an imported (or linked) table full of gibberish. If you do, check the format of the source file. For example, if the source is a text file and you get gibberish, you may need to confirm that the text file was saved as a *delimited* file (with a character — a comma, for example — placed between fields). It's also possible that the source file isn't in the correct format (for example, you may think it's an Excel spreadsheet but it's not).

TIP

If you expect to import or link to this data format often, click the Save Import Steps check box. (The check box will be located on the last screen of the wizard.) After you check the box, you'll be prompted for a name for your import and a description of it, as shown in Figure 9-3.

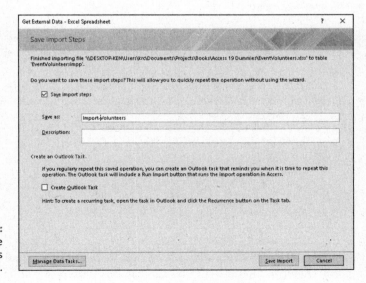

FIGURE 9-3:
Saving the
Volunteers
import steps.

STORING DATA FROM EXTERNAL DATA SOURCES

When you select a method of data storage, most of the Get External Data dialog boxes ask you to select from the following storage methods:

Import the source data into a new table in the current database. This means creating a new table from the imported data.

Access warns you that this choice could overwrite an existing table with the same name as the imported data's filename. For example, if you have a Volunteers table in your database and an Excel spreadsheet with Volunteer data (the first tab name is Volunteers in the spreadsheet), then Access will prompt you to overwrite (replace) the existing table. So, be careful when importing!

Append a copy of the records to the table. This choice adds the imported data to the end of existing records in an existing table.

When you append, make sure that the import file and the existing table have

- The same number of columns
- The same order of columns
- The same data types
- The same field names

Link to the data source by creating a linked table. Access creates a table that manages the data in the external file. Depending on the source, the link may be either of the following:

- *Two-way link.* Edits in *either* data source (the internal Access file or the external data source) automatically appear in *both*.

  A link to another Access data source is an example of a two-way link.

- *One-way link.* You can change the data in the external source but not in Access.

  A spreadsheet link is a one-way link. You can change the data in the spreadsheet but not in the Access table linked to the spreadsheet.

TIP

The External Data tab's Import group on the Ribbon contains a button called Saved Imports. (Refer to Figure 9-1.) You can use this button to call up saved imports and run them as often as you like. (See Figure 9-4.) Data sources must remain in their original locations with their original names to rerun a saved import.

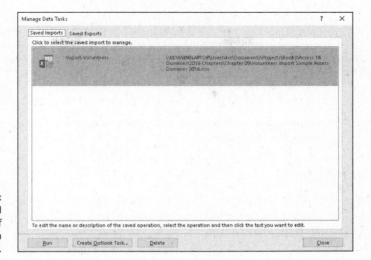

FIGURE 9-4:
The Saved
Imports tab of
the Manage Data
Tasks dialog box.

Troubleshooting

During the import or linking process, Access may have difficulties. If it does, you'll know — either the import or linking process will take a noticeably long time to finish or Access will display an error message. This section describes some common problems that crop up during importing and linking — and how to fix these problems.

SLOW IMPORTS AND LINKS

If importing is taking forever, Access is probably struggling with errors in the inbound data. Follow these steps to troubleshoot the problem:

1. **Press Ctrl+Break to stop the import process.**

   If your device does not have a Break key, consult its documentation for the proper key sequence to implement the Break command. For example, on some laptops it's the Fn+F6 key, so to stop the import process, you'd press Ctrl+Fn+F6.

2. **Open the source file in its native application and check the data that's being imported for problems, such as**

   - *Corrupt data.* The file you're attempting to import may be unusable.

   - *Badly organized spreadsheet data.* See the Spreadsheets section of the "Translating data formats" section earlier in this chapter for tips on a properly organized spreadsheet.

- *An invalid index.* Sometimes database indexes become corrupt, making the data within the table with the corrupt index unusable. Access will usually holler at you when you open the source table that contains the invalid index. For more on indexes, see Chapter 5.

3. **Make any necessary changes, and then save the corrected source file.**

4. **Start the import or linking process again, as outlined in the previous section of the chapter.**

BAD DATA

If the imported table barely resembles the source, delete the imported table from Access, open the source file in its native program, and clean up the data before importing again.

TIP

Follow the tips in the earlier section, "Translating data formats," to clean up your data.

Hit the Road, Data

Every Access object can be exported; the most common export tasks are exporting data in a table or query to another program (such as a spreadsheet) and exporting a report as a Portable Document Format (commonly known as a PDF). Therefore, this section concentrates on exporting table and query data to other file formats and exporting reports.

Exporting a table or query involves reorganizing the data it contains into a different format. As with importing, Access can translate the data into a variety of file formats, depending on your needs.

REMEMBER

Because every Access object can be exported, the External Data tab on the Ribbon presents you with all the file formats in which the object can be exported. If you can't export it to a certain format, that format's button is disabled.

Export formats

Access exports to the same formats that it imports (as listed earlier in the chapter). Access also exports to PDF (Adobe Acrobat files), XPS (XML Paper Specification), Microsoft Word, and to an email attachment.

Exporting table or query data

The steps to exporting a table or query are simple:

1. **With the database open, click the table or query that you want to export. All database objects are located in the Navigation pane.**

   The table or query name is highlighted.

2. **Click the External Data tab on the Ribbon.**

   The Export button group appears on the Ribbon. (See Figure 9-5.) Note the following features of the Export button group:

   - The common exporting tasks have their own buttons.
   - The seldom-used formats are lumped together; you can get at them with the More button.

Export group

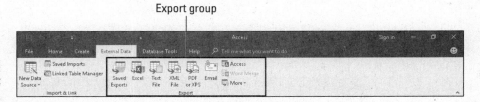

FIGURE 9-5:
The Export button group.

3. **Click the button that matches the program to which you'll export your data.**

   An Export dialog box (see Figure 9-6) customized to your format of choice appears.

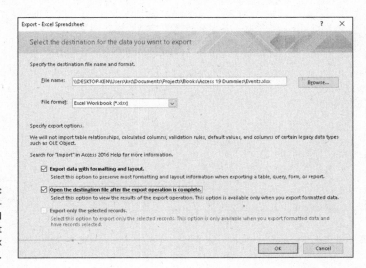

FIGURE 9-6:
The Export – Excel Spreadsheet dialog box completed.

4. Follow the steps in the Export dialog box to complete the export.

The Export dialog box displays the choices for your export file's format:

- Every choice asks for a filename (including path) for your exported data.

- Some export processes also ask whether you want to open your new file after the export is complete.

  This latter feature can prevent a frustrating search after you save the file. Try it, you'll like it!

TIP

5. Select the Save Export Steps check box if you know you'll do this export again.

The check box is located on the last screen of the Export Wizard. After you check the box, you'll be prompted for a name for your export.

The Ribbon contains a button called Saved Exports. (Refer to Figure 9-5.) Use this button if you want to make the frequent export of a table or query easier. Figure 9-7 shows a table exported from Access as it appears in Excel. When you run a saved export more than once, Access tells you that the destination file already exists.

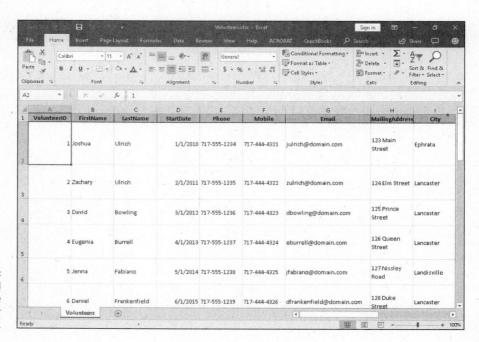

FIGURE 9-7:
The exported Volunteers table in Excel, ready for anything.

Exporting a report to PDF

Follow these steps to export a report to PDF:

1. **With the database open, click the report that you want to export. All database objects are located in the Navigation pane.**

   The report name is highlighted.

2. **Click the External Data tab on the Ribbon.**

   The Export button group appears on the Ribbon.

3. **Click the PDF or XPS button in the Export group.**

   The Publish as PDF or XPS dialog box appears (see Figure 9-8).

4. **Browse to the folder you'd like to store the file in and type a file name in the File name box.**

5. **Click Publish.**

   The report is saved as a PDF to the folder and with the file name you specified.

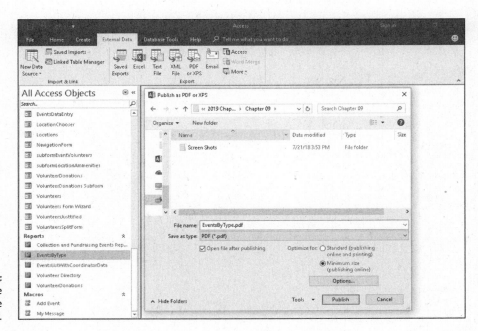

FIGURE 9-8:
Exporting the Events by Type report to PDF.

» Replacing data automatically

» Finding unwanted duplications in your data

Chapter 10

Automatically Editing Data

Correcting an incorrect entry in an Access table is pretty easy: A few clicks, some typing, and voilà — the problem is gone. But what if you need to correct 26,281 records? Manually editing so many records would involve an eternity of clicking and typing and hardly qualifies to end in a victorious "Voilà!"

Fortunately, Access offers some handy, large-scale editing tools you can use to make big changes to your database — all without wearing out your keyboard, mouse, or fingertips.

Please Read This First!

WARNING

After a heading like that, it cannot be a mystery to you that I think you really need to read this section. Why? Because the fact that you're reading this tells me you're a careful person who follows advice and instructions. These traits are the key to managing thousands of records, keeping them accurate and up-to-date, and making the types of corrections I talk about in this chapter.

Why do I sound so serious, all of the sudden? Well, when you're making large-scale changes to a database, things can go wrong and mistakes can be made. If you're going to do anything major to your database — especially if you're editing and/or deleting a whole lot of records — you want a backup there behind you; if you do make a mistake and wipe out the wrong records, or edit something that should have been left alone, you can easily go back to the original version of the database and start over.

It's a wise Access user who makes a backup of his or her database table or tables before starting any task that involves a margin for error. Here's how you back up the table you want to edit:

1. Open the database file that contains the table you want to edit.

The list of tables in the database appears on the left side of the window.

2. Right-click the table name in the All Access Objects list on the left.

3. Choose Copy from the pop-up menu that appears (see Figure 10-1).

Access places a copy of the table on the Windows Clipboard.

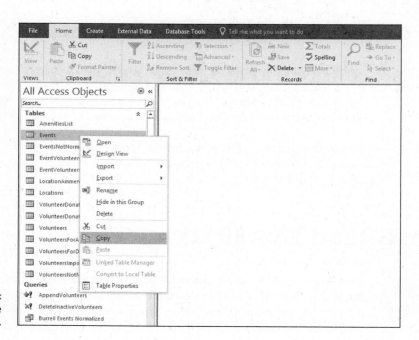

FIGURE 10-1:
Copy that table
for safekeeping.

4. Right-click anywhere below the list of tables, reports, and so on in the left-side panel (as shown in Figure 10-2).

A pop-up menu appears.

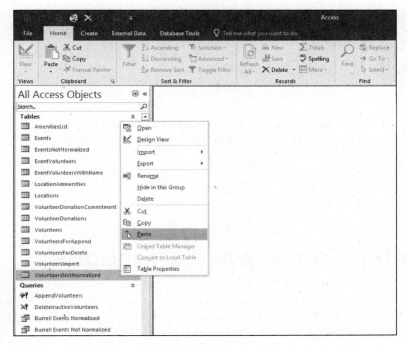

FIGURE 10-2:
Choose Paste to make a backup version of the table.

5. **Choose Paste from the pop-up menu.**

The Paste Table As dialog box appears, as shown in Figure 10-3. It offers choices for how to paste your copied table data, but you don't really need to worry about them at this point.

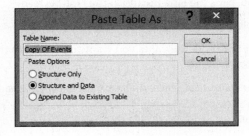

FIGURE 10-3:
The Paste Table As dialog box.

6. **Type a name for the new table into the dialog box's Table Name field.**

Access suggests "Copy of ____," where the blank is the current table name (which might be a good choice).

7. **Click OK.**

TIP

Don't worry about the options in the dialog box. The default setting (Structure and Data) works just fine.

The dialog box closes, and you now have a copy of the original table.

With your table copy there to support you, you now have a backup — something to go back to should any of the steps in the rest of this chapter go awry when you apply them to your data.

Backup at the ready, it's time to move on and start editing your database — automatically.

Creating Consistent Corrections

Automated editing queries have a lot of power. But before you haul out the *really* big guns, here's a technique for small-scale editing. The technique may seem simplistic, but don't be fooled; it's really very handy.

You can practice small-scale editing by using the Replace command as follows:

1. **Open a table in Datasheet view.**

2. **Click in the field you want to edit — it doesn't matter which row you're in; just be in any record, in the field you want to edit.**

3. **On the Home tab, click the Find button in the Find section.**

The Find and Replace dialog box appears, as shown in Figure 10-4.

4. **In the Find What box, type the value you want to change. In the Replace With box, type a new value.**

With this information in place, you're ready to start making changes. Note that the Look In setting defaults to Current Field, which is why you clicked as instructed in Step 2.

5. **(Optional) Click the Look In drop-down list to choose a different field in which to search.**

The Find and Replace dialog box assumes you want to search and make changes to the active table (or form, report, or query, whatever's the open and active part of your database). As mentioned previously, it defaults to searching the current field, but you can click the Look In drop-down list and choose Current Document instead, which means to search all fields in the active table, form, report, or query.

6. **Click one of the buttons on the right side of the dialog box to apply the changes to your table.**

   - **To find the next record to change, click Find Next.** The cursor jumps to the next record in the table that contains the text you entered in the Find What box. No changes get made at this point — Access only finds a matching candidate. To make a change, click the Replace button, explained next.

   - **To apply your change to the current record, click Replace.** This makes the change *and* moves the cursor to the next matching record in the database. Click Replace again to continue the process. To skip a record without changing it, click Find Next.

   - **To make the change *everywhere* in the current field, click the Replace All button.** Access won't ask about each individual change. The program assumes that it has your permission to correct everything it finds. Don't choose this option unless you are *absolutely certain* that you want the change made everywhere.

WARNING

The moment you click either the Replace or Replace All button, Access *permanently* changes the data in your table. Access lets you undo only the last change you made, so if you clicked Replace All and updated 12,528 records, Access lets you undo only the very last record that you changed — the other 12,527 records stay in their new form. This, dear reader, is why we started out making a backup!

7. **When you finish, click Cancel or the X button in the top right corner of the dialog box.**

   The Find and Replace dialog box closes.

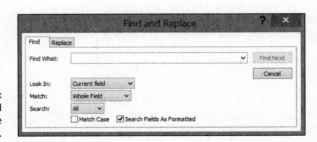

FIGURE 10-4:
The Find and Replace dialog box.

TIP

One of the most common reasons to use Find and Replace is to correct a misspelling. We all hate it when we make such a mistake, but we hate it less when the solution is as simple as making Access go look for the error and replace it with the correction, utilizing the very powerful Find tools we've been discussing in this section. So . . . if you misspell a word, any word, throughout your data and need to change all its occurrences to the proper spelling, follow these steps:

1. **Open the Find and Replace dialog box.**

2. **On the Find tab in the dialog box, type the incorrect spelling in the Find What box.**

3. **Type the proper spelling in the Replace With box.**

4. **Click the Replace All button.**

   Your computer goes off and does your bidding, changing each instance of the word in the Find What box to the word in the Replace With box.

Access gives you a lot of control over the process. In addition to the options of the Find command (discussed in Chapter 12), Replace allows you to change what you found to what you need in its place, making use of the following options to fine-tune what's found:

» **Match Whole Field:** Selected by default, Whole Field (in the Match drop-down list) makes Access look only for cases in which the information in the Find What box *completely matches* an entry in the table. That is, if the data in your table includes any additional characters in the field — even a single letter — Match Whole Field tells Access to skip it.

» **Match Any Part of Field:** If you select Any Part of Field from the Match drop-down list, Access performs the replace action whenever it finds the text in *any portion* of the matching text in the field. For example, this setting picks the area code out of a phone number. Unfortunately, it also replaces those same three numbers if they appear anywhere else in the phone number, too.

» **Match Start of Field:** If you choose Start of Field from the Match drop-down list, Access replaces the matching text only if it appears at the beginning of the field. This option could replace only the area code in a series of phone numbers without touching the rest of the numbers.

WARNING

If your editing goes awry, remember that the wonderful Undo option corrects only the *very last record* that Access changed. Just click the Undo button on the Quick Access Toolbar or press Ctrl+Z.

Using Queries to Automate the Editing Process

Queries, especially those created through the Query Wizard, are exceptionally easy to create (as you discover in Chapter 13). In this chapter, you create a very simple and specific query not created elsewhere in the book — a query designed specifically to look for duplicate records.

But what about correcting those 26,281 records? If Find and Replace doesn't solve the problem, you're looking at some serious querying (a topic covered in Chapters 12 through 17), and you may find that creating a single query that fixes all the problems is impossible.

Therefore, be prepared to use a combination of things: Create a query that seeks out certain issues, do some editing of individual records, and use Find and Replace procedures to locate consistent errors and replace them with something you can spot easily, like every place someone doing data entry placed an "X" to indicate they didn't know what to enter or didn't have the data to enter for a given field. This is kind of a twist on using Find and Replace to fix spelling errors (covered previously in this chapter), but instead of fixing an error, you're using Replace to flag certain records for editing.

Generally, however, Find and Replace will do what you need because a universal misspelling, a bunch of zip codes entered accidentally into the wrong numeric field — or any repeated error of that sort — can be fixed pretty quickly by searching for the erroneous content and replacing it with what should be there instead. With a backup copy of your table preserved for safekeeping (you *did* read the "Please Read This First!" section, didn't you?), feel free to experiment with Find and Replace and even some queries that you make on your own.

Looking for duplicate records

Let's get back to that duplicate records query. What, exactly, *is* a duplicate record? You will have duplicated data in your database — people who live in the same city, for example, will have the same city in their records in the `City` field. Products that have the same price, or that come in the same colors, will have the same data in some or nearly all of their fields. What I mean here by a duplicate *record* is an entire record that is an exact duplicate — every field is the same in one record as it is in another record (or in several others, as the case may be).

How do duplicate records get made? It can happen quite easily:

>> It happens a lot when more than one person is doing data entry; two or more people might have the same list or stack of cards or other source of data that's being keyed into your Access table.

>> If you're relying on an Excel worksheet as the source of the table data, or if some other electronic source is providing the records, accidental duplication is still a common risk; it's just as easy to paste the same rows of data into the table twice as it is to enter the same records twice manually. Maybe easier.

TIP

Duplicate records waste time and money. If you think that it's no big deal to have the same person entered into your database three times, or that the record for your Green Widget with the Deluxe Carrying Case is in the database twice, consider the extra postage you would spend mailing a catalog more than once to the people who appear in the database multiple times, or the confusion when only one instance of a product is updated to reflect a price increase. Which record is correct after they're no longer identical? So it's a good idea not only to be vigilant about avoiding duplicates from the beginning, but also to ferret them out and get rid of them whenever they're found.

Running the Find Duplicates Query Wizard

The Find Duplicates Query Wizard can help you spot that common curse of the database: duplicate records. Duplicates waste time and money, especially when the database is used for mailings or some similar business activities. This wizard can help your database clean up its act.

To run the Find Duplicates Query Wizard, follow these simple steps:

1. **Click the Ribbon's Create tab.**

   The Create tab's sections — Templates, Tables, Queries, Forms, Reports, and Macros & Code — appear.

2. **Click the Query Wizard button, found in the Queries section.**

   The New Query dialog box opens, as shown in Figure 10-5.

3. **Choose the Find Duplicates Query Wizard from the list of available wizards.**

   A description of the wizard's function appears on the left side of the dialog box.

4. **Click OK.**

   The original Query Wizard dialog box closes and is replaced by the Find Duplicates Query Wizard dialog box, shown in Figure 10-6.

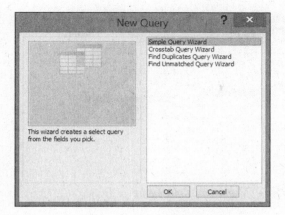

FIGURE 10-5:
The Query
Wizard is here
to help you.

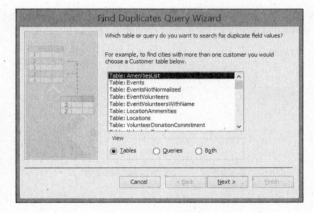

FIGURE 10-6:
The Find
Duplicates
Query Wizard
takes you
through
duplicate-finding
steps.

5. **Choose the table in which you want to search for duplicates.**

- Notice that in the View area, you can choose to see Tables, Queries, or Both, so if this isn't your first query or if another user has created one for you, you can certainly search an existing query's results for duplicates, too.

- If this is your first query, and your data is only in tables that you or someone else made, simply leave Tables selected in the View area.

You'll also see your backup copy of the table in this list, so be sure you pick the right table and don't start operating on your backup!

TIP

6. **Click Next.**

In the Available Fields list (see Figure 10-7), double-click those fields you're worried could have duplicate entries in them. Skip fields that are supposed to have duplicates anyway or where duplicates, however unlikely, are no problem — such as cities, states, zip codes, or last names. You can also skip your primary key field, because by its very nature (as a field containing unique data for each record), it won't have any duplicate values.

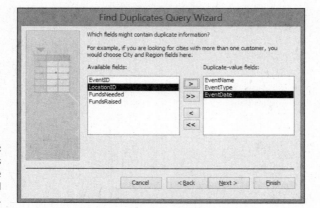

FIGURE 10-7:
Pick the fields
that might have
unwanted
duplicate entries.

7. **When the Duplicate-Value Fields list is populated with those fields that you want the query to look in, click Next.**

   The next step in the wizard appears, as shown in Figure 10-8.

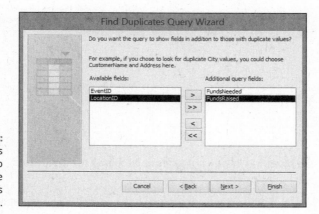

FIGURE 10-8:
Pick the fields
that will help
you choose
which duplicates
to keep.

8. **From the Available Fields list, double-click those fields you want to include in the query's results in addition to those with duplicate values.**

   Such fields typically include those that help you identify records that are harboring duplicate data, such as First Name if you're looking for records that might have identical Last Names, or Product Numbers if you're looking for products that have the same description or price. In this example, I am looking for duplicate records in a customer table, which will prevent mailings going out to anyone more than once (or at an old and a new address for the same person).

9. **Click Next.**

   The last step in the Find Duplicates Query Wizard appears, as shown in Figure 10-9. Here's where you decide on a name for your new query.

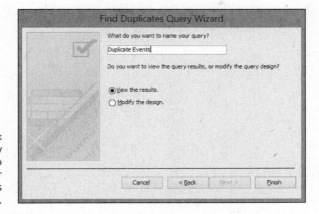

FIGURE 10-9:
Name your query and finish it so you can see your duplicates onscreen.

10. **If you don't like the default name Access gave your query, just enter a new name into the text field.**

    Preferably, the name should be short but should identify the query's purpose — Duplicate Names Query is a good name for this example. The default query name that Access offers will be "Find duplicates for ____," where the blank is the name of the table searched for duplicates.

11. **Click Finish.**

    The results of your query appear onscreen, as shown in Figure 10-10.

Now that you know which records have duplicate data within them, you can

>> **Edit them individually.** Just click within the records shown as duplicates and make changes to names, addresses, or whatever else might be incorrect, if an error is the cause of the duplication.

>> **Use Find and Replace.** Use on the query results to make more targeted changes, such as taking all records with a particular word in a particular field and either

   • Change that word to something else

   or

   • Append a character or digit to that entry to make it different from the others.

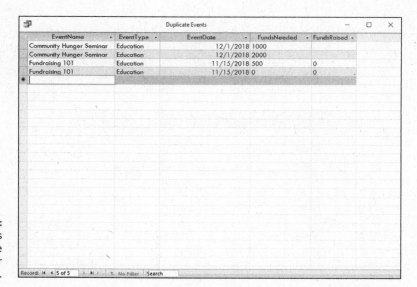

FIGURE 10-10: All these records have duplicate entries in one or more fields.

>> **Delete the unwanted records.** To do so, simply click the leftmost cell in the row for the unwanted record (the entire record/row will be selected) and then press the Delete key. Of course, be careful not to delete both records — you only want to delete the unwanted duplicate!

You'll be asked to confirm your deletion, and you can choose Yes if you do want to get rid of the extra record.

Chapter **11**

Access and the Web

Access can be a great resource for Internet and intranet information. If the data you're working with really needs global exposure — or if you simply want to reach your data from anywhere you might be — Access 2019 (and the entire Office suite, for that matter) is ready to help. In fact, a connection to all things web-related has been a priority for Microsoft as each new version of Office has been released over the years, and Office 365 takes that to a whole new level with the suite's new connection to the cloud.

In this chapter, I explain the Office connection to the cloud and discuss the overall capabilities of Access with regard to the web. Then you'll find out how to build and use a web app, and finally, how to use hyperlinks within your Access desktop application. The hyperlink section of this chapter applies to the desktop version of Access 2019.

How Access Works with the Web

It's almost a requirement these days that software be web-ready, or at least web-friendly. Even word processors — which should never be used to create a web page — contain "Save for Web" commands, and graphics software can help you create web-ready images.

Of course, Access is a natural fit for the web because data is something we've all come to expect to find online. Access makes it easy to both export your data to the web, using External Database Tools, and to embed Web content on Access forms or reports, or simply upload your existing desktop database tables. By putting your tables on the Web, you can link back to them in your desktop database. Your data now sits in the cloud available to any computer with an Internet connection.

TECHNICAL
STUFF

To make Access do its Internet tricks, you should have or be able to obtain:

>> A connection to the Internet

>> A subscription to Office 365 for Business that includes SharePoint Online for each user of the database

>> The web address to the SharePoint Online site that will host your data

TECHNICAL
STUFF

Don't know how to set up a SharePoint Online site? Search the web for *create a SharePoint Online team site*. The first page in the search results should be from support.microsoft.com which will have what you need. After you set it up, note the name of the team site because you'll need it later.

Understanding Office 365

Office 365 is not the same thing as Office 2019. Office 2019 is just the combined suite of applications — Word, Excel, PowerPoint, Outlook, and Access for the desktop computer. Office 365 is a subscription-based set of tools that enables companies to collaborate and share their data online. Most Office 365 subscriptions come with all the desktop office applications but not the other way around.

Microsoft offers a variety of monthly fee-based plans for businesses of all shapes and sizes, providing a variety of options. You can investigate these plans by searching the web for "compare office 365 plans" and choosing the right plan for you.

Now, this is not to say that you have to use Office 365, because you absolutely do not. You can use Office 2019's applications without setting foot on the cloud, and install the applications locally. You don't need to put your Office data (documents, worksheets, presentations, and so on) in the cloud if you don't want to. You can store your data locally, just as you always have. In fact, everything done in this book was done with a locally installed copy of Access 2019.

TECHNICAL STUFF

Whether you're planning to use it or not, you're probably asking, "What is the cloud?" The term *the cloud* simply describes services that are hosted outside of your organization, using the web. You may already be using the cloud, because lots of services you use all the time are part of the cloud — things like social media, web-based email, mobile banking, and online data storage services. Because this data is located online, you can access it from just about anywhere, using any PC, laptop, tablet, or mobile device.

When it comes to Office 365, the cloud also provides online versions of your software, meaning that you can work with most of the Office applications online, instead of from locally installed copies. This is where the fee-based subscription plans come into play — along with sharing options for online collaboration with co-workers and clients anywhere in the world. Office 365 makes it easy to collaborate on and share a Word document or Excel spreadsheet. Oddly, Access is not one of those applications with a companion online version. Access does make use of the web, however, as you'll soon see.

TECHNICAL STUFF

Perhaps you've heard about Access web apps (a type of Access database that sits in the cloud) and are wondering what happened to them. In early 2018, Microsoft eliminated support for Access web apps and instead recommends using Power-Shell. Creating a PowerShell application is beyond the scope of this book.

Connect Office 365 to Access 2019

As mentioned earlier, you can host your Access data on an Office 365 SharePoint site in the cloud. To begin, connect Access 2019 to your Office 365 account.

1. **Click Sign in to get the most out of Office near the right end of the screen (see Figure 11-1).**

The Sign in dialog box appears.

2. **Type the email address associated with your Office 365 account and click Next.**

3. **Type the password associated with the account and click Sign In.**

You'll see the name associated with the account at the right end of the Ribbon in place of the words *Sign In*. Now you're ready to upload your data.

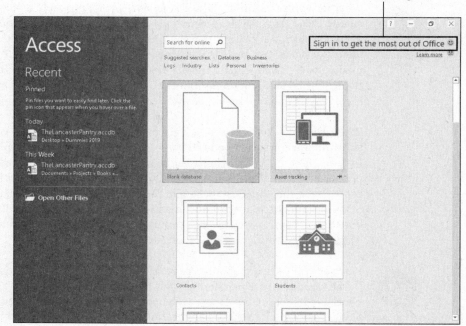

Click here to sign in.

Your data and the cloud

It is possible to upload tables to the cloud from your desktop database and then link to those tables. This means your data is in one place (cloud) and you can access it from the desktop database on your computer, and others in your organization can access that data from their computers. This is a very important piece of information to know before planning and building your database. If you have multiple people using your database and one or more of them are often out of the office, putting your data in the cloud might be just right for you. Just find an internet connection and your data will always be there on the road with you and everyone else using the database. If your data is not in the cloud, each user will either need to be in the office or remotely connected to a computer that is in the office to use your database.

WARNING

Putting your data in the cloud means that it will have to travel over the information highway to and from your computer. This will slow the performance of your database. If your tables contain tens of thousands of records or your database crunches lots of data, SharePoint may not be the way to go for you.

Upload your Access desktop data to the cloud

Enough of the chatter, right? Here's how to upload desktop database tables to SharePoint Online:

1. **Open the desktop database that contains the tables you want to upload to the cloud.**

2. **Select the Database Tools tab on the Ribbon.**

3. **In the Move Data group, click SharePoint.**

   The Export Tables to SharePoint Wizard dialog box opens (see Figure 11-2).

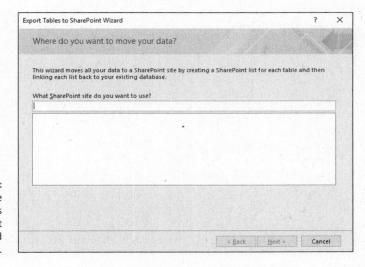

FIGURE 11-2:
Please welcome the Export Tables to SharePoint Wizard dialog box.

4. **In the What SharePoint Site Do You Want to Use text box, type the address (URL) to your SharePoint Online site (see Figure 11-3).**

   The SharePoint Online URL will typically be the name you gave to your SharePoint Online team site followed by sharepoint.com. For example, if your team name is AccessDummies, your SharePoint Online URL will be access-dummies.sharepoint.com.

TECHNICAL STUFF

   SharePoint Online calls a table a list. From my way of thinking, a table should just be a table but in the SharePoint world, it's not. It's a list. What can I say?

5. **Click Next.**

   Things start happening! The wizard begins moving tables from your desktop database to the cloud (see Figure 11-4).

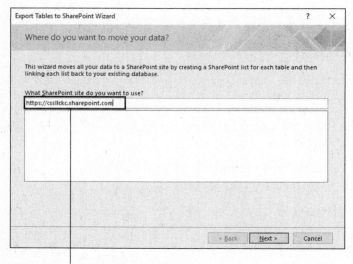

FIGURE 11-3:
Enter your
SharePoint
Online URL.

Enter your SharePoint site URL here.

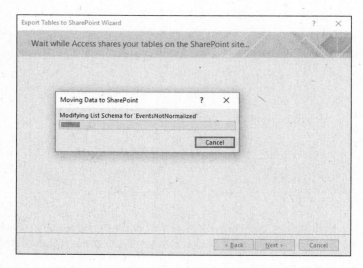

FIGURE 11-4:
Tables floating up
to the cloud!

6. **Click the Show Details check box.**

The wizard summarizes what it did (see Figure 11-5).

TECHNICAL
STUFF

Besides moving your tables to the cloud, the wizard creates a backup copy of
your original database, using the same file name as the original, then cleverly
adding "_backup" to the end of the name. It then deletes the tables in your
original database and links to the new tables in the cloud all without you lifting
a finger. What a wizard indeed!

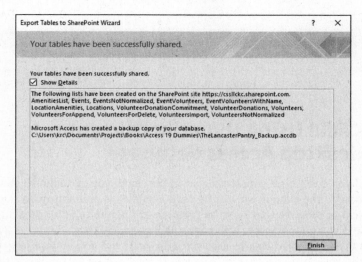

7. **Click Finish.**

   The new database opens. It's connected to the cloud! (see Figure 11-6).

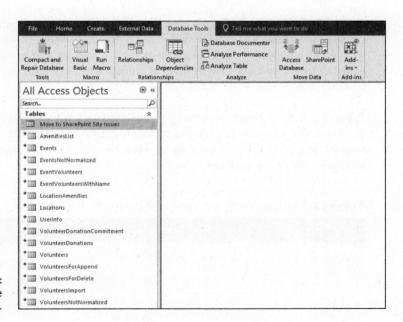

TIP

When the Wizard is done, you may see a new table in your database called Move to SharePoint Site Issues (see the highlighted table in Figure 11-6). Open it to see what the Wizard had trouble with and why (see Figure 11-7 for a sample of what's inside the table).

FIGURE 11-7:
Bad news from
the SharePoint
export wizard

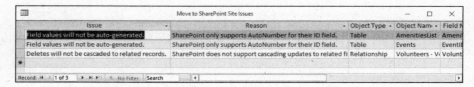

Click! Using Hyperlinks in your desktop Access database

If you don't need your data to sit in the cloud, you can connect your desktop database to the outside world. The term *hyperlink* is probably quite familiar — it's the text or pictures that serve as jumping-off points to other data. Click a hyperlink, and you go to another web page. Click an image that's set up as a hyperlink (your mouse pointer turns to a pointing finger), and you go to a larger version of the image — or to another website where information pertaining to the subject of the image can be found. Underlined text (or text in a different color or that changes color when you point to it) is the typical sign of the existence of a hyperlink.

So what's this *hyperlink* stuff? Although *hyperlink* makes it sound like a link that's had way too much coffee, within the context of Microsoft Office (of which Access is a part), it's actually a special storage compartment for storing the address of a resource on either the Internet or your local corporate network (or a file stored on your local computer). Hyperlinks start with a special identification code that explains to the computer what kind of resource it's pointing to and where that resource is.

Table 11-1 lists the most common *protocol codes* (a harmless but scary-sounding term that simply refers to portions of the programming code that allow a browser to use a hyperlink). You'll find, along with the code itself, an explanation of the kind of resource the code refers to.

TABLE 11-1 ## Types of Hyperlink Protocol Codes in Access

Protocol Code	What It Does
file://	Opens a local or network-based file
ftp://	File Transfer Protocol; links to an FTP server
http://	Hypertext Transfer Protocol; links to a web page
mailto:	Sends email to a network or Internet address

TIP

For more information on links and how Access understands and uses them, press F1 or click the handy Help icon (the question mark in the upper right corner of the Access screen) to open the Access Help system and then search for the term *hyperlink.*

If you surf the web regularly, many of these terms and concepts should be familiar. Although most of them are geared to Internet or intranet applications, Access can also use hyperlinks to identify locally stored documents (that's what `file://` does). This enables you, for example, to create a hyperlink in your Access table that opens a Word document, an Excel spreadsheet, or a JPEG image file. This technology is so flexible that the sky's literally the limit.

Adding a Hyperlink field to your desktop database table

Access provides a handy field type specifically designed for this special type of data. As you probably guessed, this type is called the *Hyperlink field.*

Adding a Hyperlink field to a table doesn't require special steps. Just use the same steps for adding *any* field to a table — get to Design view for your table and use the Data Type column to choose the Hyperlink data type, as shown in Figure 11-8.

The Hyperlink data type is no different from the other field types in terms of applying it. When you hop back to Datasheet view, you'll see that your entries (if any) in the Hyperlink field are underlined, looking just like link text on a web page.

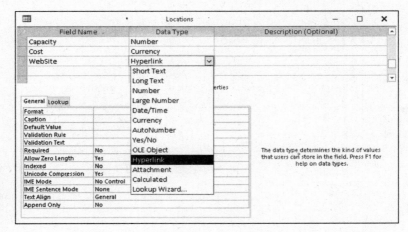

FIGURE 11-8: In Design view, choose Hyperlink from the list of data types.

TIP

To switch between Design and Datasheet views of your data, click the View button on the Ribbon's Home tab or its Design tab. It's the first button, and appears either as:

>> A table icon (a small grid)

>> An icon combining images of pencil, ruler, and angle

Fine-tuning your hyperlinks

Once you've created your hyperlink field, enter your hyperlinks into the field with the Edit Hyperlink menu. Follow these steps to enter a hyperlink:

1. Right-click the hyperlink field you want to change in your table.

2. Choose Hyperlink and then select Edit Hyperlink from the pop-up menu, shown in Figure 11-9.

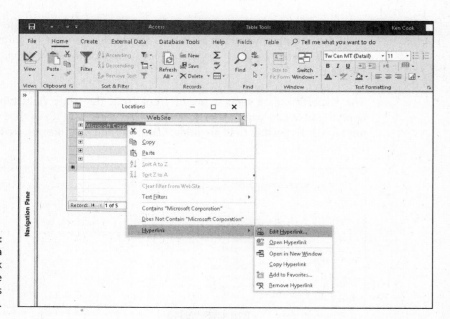

FIGURE 11-9:
Right-click a stored hyperlink within the table and access tools for editing it.

The clever little dialog box shown in Figure 11-10 appears.

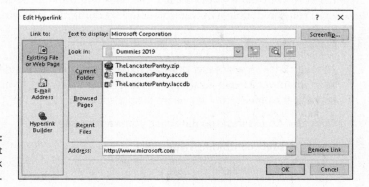

FIGURE 11-10:
The Edit
Hyperlink
dialog box.

3. **Use the dialog box to fill in the following information:**

   - The text that's displayed.

   - The ScreenTip (the little text that pops up when your mouse pointer hovers over a web address). To create one, click the ScreenTip button and use the resulting Set Hyperlink ScreenTip dialog box to create your tip — then click OK to return to the Edit Hyperlink dialog box.

   - Links for documents, spreadsheets, graphics, or even email addresses in an Access database.

   - The site address.

4. **Click OK.**

   Your hyperlink is edited, showing the text you choose to display and pointing to the web address (document or other file) that you designate. If you choose to create a ScreenTip, you can test the new tip in Datasheet view by rolling the mouse over your hyperlink and seeing what appears.

Pretty cool, huh? Experiment with the dialog box a little to find out how everything works. It takes only a moment.

REMEMBER

Although most hyperlinks store web or other Internet addresses, they can point to just about anything in the cyberworld. Thanks to their flexible tags, hyperlinks understand web pages, intranet servers, database objects (reports, forms, and such), and even documents on your computer or another networked PC.

Testing links

Hyperlinks in your table work just like the ones you find on the web — just point and click. You can double-check for yourself by doing the following:

1. Make sure you're connected to the Internet.

Although Edge (or whichever browser you've designated as your default) will open whenever a hyperlink that points to a website is clicked, if you're not online at the time, it won't go where the hyperlink points.

2. Open the Access desktop database you want to use.

3. Open the table containing hyperlinks.

The fun is about to begin!

4. Click the hyperlink of your choice.

- If the hyperlink leads to a web page, your web browser leaps onto the screen, displaying the website from the link.

- If the link leads to something other than a website, Windows automatically fires up the right program to handle whatever the link has to offer.

4

The Power of Questions

Contents at a Glance

Chapter **12**

Finding, Filtering, and Sorting Your Data — Fast

You probably already know that your database helps you store, organize, view, and document the information that's important to you — your personal information, your business-related information, any kind of information you need to keep track of.

Of course, this is not a new concept. People have been storing information for as long as there've been people. From making scratches in the dirt to keep count of the number of sheep in the flock to handwritten census information kept in huge ledgers to metal filing cabinets filled with typed lists and reports, man has been using some form of database for a long, long time.

Over the years — make that decades, even centuries — the process of storing information has gotten easier, even if it's more technologically complicated than writing things down and putting the paper you wrote it on in a box or drawer.

Thanks to the advent of database software and the Internet, you can store millions of records in a single computer, and people all over the world can access them, assuming they have permission. Farmers can keep track of their sheep, countries can keep track of their populations, and you can keep track of your friends, family, employees, products, and holiday card lists — anything your little data-driven heart desires.

But what is all this "keeping track" of which I speak? It's not just storing the data; it's getting at it when you need it. Thanks to the magic of the Find, Sort, and Filter commands, Access tracks and reorganizes the stuff in your tables faster than ever, putting it literally at your fingertips whenever you need to locate one or more of the pieces of information you're storing. When you need a quick answer to a simple question, these three commands are ready to help. This chapter covers the commands in order, starting with the speedy Find, moving along to the organizational Sort, and ending with the flexible Filter.

Find, Sort, and Filter do a great job with *small* questions (such as "How many customers who bought something in July didn't give us an email address?"). Answering big, complex questions (such as "How many people attended Major League Baseball games in July and also bought a team hat in the stadium store?") still takes a full-fledged Access query (in this case, querying a database of baseball-game attendees and the database of items sold in the team store). Don't let that complexity worry you, though, because you can flip back to Chapter 10, which explains queries in exciting detail.

Using the Find Command

When you want to track down a particular record *right now,* creating a query for the job is overkill. Fortunately, Access has a very simple way to find one specific piece of data in your project's tables and forms: the Find command.

Find is found — big surprise here — in the Find section of the Home tab, accompanied by a magnifying glass icon. You can also get to Find by pressing Ctrl+F to open the Find dialog box.

Although the Find command is pretty easy to use, knowing a few tricks makes it even more powerful, and if you're a Word or Excel user, you'll find the tricks helpful in those applications, too — because the Find command is an Office-wide feature. After you get through the Find basics (covered in the next section), check the tips for fine-tuning the Find command in the "Shifting Find into high gear" section, later in this chapter.

Finding anything fast

Using the Find command is a very straightforward task. Here's how it works:

1. **Open the table or form you want to search.**

   Note that the Find command works in Datasheet view and with Access forms and becomes available as soon as a table or form is opened.

   If you want to dive into forms right now, flip back to Chapter 8.

2. **Click in the field that you want to search.**

   The Find command searches the *current* field in all the records of the table, so be sure to click the correct field before starting the Find process. Access doesn't care which record you click; as long as you're on a record in the correct field, Access knows exactly which field you want to Find in.

3. **Start the Find command.**

   You can either click the Find button in the Find section of the Home tab or press Ctrl+F.

   The Find and Replace dialog box opens, ready to serve you.

4. **Click the Match drop-down list and choose Any Part of Field if you don't want to or can't supply the entire value, such as a complete company name or specifying a Street, Road, or Lane in the Address field.**

5. **Type the text you're looking for in the Find What box, as shown in Figure 12-1.**

   Take a moment to check your spelling before starting the search. Access is pretty smart, but it isn't bright enough to figure out that you actually meant *plumber* when you typed *plumer*.

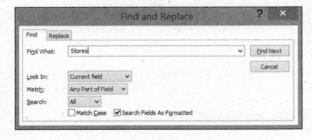

FIGURE 12-1:
The Find and Replace dialog box.

6. **Click Find Next to run your search.**

   - If the data you seek is in the active field, the Find command immediately tracks down the records that contain what you typed in the Find What box.

   The cell containing the data you seek is highlighted.

What if the first record that Access finds isn't the one you're looking for? Suppose you want the second, third, or the fourteenth *John Smith* in the table? No problem; that's why the Find and Replace dialog box has a Find Next button. Keep clicking Find Next until Access either works its way down to the record you want or tells you that it's giving up the search.

- If Find doesn't locate anything, it laments its failure in a small dialog box, accompanied by this sad statement:

  Microsoft Access finished searching the records. The search item was not found.

If Find didn't find what you were looking for, you have a couple of options:

>> You can give up by clicking OK in the small dialog box to make it go away.

>> You can check the search and try again (you'll still have to click OK to get rid of the prompt dialog box). Here are things to check for after you're back in the Find and Replace dialog box:

- Make sure that you clicked in the correct field and spelled everything correctly in the Find What box.

  You can also check the special Find options covered in the following section to see whether one of them is messing up your search.

- If you ended up changing the spelling or options, click Find Next again.

Shifting Find into high gear

Sometimes just typing the data you need in the Find What box doesn't produce the results you need:

>> You find too many records (and end up clicking the Find Next button endlessly to get to the one record you want).

>> The records that match aren't the ones you want.

The best way to reduce the number of wrong matches is to add more details to your search, which will reduce the number of matches and maybe give you just that one record you need to find.

Access offers several tools for fine-tuning a Find. To use them, open the Find and Replace dialog box by either

>> Clicking the Find button on the Home tab

or

>> Pressing Ctrl+F

The following sections describe how to use the options in the Find and Replace dialog box.

If your Find command isn't working the way you think it should, check the following options. Odds are that at least one of these options is set to *exclude* what you're looking for.

Look In

By default, Access looks for matches only in the *current* field — whichever field you clicked in before starting the Find command. To tell Access to search the entire table instead, choose Current Document from the Look In drop-down list, as shown in Figure 12-2.

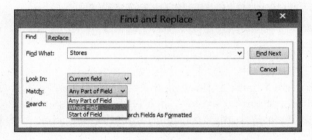

FIGURE 12-2: To search the entire table, change Look In.

Match

Your options are as follows:

>> **Any Part of Field:** Allows a match anywhere in a field (finding *Richard, Ulrich,* and *Lifestyles of the Rich and Famous* if the Find What box contains *Rich*). This is the default.

>> **Whole Field:** This requires that the search terms (what you type in the Find What box) be the entirety of the field value. So *Rich* won't find *Ulrich, Richlieu, Richard,* or *Richmond.* It finds only *Rich.*

>> **Start of Field:** Recognizes only those matches that start from the beginning of the field. So *Rich* finds *Richmond,* but not *Ulrich.*

This option allows you to put in just part of a name, too, especially if you know only the beginning of a name or the start of an address.

To change the Match setting, click the down arrow next to the Match field (see Figure 12-3) and then make your choice from the drop-down menu that appears.

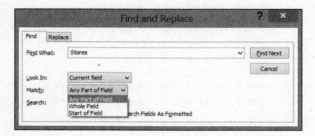

FIGURE 12-3:
Using the
Match option.

Search

If you're finding too many matches, try limiting your search to one particular portion of the table with the help of the Search option. Search tells the Find command to look either:

>> At all the records in the table (the default setting)

or

>> Up or down from the current record

Clicking a record halfway through the table and then telling Access to search Down from there confines your search to the bottom part of the table. Once the search hits the last record, it continues from the beginning, with the first record.

Fine-tune your Search settings by clicking the down arrow next to the Search box and choosing the appropriate offering from the drop-down menu.

Match Case

Checking the Match Case check box makes sure that the term you search for is *exactly* the same as the value stored in the database, including the same uppercase and lowercase characters.

This works really well if you're searching for a name, rather than just a word, so that *rich custard topping* is not found when you search for (capital *R*) *Rich* in the entire table.

Search Fields as Formatted

This option instructs Access to look at the formatted version of the field rather than the actual data stored in the field. By "formatted" we mean with formatting applied to the content — numbers formatted as percentages, dates set as short dates versus medium dates, and so on.

Limiting the search in this way is handy when you're searching for dates, inventory unit IDs, or any other field with quite a bit of specialized formatting.

Turn on Search Fields as Formatted by clicking the check box next to it.

This setting doesn't work with Match Case, so if Match Case is checked, Search Fields as Formatted appears dimmed. In that case, uncheck Match Case to bring back the Search Fields as Formatted check box.

Most of the time, this option doesn't make much difference. In fact, the only time you probably care about this particular Find option is when (or if) you search many highly formatted fields.

Sorting Alphabetically and Numerically

Very few databases are organized into nice, convenient alphabetical or numerical lists. You don't enter your records in any particular order; you enter them in the order they come to you. So what do you do when you need a list of products in product-number order or a list of addresses in zip code order or a list of clients by last name, right now?

Sorting by a single field

The solution lies in the sort commands, which are incredibly easy to use. The sort commands are on the Ribbon's Home tab, in the Sort & Filter section. The two buttons (Ascending and Descending) do the job quite well:

>> Sort Ascending sorts your records from top to bottom:

- Records that begin with *A* are at the beginning, and records that begin with *Z* are at the end.

- If your field contains numeric data (whether they're true numbers or Short Text fields storing zip codes or Currency fields storing prices), an Ascending sort puts them in order from lowest number to highest.

- Date/Time fields will offer Sort Oldest to Newest or Sort Newest to Oldest.

>> Sort Descending sorts your records from bottom to top:

- Records that begin with Z are at the top, and records that begin with A are at the bottom of the list.

- If your field contains numeric data, a Descending sort puts the records in order from highest number to lowest.

If, after sorting in Ascending or Descending order you want to put things back the way they were — in the order just prior to clicking either of those buttons — click the Remove Sort button, located just below the Ascending and Descending buttons in the Sort & Filter group.

TIP

You can initiate a sort in Datasheet view by right-clicking any cell in the field you want to sort by, and Access offers up the right sorting options for you, based on the field's data type. If you right-click a field that contains text values (Short Text or Long Text), your options in the resulting pop-up menu include Sort Ascending and Sort Descending, just like the Home tab options. If you right-click a field containing numeric data, the options in the pop-up menu are Sort Smallest to Largest or Sort Largest to Smallest.

Sorting on more than one field

What if you want to sort by multiple fields — such as by zip code, and then within that sort, you want all the people with the same zip code to appear in Last Name order? Or maybe you want to sort all your customers by a Status field and then within each group of customers that creates, to sort by current balance? You'd need to use the following steps to nest one sort inside another.

You can sort by more than one column at a time like this:

1. Click the heading of the first column to sort by.

The entire column is highlighted.

2. Hold down the Shift key and click the heading of the last column to sort by.

All columns from the first one to the last one are highlighted.

3. Choose either Sort Ascending or Sort Descending.

The sort is always performed from left to right.

In other words, you can't sort by the contents of the fourth column and within that by the contents of the third column.

Sorting has its own peculiarity when working with numbers in a text field. When sorting a field that has numbers mixed in with spaces and letters (such as street addresses), Access ranks the numbers as though they were *letters,* not numbers. This behavior means that Access puts (say) "1065 W. Orange Street" before "129 Mulberry Street." (Thanks to the peculiar way that your computer sorts information, the 0 in the second position of 1065 comes before the 2 in the second position of 129.)

Fast and Furious Filtering

Sometimes you need to see a group of records that share a common value in one field. Perhaps they all list a particular city, a certain job title, or they're all products that have the same cost. Always willing to help, Access includes a special tool for this very purpose: the Filter command.

Filter uses your criteria and displays all matching records, creating a mini-table of only the records that meet your requirements. It's like an instant query without all the work and planning. Of course, it's not as flexible or powerful as a query, but it's all you need when you're looking for a fairly simple answer.

The Filter tool appears in the Sort & Filter section of the Ribbon's Home tab, and you have the following choices for a simple filter:

» Filter

» Selection

» Advanced Filter by Form

» Advanced Filter/Sort

» Toggle Filter

Each type of filter performs the same basic function, but in a slightly different way. The following sections cover the first three options. The Advanced Filter/Sort option, found by clicking the Advanced button, opens a window that actually has you building a query — selecting tables and fields to filter, setting up criteria for the filter to use while it's finding specific records, that sort of thing. You can read about queries and familiarize yourself with the Advanced Filter/Sort tool in Chapter 13.

Filters work in tables, forms, and queries. Although you can apply a filter to a report, filtering reports can be a daunting task, one that I'm not going to get involved with here. Of course, what you read here can be applied to that process, should you want to try it on your own. And in the following sections, what you learn to apply to a table can also be applied when you're working with queries and forms.

Filtering by a field's content

The main Filter command enables you to filter your records so you view only records that meet specific criteria. Suppose, for example, that you want to see all records for people living in a particular city. Here's how to do it:

1. **In your table of interest, click the small triangle on the field name for the field you want to filter (City in this case).**

   Access displays a pop-up menu like the one in Figure 12-4.

   Don't right-click the header at the top of the column (where it says *City* in the figure). Right-clicking there displays a different pop-up menu filled with wonderful things you can do to that column of your table.

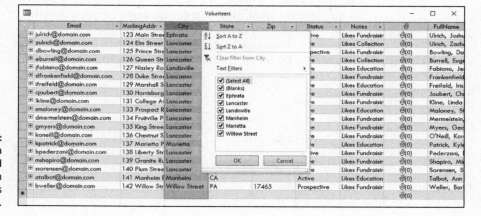

FIGURE 12-4: Filtering a single field based on that field's entries.

2. **If you want to omit some entries from your filter, remove their check marks in the pop-up menu.**

   You can either

   - Remove check marks from individual entries.

     or

   - Uncheck the Select All check box to uncheck all the items.

   Uncheck everything so you can easily check only those entries whose matching records you want to see. With all the entries checked, you see all the records.

3. **Place check marks next to those entries you want to use in constructing your filter for the field.**

   Access searches the selected field and displays only those records that meet your Filter criteria.

4. **Click OK.**

   All the records meeting the criteria set (by virtue of the items you checked) are displayed. This might be several records, a whole lot of records, or just one.

To jump back and see all the original (unfiltered) records, you can either

>> Click the Toggle Filter button in the Sort & Filter section of the Ribbon to remove the last filter applied. Click it again to reapply the filter.

   or

>> Click the field name's tiny triangle again and choose Clear Filter From *Field Name.*

   If you don't remember which fields you filtered, you can tell them by the small funnel symbol that appears next to the field name in Datasheet view.

The entire table, full of records, returns to view.

Filter by selection

The Selection command is the easiest of the Sort & Filter commands to use. It assumes that you've found one record that matches your criteria. Using the Selection filter is a lot like grabbing someone in a crowd and shouting: "Okay, everybody who's like this guy here, line up over there."

For example, imagine you want to find all the volunteers who live in Landisville. You can use the Selection filter in this manner:

1. **Click the field that has the information you want to match.**

   In this case, it's the City field.

2. **Scroll through the list until you find the field entry that will serve as an appropriate example for your filter.**

3. **Click to select the value you're searching for, right-click the cell containing the selection, and then choose Equals Whatever. (In this instance, it would be Equals Landisville, as shown in Figure 12-5.) You can also select**

the cell and then click the Selection button on the Home tab (in the Sort & Filter section) to access the same list of choices.

Access immediately displays a table containing only the records matching your selection. (Again, check out Figure 12-5, where my City filter has been applied.)

4. **Click the Toggle Filter button on the toolbar after you finish using the filter.**

Your table or form returns to its regular display.

At this stage of the game, you may want to save a list of everything that matches your filter. Unfortunately, the Filter's simplicity and ease of use now come back to haunt you. To permanently record your filtered search, you have to create a query. (See Chapter 13 for details about creating queries.)

You can also use the Filter menu that shows sorting options and the list of checked field values in the "Filtering by a field's content" section earlier in this chapter. When you display the pop-up menu, uncheck Select All and then check the value you want to look for. Then choose Text Filters from that same pop-up menu. The same list of options (Equals, Does Not Equal, Begins With, and so on) appears as a fly-out menu, and you can make your choice there.

Filter by Form

You can tighten a search by using additional filters to weed out undesirable matches, but that takes a ton of extra effort. For an easier way to isolate a group of records according to the values in more than one field, try Filter by Form.

Filter by Form uses more than one criterion to sift through records. In some ways, it's like a simple query. (What's a query? See Chapter 13.) It's so similar to a query that you can even save your Filter by Form criteria *as* a full-fledged query!

Suppose, for example, that you need a list of all the employees at your company who work in a certain department and have a particular title. You can perform two Selection filters (on the Department and Job Title fields, using the employee database as an example) and write down the results of each to get your list; or you can do just *one* search with Filter by Form and see all the records that meet your criteria (based on their entries in multiple tables) in a single step.

To use Filter by Form, follow these steps:

1. **On the Ribbon's Home tab, click the Advanced button in the Sort & Filter section.**

   A menu appears.

2. **Choose Filter By Form from the menu.**

   The table is replaced by a single row of cells, one under each field header in your table, as shown in Figure 12-6.

3. **Click in the empty cell beneath the field name for the first column that you want to filter.**

   Use the scroll bars to bring the column onscreen if it's off to the right and can't be seen.

   The down arrow jumps to the column you click.

   - Normally, Access shows a down-arrow button next to the first field in the table.

   - If you previously used a Filter command with the table, Access puts the down-arrow button in the last field you filtered. (Again, refer to Figure 12-6.)

4. **Click the down arrow to see a list of values that the field contains, as shown in Figure 12-7.**

5. **In the list of values, click the value that you want to use in this filter.**

   For example, if you select Landisville from the drop-down list in the City field, "Landisville" moves into the City column. Access adds the quotes automatically — one less detail that you have to remember!

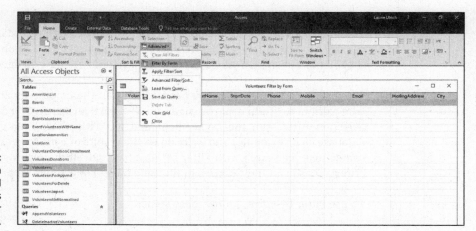

FIGURE 12-6:
Filter by Form
offers a grid and
drop-down lists
to set criteria for
each field.

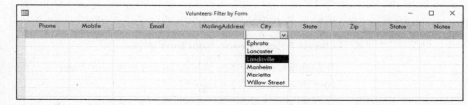

FIGURE 12-7:
The drop-down
list shows all
unique values in
a field.

6. **To add another filter option for the chosen field, click the Or tab in the lower left corner of the table.**

A new Filter by Form window appears, letting you add an alternate search condition. Access also offers an Or tab to the lower left corner of the display, as shown in Figure 12-8.

The Filter by Form command likes to answer simple questions, such as "Show me all the volunteers who live in Landisville." It also provides answers to more complex questions like "Show me all the records containing "Active" in the Status field and who have Landisville in the City field," and it performs both tasks easily.

Asking a more complex question (such as "Show me all the volunteers in Lancaster who like fundraising") requires a query. To find out about queries, flip ahead to Chapter 13.

FIGURE 12-8:
Click the Or
tab to further
define the
criteria.

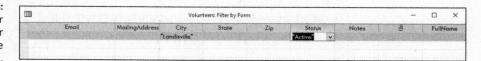

7. **For each additional field you want to filter, click the Or tab and repeat Steps 3 through 6.**

   In this example, the second field to be filtered is Status, and **Active** was typed into the field's box.

8. **When you finish entering all the criteria for the filter, click the Toggle Filter button.**

   Figure 12-9 shows the results.

FIGURE 12-9:
Access finds all
the Active
volunteers who
live in Lancaster
or Landisville.

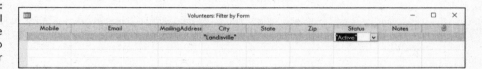

A final thought about Filter by Form: Although you can get fancy by adding Or searches to your heart's content, keeping track of your creation gets tough in no time at all. Before you go too far, remind yourself that queries work better than filters when the questions get complex. Flip to Chapter 13 for the lowdown on queries.

When you finish fiddling with your filter, click the Toggle Filter button. At that point, your table returns to normal (or at least as normal as data tables ever get). The filter is still in place, however, and clicking the Toggle Filter button again reapplies it. To really get rid of a filter, click the Advanced button and choose Clear All Filters from the drop-down list.

Unfiltering Filter by Form

What do you do when you enter criteria by mistake? Or when you decide that you really don't want to include Lancaster in your filter right after you click Lancaster? No problem — the Clear Grid command comes to the rescue!

When you click the Clear Grid command (found in the Sort & Filter section's Advanced menu), Access clears all the entries in the Filter by Form grid and gives you a nice, clean place to start over again.

Filter by excluding selection

The Selection filter can also be used to exclude certain records. This works great for times when you want to briefly hide a bunch of records that all share a unique attribute (a particular state, city, or zip code). In the following sample, I searched for the volunteers who are either Active or Inactive, by choosing Does not equal "Prospective".

Here's how to make the Selection filter exclude records for you:

1. **Scroll through the table until you find the value you want to exclude.**

2. **Right-click the field containing the value and then choose Does Not Equal _____ (where the blank represents the value you've right-clicked) from the menu that appears, as shown in Figure 12-10.**

   Those records matching the value you've chosen get out of the way so you can concentrate on the records that really interest you.

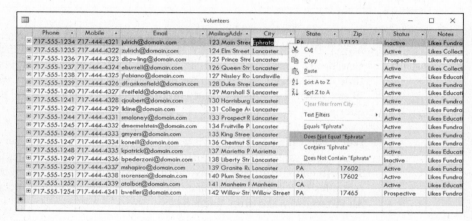

FIGURE 12-10:
With one click, Access hides all volunteers whose City field value is Ephrata.

You can also click the Selection button (in the Sort & Filter section of the Home tab) and choose Does Not Equal from the menu there. You'll also notice the Contains and Does Not Contain commands. These are handy for culling records that have something in common, such as a particular word or number within them. You can also combine filters, excluding not only (for example) volunteers who are Prospective, but the Prospective volunteers who live in a certain City or State.

Chapter **13**

I Was Just Asking . . . for Answers

Y
ou know the old saying, "The only stupid question is the one you didn't ask." It's supposed to mean that if you have a question, ask it — because if you don't, you'll be operating in the dark, and that's far sillier than your question could ever have been. Although you don't ask "meaning of life" questions of a database, you do pose questions such as, "How many customers in London do we have?" or "What's the phone number of that guy who works for Acme Explosives?" Either of those questions, if you didn't ask it, would require you to scroll through rows and rows of data to find the information. (That's the silly approach, obviously.)

This chapter introduces you to the art of asking questions about the information in your database using *queries.* You discover how to use the Query Wizard to pose simple questions, and then you find out about creating your own simple-yet-customized queries by using the bizarrely and inaccurately named Advanced Filter/Sort tool. After that, you discover how to combine multiple tables (from the same database) in your query — which can yield interesting answers to the questions you have about your data. Suffice it to say that by the end of this chapter, you'll be a veritable quizmaster, capable of finding any record or group of records you need.

TIP

Don't worry if your first few queries produce odd or unexpected results — including no results at all. As with anything new, queries (along with their inherent procedures and concepts) take a little getting used to. Because they're so powerful, they can be a little complicated, but it's worth taking the time to figure things out (with the help of this book!). Take your time, be patient with yourself, and remember that old saying: "The only stupid question is the one you didn't ask."

Simple (Yet Potent) Filter and Sort Tools

Wait a minute. We were just talking about queries, and the heading above says something about *filter* and *sort*. What happened to querying? Well, sorting and filtering are queries unto themselves; using them, you can more easily find a record — say, for a particular person if your list is in alphabetical order by the LastName field. Filtering, on the other hand, says "Give me all the records that have *this* in common" (*this* being the criterion you set your filter to look for). It's kind of like playing Go Fish with your database.

It's all related, and it's all about asking questions. There are really two ways to find a particular record:

>> *Queries* use a *set* of criteria — conditions that eliminate many, if not all but one, of your records — that you present to the database and that says, "Look here, here, and here, and find THIS for me!"

>> *Filters* use one criterion, saying (in effect), "Sift through all these records and find the one(s) with THIS!"

Of course, the exclamation point is optional (depending on your level of excitement about the data involved) — and so is the method you use. You can query *or* filter for any record or group of records you want. And you can sort the results of your filter. But it's still all about asking questions.

Filter things first

I begin by explaining filters because they're more straightforward, procedurally, than queries. By starting with filters, too, you can get your feet wet with them while preparing for the deeper waters of querying.

FAST FILING WITH ACCESS

Back before computers, people filed information in file folders and stored them in file cabinets.

- The file folders had useful information on their tabs — such as letters of the alphabet, dates, or names, indicating what kind of information could be found inside.

- The file-cabinet drawers had information on them, too — little cards with names, numbers, or letters on them, indicating which folders were stored inside the drawers.

The figures on the file drawers and file folders helped people find information:

- Need an order from April 10, 2018? Go to the Order cabinet, open the 2018 drawer, and pull out the folder for April's orders. After a little leafing through, voilà! You've got the order from April 10.

- Need to know how much a particular customer spent in the last quarter of 2017? Go to the 2017 cabinet, open the drawer of customer orders, pull the folder for the customer you're interested in, and begin tallying the orders for that year, for that customer.

  In a sans-computer environment, you'd also need a calculator, abacus, or scrap paper and a pencil to do this. Sound tempting? Didn't think so.

Querying in Access is similar to the process of opening a file drawer, looking at folder tabs to figure out which folder is needed, and then leafing through the pages in the folder, at least in terms of the progression of steps. The process just happens a lot faster, and you don't get any paper cuts!

- The data stored in an Access table can be found by using a query that goes to a particular table, looks in particular fields, and pulls out certain records, based on the criterion set for the query, such as "Show me all the customers with *Lancaster* in the City field."

- You can even perform calculations with queries (such as tallying the orders for a particular customer). Chapter 16 shows you how.

How filters work

Filters quickly scan a single table for whatever data you seek. Filters examine all records in the table and then hide those that do not match the criteria you seek.

The filtering options are virtually unlimited, but simple:

>> Want every volunteer in Lancaster? Filter the `City` field for Lancaster.

>> Want to see all the fundraising events that occurred in the first quarter of 2018? Filter for `EventDate` (between 1/1/2018 and 3/31/2018) and the `EventType` field for Fundraising, and there you go.

>> Want all the Locations that have Wi-Fi, but that are also Outdoor locations? Filter for Yes on the `Wi-Fi` field and Outdoor in the `LocationType` field.

There's a price to pay for ease and simplicity, however. Filters are neither *smart* nor *flexible*:

>> You cannot filter multiple tables without first writing a query that contains — *brings together* — the tables.

>> A filter cannot be the basis for the records seen on a report or form.

>> If you want to filter on two fields using the OR operator, you'll need a query, not a filter — when using multiple fields with a filter, the criteria must work with AND as the operator.

Chapter 12 covers filters in their limited-but-useful glory.

What about queries?

Queries go far beyond filters. But to get to that great "beyond," queries require more complexity. After all, a bicycle may be easy to ride, but a bike won't go as fast as a motorcycle. And so it goes with queries. Queries work with one or more tables, let you search one or more fields, and even offer the option to save your results for further analysis, but you can't just hop on and ride a query with no lessons.

TECHNICAL STUFF

For all the differences between filters and queries, the most advanced filter is, in reality, a simple query — which makes some bizarre sense: Your first step into the world of queries is also your last step out of the domain of filters. Welcome to Advanced Filter/Sort, the super-filter of Access, masquerading as a mild-mannered query.

Advanced Filter/Sort

Advanced Filter/Sort is more powerful than a run-of-the-mill filter. It's so powerful that it's like a simple query:

>> You use the same steps to build an Advanced Filter/Sort as you do to create a query.

>> The results look quite a bit alike, too.

TECHNICAL STUFF

Advanced Filter/Sort looks, acts, and behaves like a query, but it's still a filter at heart and is constrained by a filter's limits, including these:

>> Advanced Filter/Sort works with only one table or form in your database at a time, so you can't use it on a bunch of linked tables.

>> You can ask only simple questions with the filter.

Real, honest-to-goodness queries do a lot more than that.

>> The filter always displays all the columns for every matching record.

With a query, *you* choose the columns that you want to appear in the results. If you don't want a particular column, leave it out of the query. Filters aren't bright enough to do that.

Even with these limitations, Advanced Filter/Sort makes a great training ground to practice your query-building skills (that's why I'm starting with this feature, despite the word "Advanced" in its name).

TECHNICAL STUFF

Although this section talks about applying filters only to tables, you can also filter a query. There's a good reason to filter queries: Some queries take a long time to run, so it's faster to *filter* the query results than to *rewrite and rerun* the query. Suppose (for example) that you run a complicated sales-report query and notice it includes data from *every* state instead of the individual state you wanted. Rather than modify the query and run it again, you can apply a filter to your query's results. *Poof!* You get the results you're after in a fraction of the time.

Fact-finding with fun, fast filtering

Before you use the Filter window, you need to take a quick look at its components and what they do. In the section that follows this one, you find out how to access and use the Filter window.

The Filter window is split into two distinct sections, as shown in Figure 13-1:

>> **Field list (the Volunteers box in Figure 13-1):** The Field list displays all the fields in the *current table* or *form* (the table or form that's open at the time). Not sure about forms? Check out Chapter 8!

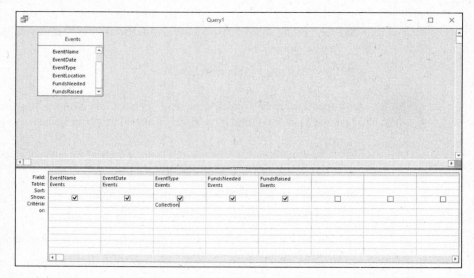

FIGURE 13-1:
Query Design View window allows you to choose the field(s) on which to filter your data in the current table.

TIP

At this point, don't worry about the upper half of the window. The Field list comes more into play when you start working with full queries. The table you were working on is already shown in the upper half of the window, so you don't have to do anything with this part of the window now.

>> **Query grid (the lower half of the screen):** When you use the Advanced Filter/Sort command, you are presented with a blank *query grid* for the details of your filter.

TECHNICAL STUFF

You're building a filter, but Access calls the area at the bottom of the screen a query grid because you use the same grid for queries. (You also see it later in the chapter, in the section about building real queries.)

To build the filter, you simply fill in the spaces of the query grid at the bottom of the window you see in Figure 13-1. Access even helps you along the way with pull-down menus and rows that do specific tasks. The procedure for filling in these spaces appears in the next section, along with details about each part of the grid and how it all works.

Here's the "advanced" part

TIP

The Advanced Filter/Sort tool also works on *forms.* If you feel particularly adventuresome (or if you mainly work with your data through some ready-made forms), try the filter with your form. Filtering a form works like filtering a table, so you can follow the same steps.

The following sections show how to design and use filters.

Starting the process

Start your filter adventure by firing up Access's basic query tool, the Advanced Filter/Sort.

1. **Decide what question you need to ask and which fields the question involves.**

    Because it's your data, only you know what information you need and which fields would help you get it. You may want (for example) a list of volunteers who live in a particular state, donors who've donated in excess of a certain amount to your organization, cities in a particular state, books by your favorite author, or people whose birthdays fall in the next month (if you're painfully organized, in which case I commend you).

    Whatever you want, decide on your question first and then get ready to find the fields in your table or form that contain the answer.

    REMEMBER

    Don't worry if your question includes more than one field or multiple options. Both filters and queries can handle multiple-field and multiple-option questions.

2. **Open the table (or form) that you want to interrogate.**

    Assuming you have the correct database open, your table or form pops into view.

3. **Click the Ribbon's Home tab at the top of the Access workspace.**

4. **In the Sort & Filter section of the Ribbon's Home tab (see Figure 13-2), choose Advanced ⇨ Advanced Filter/Sort.**

    The Filter window appears, ready to accept your command. What you see depends on the following considerations:

    - If you previously used a filter of any kind with this table, Access puts that most recently used filter information into the new window.

    - If no filter was done previously — or you cleared the previous filter — the Filter/Sort window looks pretty blank — for now.

    REMEMBER

    The Filter window is nothing but a simplified query window. The filter looks, acts, and behaves a lot like a real query. More information about full queries comes later in the chapter, so flip ahead to the next section if that's what you need.

After you open the Filter window, you're ready to select fields and criteria for your filter. The following section shows you how.

Advanced button

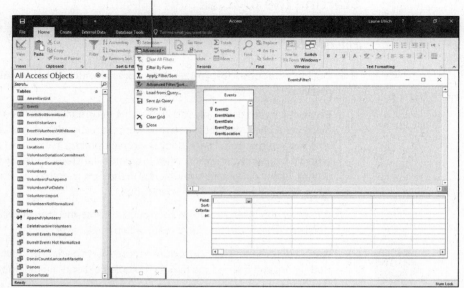

FIGURE 13-2:
Click the
Advanced
button to
choose
Advanced
Filter/Sort.

Selecting fields and criteria

As you begin selecting the fields you want to use in your filter and set up the criteria against which your fields' content will be compared, be sure to follow these steps carefully:

1. Click the first box in the Field row (in the query grid) and then click the down arrow that appears to the right of the box.

The drop-down menu lists all the fields in your table (or form).

2. Click the field (as identified in the preceding section) that you want to query.

Access helpfully puts the field name in the Field box on the query grid. So far, so good.

TIP

If you want to see the results of your filter in the same order that your data always appears in, skip to Step 4.

3. If you want to sort your filter results by this particular field, follow these steps:

a. *Click the Sort box.*

b. *Click the down arrow that appears.*

c. *Select Ascending or Descending from the drop-down menu.*

TIP

Ascending order is lowest to highest (for example, *A, B, C . . .*). *Descending* order is highest to lowest (for example, *Z, Y, X . . .*). If you don't want to stop and click the drop-down arrow to choose a sort method, just type an "a" or a "d" and Access fills it in for you, and you can move on to the `Criteria` field to specify what you're looking for.

4. **Set up your criteria for the field.**

Follow these steps:

a. Click the Criteria box under your field.

b. Type each criterion (such as =value, where "value" refers to a specific word or number that is represented within your data or < or > followed by a value).

REMEMBER

Setting criteria is the most complex part of building a query — it's the most important part of the entire process. The criteria are your actual questions, formatted in a way that Access understands. Table 13-1 gives you a quick introduction to the different ways you can express your criteria.

TIP

If you're making comparisons with logical operators, flip to Chapter 14 for everything you need to know about Boolean logic, the language of Access criteria.

c. If your question includes more than one possible value for this field, click the Or box and type your next criterion in the box to the right of the word Or.

TIP

If you move on to a new box, the criterion you entered is automatically placed in quotes. Don't worry. This is just Access acknowledging that you've given it a specific value to look for, to

● Make an exact match.

● Use the value with a greater-than or less-than symbol for comparison.

TIP

If your question involves more than one field, repeat the preceding Steps 1 through 4 for each field. Just use the next column in the grid for the additional field or fields you want to use in your filter.

With all the fields and criteria in place, it's time to take your filter for a test drive. Figure 13-3 shows an example that uses two criteria: the Volunteers table filtered for Active Status volunteers whose start date is before 2011, indicating they're long-time volunteers whom the organization can count on.

TABLE 13-1 ## Basic Comparison Operators

Name	Symbol	What It Means	Example
Equals	=	Displays all records that exactly match whatever you type.	To find all items from customer 37, type **37** in the Criteria row.
Less Than	<	Lists all values that are less than your criterion.	Typing **<50000** in the Salary field finds all employees who earn less than $50K.
Greater Than	>	Lists all values in the field that are greater than the criterion.	Typing **>50000** in the Salary field finds all employees I'll be hitting up for a loan because they earn more than $50K.
Greater Than or Equal To	>=	Works just like Greater Than, except it also includes all entries that exactly match the criterion.	**>=50000** finds all values from 50,000 to infinity.
Less Than or Equal To	<=	If you add = to Less Than, your query includes all records that have values below or equal to the criterion value.	**<=50000** includes not only those records with values less than 50,000, but also those with a value of 50,000.
Not Equal To	<>	Finds all entries that don't match the criterion.	If you want a list of all records except those with a value of 50,000, type **<>50000**.

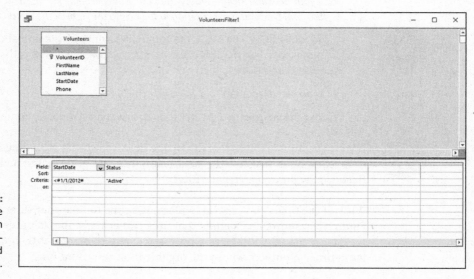

FIGURE 13-3:
Two fields are
queried in
this example —
Status and
StartDate.

Running the filter

After completing the process of choosing fields and setting criteria, you're ready to run the filter. Click the Toggle Filter button in the Sort & Filter section of the Ribbon.

Access thinks about it for a moment, and then the record or records that meet your criteria appear. This is shown in Figure 13-4. Pretty cool, eh? Note the little Filter symbols on the Field Name headers for the two fields by which this particular table was filtered — a tiny arrow and a Filter icon — to remind you which fields your filter used.

Note also that I've hidden the columns between StartDate and Status so you can see them both in the same Figure (13-4). In your copy of the Volunteers table, if you're working along with us, you'll need to scroll to the right to verify that you're seeing Active volunteers after you see that you are in fact seeing only volunteers who joined the organization before 2011.

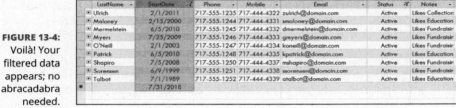

FIGURE 13-4:
Voilà! Your
filtered data
appears; no
abracadabra
needed.

TIP

There are two ways to see all the data again:

>> Click the Toggle Filter button, found in the Sort & Filter section of the Ribbon's Home tab.

The filtered records join their unfiltered brethren in a touching moment of digital homecoming.

>> Click the Filtered button.

This button appears at the bottom of the Access window (next to the Record buttons that you use to move through your records one at a time, and which you can see in Figure 13-4). When you click the Filtered button, your entire table comes back, and the button changes so its label says *Unfiltered*. Click again? The results of your query return. It's a quick toggle, perhaps even toggle-ier than the Toggle Filter button!

Select Queries

The basic query tool, created to make your life easier, is the *Select query* — so named because it *selects* matching records from your database and displays the results according to your instructions.

TIP

The sidebar "Secrets of the Select query" summarizes the differences that make Select queries more powerful than filters. If upon reading these secrets you suspect that the Select query sounds like the right tool for the job you have in mind, you may be able to use a query rather than a filter.

The best process for creating a Select query depends on the following:

>> If you're new to writing queries, the Query Wizard is a fast, easy way to get started. It walks you through the process of selecting tables and fields for your query — and can even add some summary calculations (such as counting records) to your query.

>> If you've already written some queries and are comfortable with the Query Design window, you'll probably want to bypass the Query Wizard and build your queries from scratch. Later in this chapter, "Getting Your Feet Wet with Ad Hoc Queries," guides you through the process.

SECRETS OF THE SELECT QUERY

Unlike its simplified little brother, Advanced Filter/Sort (shown previously in this chapter), a Select query offers all kinds of helpful and powerful options, including these:

- **Use more than one table in a query.** Because a Select query understands the relational side of Access, this query can pull together data from more than one table.

- **Show only the fields you want in your results.** Select queries include the ever-popular Show setting, which tells Access which fields you really care about seeing.

- **Put the fields into any order you want in the results.** Organize your answer fields where *you* want them without changing the order of the fields in your original table(s).

- **List only as many matching entries as you need.** If you need only the top 5, 25, or 100 records, or a percentage, such as 5% or 25%, use the *Top Value* setting. (This and other query options are covered in Chapter 14.)

- **You can save your query for future use.** A Select query can be given a name and run over and over, whenever you need it.

Solid relationships are the key to getting it all (from your tables)

In life, solid relationships make for a happier person; in Access, solid relationships make for a happier query experience.

REMEMBER

To query your database effectively, you need to know the following about its table structure:

>> Which tables do you need to use?

>> How are the tables you need to use related to each other?

>> Which fields contain the data you want to know about?

>> Which fields do you need in the solution?

TECHNICAL STUFF

Access maintains relationships between the tables in your database. Usually you (or your Information Systems department) create these relationships when you first design the database. When you build the tables and organize them with special key fields, you actually prepare the tables to work with a query.

Key fields relate your Access tables to each other. Queries use key fields to match records in one table with their related records in another table. You can pull data for the item you seek from the various tables that hold this data in your database — provided they're properly related before you launch the query.

Want to refresh your memory on creating relationships between the tables in your database? Check out Chapter 4, where all those secrets are revealed.

REMEMBER

If you don't relate your tables via the Relationships window, you'll have to do so for each multiple-table query you build in Access. As a general rule, put in the time to properly design and relate your tables. With proper table design and relationships, you'll get the results you want in a shorter amount of time.

Running the Query Wizard

You can rely on the Query Wizard — and the Simple Query Wizard found within it — for a real dose of hands-free filtering. With the Simple Query Wizard, you enter *table and field information*. The wizard takes care of the behind-the-scenes work for you.

Access isn't psychic (that's scheduled for the next version); it needs *some* input from you!

To create a query with the Query Wizard's Simple Query Wizard, follow these steps:

1. **On a piece of paper, lay out the data you'd like in your query results.**

A query returns a datasheet (column headings followed by rows of data), so make your layout in that format. All you really need are the column headings so you'll know what data to pull from the database.

2. **Determine the table location of each piece of data (column heading) from your paper.**

Write down the table and field name that contain the data matching the column heading on the paper above the column heading.

3. **In the Database window, click the Create tab on the Ribbon and then click the Query Wizard button from the Queries section.**

The New Query Wizard dialog box appears, asking you what kind of Query Wizard you'd like to run. Choose Simple Query Wizard and click OK.

4. **Choose the first table you want to include in the query (see Figure 13-5).**

You'll use the Tables/Queries drop-down menu, which shows all the tables (and any existing queries) in your database. Here are the specifics:

a. Click the down arrow next to the Tables/Queries drop-down menu (as shown in Figure 13-6).

b. Click the name of the table or query to include in this query.

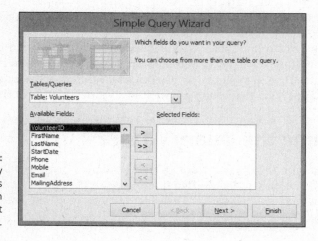

FIGURE 13-5:
The Simple Query Wizard starts and asks which table(s) you want to query.

5. **Select the fields from that table or query for your query.**

Repeat these steps to select each field you want included in your query:

a. *Click the name of the table or query to include in this query.*

The Available Fields list changes and displays the fields available in the table.

b. *In the Available Fields list, double-click each field from this table or query that you want to include in the query you're creating.*

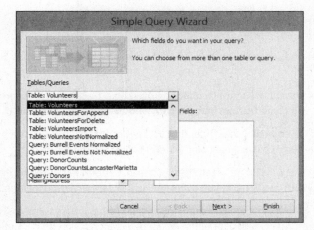

FIGURE 13-6:
The Tables/
Queries
drop-down list.

TIP

If you add the wrong field, just double-click it in the Selected Fields list. It will go back home. If you just want to start all over, click the double-left chevron (that's what you call the symbol that looks like a less-than sign) and all the selected fields go away.

6. **After you select all the fields, click Next.**

If the wizard can determine the relationships between the tables you selected, the window in Figure 13-7 appears.

If you don't see the window, not to worry. Access just wants you to name the query instead. Skip to Step 8.

TIP

If you include fields from two tables that aren't related, a warning dialog box appears. The dialog box reminds you that all the selected tables must be related before you can run your query — and suggests that you correct the problem before continuing. In fact, it won't let you go any further until you appease it in one of two ways:

- Remove all the fields selected for your query from the unrelated tables.

- Fix the relationships so that all tables you've selected in your query are related.

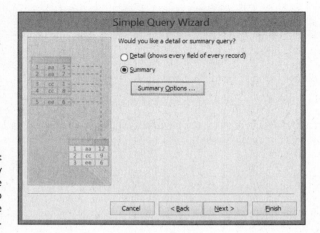

FIGURE 13-7:
The Query
Wizard may give
you the chance to
summarize
your data.

7. **If the wizard asks you to choose between a Detail and a Summary query, click the radio button next to your choice and then click Next.**

   - *Detail* creates a datasheet that lists all records that match the query. As the name implies, you get all the details from those records.

   - *Summary* tells the wizard that you aren't interested in seeing every single record; you want to see a summary of the information instead.

     TIP

     A summary query can perform calculations (such as sums and averages) on numeric fields. If text fields are selected, Access can count the records or pull the first and last item from the set of fields alphabetically.

     If you want to make any special adjustments to the summary, click Summary Options to display the Summary Options dialog box shown in Figure 13-8. Select your summary options from the check boxes for the available functions — Sum, Avg, Min, and Max — and then click OK.

   If you're curious about how the wizard decides whether to display the Detail or Summary step, the sidebar "To summarize or not to summarize" tells the story.

8. **In the wizard page that appears, select a radio button for what you want to do next:**

   - *If you want to make your query snazzy:* Select the Modify the Query Design option.

     The wizard sends your newly created query to the salon for some sprucing up, such as the inclusion of sorting and totals.

   - *If you want to skip the fancy stuff:* Select the Open the Query to View Information option to see the Datasheet view.

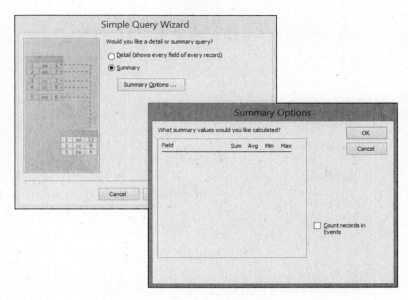

FIGURE 13-8:
Access offers
different ways of
summarizing
the data.

The wizard runs the query and presents the results in a typical Access datasheet.

9. **Type a title for your query in the text box and then click Finish.**

   The wizard builds your query and saves it with the title you entered; then Access displays the results, as shown in Figure 13-9.

   Congratulations! You've given birth to a query, and in this case, it shows the volunteers who started before 2011, who are Active, and are running events (based on the VolunteerID value in the EventCoordinator field in Events). The events with FundsRaised and/or FundsNeeded values make the cut and only those events — and the volunteers running them — appear in the results.

TECHNICAL STUFF

When you finish the steps in this section, the Query Wizard saves your query automatically with the name you typed.

FIGURE 13-9:
The results of a
query built with
the Query Wizard.

FirstName	LastName	StartDate	Mobile	Email	Status	EventName	Event Date	EventType
Mimi	Shapiro	7/5/2008	717-444-4337	mshapiro@domain.com	Active	Food Drive	6/30/2019	Collection
Zachary	Ulrich	2/1/2011	717-444-4322	zulrich@domain.com	Active	Battle of the Bands	9/20/2018	Collection
David	Mermelstein	6/5/2010	717-444-4332	dmermelstein@domain.com	Active	Christmas in July	7/25/2019	Fundraising

Volunteers Query

TO SUMMARIZE OR NOT TO SUMMARIZE

How does the wizard choose whether it feels like summarizing things? Well, computers are a lot like people that way: Choices that seem arbitrary usually have reasons behind them.

The wizard displays the Detail or Summary step (shown previously in Figure 13-7) if either of these statements is true:

- Fields for your query are selected from two tables that have a *one-to-many* relationship with each other. (Chapter 5 explains one-to-many relationships.)

- A selected field contains numeric data.

BUT WHAT ABOUT THE OTHER QUERY WIZARDS?

Besides the Simple Query Wizard, Access offers three other query wizards.

- *Crosstab Query Wizard* summarizes multiple rows of data into a spreadsheet-like format.

  A Crosstab is similar to an Excel PivotTable.

- *Find Duplicates Query Wizard* helps you locate duplicate records in a table or query.

  This wizard locates all records in the customer table that have the exact same content in the fields specified during the query's creation. After it finds the duplicates, you can decide whether the records in question are truly redundant or simply have a lot in common.

- *Unmatched Query Wizard* finds unrelated records in two tables that share a common field.

  If an Orders table contains orders for a customer who isn't in the Customers table, you have yourself a problem — orders in the system and no one to bill. Sounds like a recipe for the unemployment line! How can such a thing happen? *Referential integrity* prevents a child table from containing a record that has no corresponding record in the parent table. (Chapter 5 covers referential integrity.) If you don't turn Referential Integrity on, it's quite possible to put in an order for a nonexistent customer. The Find Unmatched Query Wizard can find records with reference problems and help you get to the bottom of such a dilemma.

TIP

Use the following list to modify or use a query created with the Query Wizard:

>> To write complex AND and OR criteria, see Chapter 14.

>> To add calculations like sums and averages, see Chapter 15.

>> To add custom formulas (like a sales tax calculation), see Chapter 16.

>> To attach the query to a report, see Chapter 18.

Getting Your Feet Wet with Ad Hoc Queries

If you use Access regularly, you need to know how to build a query from scratch. This is where Design view comes into play. Design view may look a little complicated — check out Figure 13-10 — but it's really not that bad, and you have seen it before, when building the filters you just looked at. You'll be all right, I promise!

>> The top section of the view – the portion of the Query Design space that's above the grid – is where you place the tables or previously created queries you want to include in this new query.

>> The bottom half is called the Query Design grid; it contains the Field, Table, Sort, Show, Criteria, and Or rows used to generate the results.

TIP

You'll notice that a new tab appears on the Ribbon as soon as you enter a Design task. The contextual Design tab appears under a Query Tools heading, as shown at the top of the window in Figure 13-10.

FIGURE 13-10:
A query that will allow you to see only Fundraising Events (and the volunteers assigned to run them) scheduled to occur in the summer.

EventName	EventDate	EventType	FirstName	LastName	Mobile	FundsNeeded	FundsRaised
Swim-a-Thon	8/15/2018	Fundraising	Joshua	Ulrich	717-444-4321	1500	
Food Drive	6/30/2019	Collection	Mimi	Shapiro	717-444-4337	5000	6000
Christmas in July	7/25/2019	Fundraising	David	Mermelstein	717-444-4332	10000	

To build a multiple-table query by hand in Design view, follow these steps:

1. **Click the Create tab on the Ribbon.**

   A series of buttons organized by object type appears on the Ribbon.

2. **From the Queries section, click the Query Design button.**

   The Show Table dialog box appears, listing all tables and queries available for your new query.

   Yes, you can query a query.

TECHNICAL STUFF

3. **Add the tables you want in your query:**

   a. *In the Show Table dialog box (see Figure 13-11), double-click the names of each table or query you want.*

      After you double-click a table, a small window for that table appears in the Query Design window.

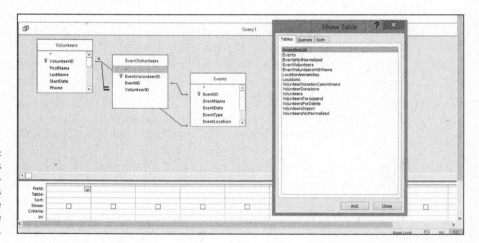

FIGURE 13-11:
The Volunteers and Event-Volunteers tables are added to the ad hoc query.

   b. *After you add the last table you want, click Close.*

      The Show Table dialog box is dismissed.

   In the Query Design window, lines between your tables (as shown in Figure 13-12) show *relationships* between the tables. The sidebar "Get the right tables" explains how these relationships are essential to the proper building and execution of your query.

TECHNICAL STUFF

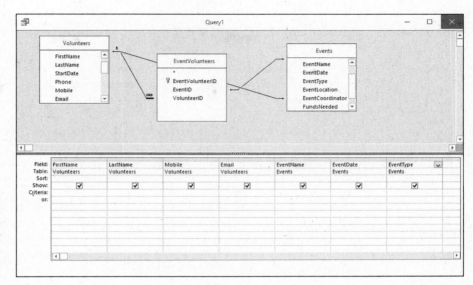

FIGURE 13-12:
Access knows how the Volunteers, EventVolunteers, and Events tables are related.

4. **In the table(s) that now appear(s) in the top half of the Query window, double-click each field you want in the list at the top of the Query Design window.**

Consider the following while choosing fields:

TIP

- Choose your fields in the order you want them to appear in the query results.

- You can include fields from any or all of the tables at the top of the query window (the tables you selected in the preceding step).

If you accidentally choose the wrong field, you can easily correct your mistake:

TECHNICAL STUFF

a. *Click the field name's entry in the Query grid.*

b. *Select the Delete Columns button from the Ribbon's Query Tools Design tab.*

The field is removed from the Query grid.

Now you're ready to put the finishing touches to your query by adding functionality such as sorting. The following section shows you how.

GET THE RIGHT TABLES

If you've been a faithful reader from Page 1 of this book, you've probably established relationships between your selected tables and saved yourself an extra step when building a query.

That's one reason table relationships are important. Each time you create a new query and select multiple tables, the relationship lines will already be in place for your queries. Database geeks call these relationship lines *join lines* or just plain old *joins*. Without those relationships, you'll have to join the tables manually for each new query.

What happens if you create a query but no line appears between the tables? Access is telling you that it doesn't have a clue how to relate the tables. It's possible that you selected the wrong tables — that is, tables that don't share a common field and therefore cannot be related. If you've selected the wrong tables, follow these steps to delete the unwanted tables and add the correct tables to your query:

1. **Click the title bar of the table that doesn't belong.**

   The little * at the top of the table's Field list will highlight, indicating that the entire Table List window is selected.

2. **Tap the Delete key on your keyboard to remove the table.**

   Repeat Steps 1 and 2 for each table you'd like to remove from the query.

   To display the Show Table dialog box, click the Show Table button, found in the Query Setup section of the Ribbon while you're in Design view.

3. **Select the correct table or tables for your query.**

If you select the right tables and still get no join lines, then you can go back to the Relationships window and relate the tables correctly. Chapter 5 shows you how. (You can also join tables in Query Design view, but I don't recommend it.)

Adding the finishing touches

To sort your query results in Design view (as shown here), follow these steps:

1. **Repeat these steps for each field you want to use for sorting:**

   a. *In the Query grid, click the Sort box under the field name.*

   b. *Click the down arrow that appears at the edge of the Sort box.*

   c. *Click either Ascending or Descending (as shown in Figure 13-13).*

FIGURE 13-13:
See the resulting events in Ascending date order.

TIP

The sidebar "Just these, and in this order" shows how to arrange sort fields. For all you need to know about sorting, see Chapter 12.

2. In the Criteria row for each field you want to use as criterion, type the criterion appropriate to that field.

For example, to show only fundraising events, as shown in Figure 13-14, type **Fundraising** in the Criteria cell in the EventType column. Table 13-1, earlier in the chapter, shows some criteria examples.

FIGURE 13-14:
With the criteria set for the EventType field, only events of that type will appear in the query results.

TECHNICAL STUFF

3. If you don't want that field to appear in the final results, deselect the check box in the Show row for that field.

The Show setting really stands out in your Query grid. There's only one check box in there — the Show option.

After you tell the query how to sort and select data, you're ready to see your query results by running the query.

Saving the query

After you create your query, you're ready to save it. Follow these steps:

1. Review your work one more time. When you're sure it looks good, click the Save button on the Quick Access Toolbar to save your query.

The Save As dialog box appears.

TIP

JUST THESE, AND IN THIS ORDER

Access has a nice tool for sorting the results from a query. After all, queries don't get much easier than clicking a little box labeled Sort and then telling the program whether Ascending or Descending is your choice for sort-flavor-of-the-moment.

The only problem with this little arrangement is that Access automatically sorts the results from left to right. If you request only one sort, this order is no big deal. But if you request two sorts, the column that's closest to the left side of the query automatically becomes the primary sort, with any other field playing second (or third) fiddle. Another trick? If you want to sort by a field and also display it in a different order within the fields included in the query, include that field twice — but only show it once. Just turn off the Show check box for the column where you're using the field for sorting.

Taking control of the sort order isn't hard, but it also isn't obvious. Because Access looks at the Query grid and performs the sorts from left to right, the trick is to move the column for the main sorting instruction to the left side of the grid. Follow these steps to move a column in the grid:

1. **Put the tip of the mouse pointer in the thin gray box just above the field name on the Query grid.**

2. **When the mouse pointer turns into a black downward-pointing arrow, click once.**

   All of a sudden the chosen field is highlighted; the mouse pointer changes from a downward-pointing black arrow to an upward-pointing white arrow.

3. **While still pointing at the thin gray box just above the field name, hold down the mouse button and drag the field to its new position on the grid.**

   As you move the mouse (which includes a gray outline of a box, along with the white arrow) a black bar moves through the grid, showing you where the field will land when you release the mouse button.

4. **When the black bar is in the right place, release the mouse button.**

   The field information pops into view, safe and happy in its new home.

This moving trick also changes the order in which the fields appear in your query results. Feel free to move fields here, there, or anywhere, depending on your needs.

Is this some great flexibility or what?

TECHNICAL STUFF

2. **In the Save As dialog box, type a name for the query and then click OK.**

You're saving the design of the query and not the results returned by the query. So as records are added, edited, and deleted from your data tables, the query always returns the data *as it is at the moment the query is run*.

Running your query

After you create your query and save it, you're ready to run it. Follow these steps:

1. **Take one last look to make sure it's correct.**

Inspect the fields you've chosen and your other settings in the query grid. The sidebar "Query troubleshooting" lists common query problems.

2. **Click the Run button (the huge red exclamation point, shown second from left in the Ribbon's Design tab shown in Figure 13-15).**

Did you get the answer you hoped for? If not, take your query back into Design view for some more work. To do so, click the Design View button on the Quick Access Toolbar.

Run button

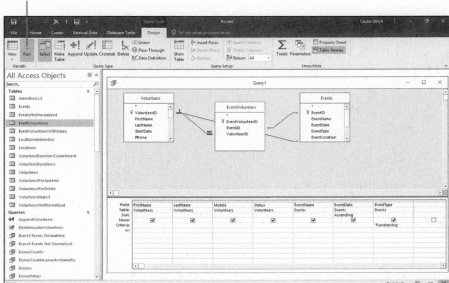

FIGURE 13-15:
Click the big red exclamation point that says "Run" underneath it to run your query.

QUERY TROUBLESHOOTING

If your query results aren't exactly what you thought you asked for (isn't that just like a computer?), double-check your query design for errors. Common design errors include

- Mixing up the greater-than (>) and less-than (<) signs
- Leaving out an equals sign (=) in your greater-than-or-equal-to statements
- Misspelling criteria such as region name, state, or postal code
- Entering criteria in the wrong field

» Working with the AND and OR operators

» Including AND and OR in the same query

Chapter **14**

I Want These AND Those OR Them

As you build larger and more complex databases with Access, your questions about the data they contain become larger and more complex. Simply changing the order of your records — sorting from A to Z and then from Z to A — and filtering it from one or more perspectives just may not be enough for your needs anymore. You want greater power to find and use data, and you need more from your database. You also need it quickly.

What to do? You can use queries that ask questions (present criteria to the database to see which records meet them) to help you find the records you need to *access* (pardon the expression) right now.

This chapter shows you how to set more specific criteria for your queries, controlling the answers to your database questions with ease and speed. You find out about two very powerful Access operators — AND and OR — what the operators do, how they do it, and (most important) when and why to use them.

TIP

If AND and OR are not the solutions to your query-building needs, Chapter 13 takes a more detailed stroll through the basics of querying, and may help point you in the right direction. You can create queries automatically, or you can build them from scratch. Chapter 13 gives you some more advanced ideas about queries and helps you craft specialized queries for your specific needs.

Working with AND and/or OR

AND and OR are the most powerful and popular of the *Boolean* terms.

In written language, you probably know when to use *and* versus *or*. If you're not sure how this knowledge can be transferred to your use of Access, read on:

>> AND is used when all the items in a list are to be chosen. For example, "bring a salad, a side dish, and a dessert to the potluck dinner" would tell the person to bring all three items to the dinner.

>> OR creates a list wherein each item is a choice — "bring a salad, a side dish, or a dessert to the potluck dinner." In this example, the person reading the instruction would know that only one item need be brought, but it's okay to bring two or more (or all) of the items.

With the OR example, you'll be spending less time in the kitchen, and with OR in your query, you'll be making it possible for more of the records to meet your criteria. Using an employee database as an example, your query might say, "Give me all the people who work in Accounting AND Operations" — and none of the employee records would meet that criterion, because nobody works in two departments at the same time. However, using OR would work: "Give me all the people who work in Accounting OR Operations" would provide a list of all the employees in the two departments.

TECHNICAL STUFF

Boolean logic (named for George Boole, the guy who invented it) allows you to use words like AND, OR, NOT, LESS THAN, GREATER THAN, and EQUAL TO to search a database. In Access, these terms are called *operators*.

REMEMBER

If you're not sure you can remember when to use AND versus OR, think of it this way:

>> AND **narrows your query.** Fewer records match.

In normal usage, *and* gives you no options. You do *everything* in the list.

>> OR **widens your query.** More records match.

In normal usage, *or* gives you more options because you can pick and choose which items from the list you want to do.

As an example, in Access, if you're searching a customer database and you say you want customers who live in a particular city *and* who live in an area with a particular zip code *and* who have purchased more than $50,000 worth of items in the past year, you're probably going to end up with a short list of customers — you'll have fewer options. On the other hand, if you want customers who are in a particular city *or* have a particular zip code *or* who have purchased more than $50,000 in goods this year, you'll get many more choices — everyone from the city, with the zip code, and over that purchasing level — probably many more customers than the *and* query will give you.

Data from here to there

One of the most common Access queries involves listing items that are between two values.

Here's an example. You may want to find all the events that occurred between June 1, 2018 and January 1, 2019. For this list of records, you use AND criteria to establish the range. Here's how:

>> Put the two conditions (on or after June 1, 2018 and before January 1, 2019) together on the same line.

>> Separate the conditions with an AND operator.

Figure 14-1 shows the query window for this range of dates.

FIGURE 14-1:
Find data that falls within a range of dates by using AND.

TIP

Don't worry about the pound signs (#) — Access puts those in automatically for you. When entering your ranges in the future, don't type them yourself; let Access do its job. You don't want it to feel unnecessary, right?

Anyway, here's what's going on in the query window:

1. **Access begins processing the query by looking through the records in the table and asking the first question in the criteria:**

Did this event take place before June 1, 2018?

- If the event occurred before this date, Access ignores the record and goes on to the next record.

- If the order was placed on or after the date, Access goes to Step 2.

2. **If the event took place on or after June 1, 2018, Access asks the second question:**

   Did this event take place before January 1, 2019?

   - If yes, Access includes the record in the results.
   - If no, the record is rejected, and Access moves on to the next record.

   Access repeats Step 1 and Step 2 for all records in the table.

3. **When Access hits the last record in the database, the query's results appear.**

Note that using the greater-than sign (>) without the equal sign (=) would include events occurring after June 1, 2018 — but not events occurring on June 1, 2018. Similarly, the second date in this query could be specified as either <1/1/2019 or ≤12/31/2018 to get the same results: records occurring before the first day of 2019.

TIP

This type of "between" instruction works for any type of data. You can list numeric values that fall between two other numbers, names that fall within a range of letters, or dates that fall within a given area of the calendar.

TECHNICAL STUFF

You could also search for dates by using the BETWEEN operator (see Figure 14-2 for an example of BETWEEN in action). The criteria BETWEEN #6/1/2018# AND #1/1/2019# selects records if the dates land on or between June 1, 2017 and January 1, 2019.

FIGURE 14-2:
The BETWEEN operator is the ultimate range finder.

Field:	EventName	EventDate		EventType	FirstName	LastName	Email	Phone
Table:	Events	Events		Events	Volunteers	Volunteers	Volunteers	Volunteers
Sort:								
Show:	☑	☑		☑	☑	☑	☑	☑
Criteria:		Between 6/1/2018 And 1/1/2019						
or:								

Using multiple levels of AND

Overall, Access lets you do whatever you want in a query — and for that reason, flexibility really adds to the application's power.

Access doesn't limit you to just *one* criterion in each line of a query — you can include as many criteria as you want, even if by adding more and more criteria you end up whittling your results down to one record, or even no records. When you add multiple criteria, Access treats the criteria as though you type an AND between each one and the next.

WARNING

All that power can backfire on you. Each AND criterion that you add must sit with the others on the same row. When you run the query, Access checks each record to make sure it matches *all* the expressions in the given Criteria row of the query before putting that record into the result table. Figure 14-3 shows a query that uses two criteria: Because they all sit together on a single row, Access treats the criteria as though they were part of a big AND statement. This query returns only events that happened between June 1, 2018 and January 1, 2019 AND that have an EventType of Education.

FIGURE 14-3:
Multiple criteria whittle down the resulting data to just those records you want to see.

When you have a very large database and want to restrict your results to a minimum of records, combining a few criteria is the most useful way to go.

TIP

Really want to whittle that list of records down? Because Access displays the query results in Datasheet view, all the tools available in Datasheet view work with the query — including filters! Just use any of the filter commands (use the Filter tool group's buttons to filter by Selection, for example) to limit your query results. (If you need a quick refresher on filters, flip back to Chapter 12.)

Establishing criteria with OR

When you want to find a group of records that match one of several possibilities (such as orders shipped from either Canada or France), you need the OR operator when you choose your criteria. It's the master of multiple options.

Access makes using OR easy. Because the OR option is built right into the Access query design window, you can just:

» Choose the field on which to query the data.

» Indicate which values to look for.

To make a group of criteria work together as a big OR statement, list each criterion on its own line at the bottom of the query, as shown in Figure 14-4. Here you see that events between June 1, 2018 and January 1, 2019 (based on the EventDate field's date range) and that are also of the Education or Collection (for the EventType field) will be the only records to meet the query's criteria.

Field:	EventName	EventDate	EventType	FirstName	LastName	Email	Phone
Table:	Events	Events	Events	Volunteers	Volunteers	Volunteers	Volunteers
Sort:							
Show:	☑	☑	☑	☑	☑	☑	☑
Criteria:		>#6/1/2017# And <#1/1/2019#	"Education"				
or:			"Collection"				

Each line can include a criterion for whichever fields you want, even if another line in the query *already* has a criterion in that field. (This is easier than it sounds.)

Of course, you can list the criteria in different columns, as shown in Figure 14-5. Here you see a query that searches for Education or Collection events that occurred in June of 2017 or June of 2018, achieved by including the EventDate field twice, each time with a different date range. Such a search might be done to isolate events that occur in a month with volatile weather, which can affect attendance or result in postponements.

FIGURE 14-5:
You can use
the OR operator
to set criteria
for data from
different field
columns in
the Query
design grid.

Field:	EventName	EventDate	EventDate	EventType	FirstName	LastName	Email
Table:	Events	Events	Events	Events	Volunteers	Volunteers	Volunted
Sort:							
Show:	☑	☑	☑	☑	☑	☑	
Criteria:		>=#6/1/2017# And <#7/1/2017#	>=#6/1/2018# And <#7/1/2018#				
or:							

Each OR criterion is on a separate line. If the criteria are on the same line, you're performing an AND operation — only records that match both rules appear.

REMEMBER

Combining AND with OR and OR with AND

When it comes to combining the use of AND and OR operators, Access can bend like a contortionist (how do they *do* that?). When the AND and OR operators by themselves aren't enough, you can combine them within a single field — or in multiple fields in one or more tables.

These logically complex queries get really complex, really fast. You can end up confused as to why certain records come back in your results — or worse, why certain records didn't make the cut. If a query grows to the point that you're losing track of which AND the last OR affected, you're in over your head, and it's time to start over again.

WARNING

Instead of adding layer upon layer of conditions into a single query, you can break down your question into a series of smaller queries that build on each other:

1. **Begin with a simple query with one or two criteria.**

2. **Build another query that starts with the first query's results.**

3. **If you need more refining, create a third query that chews on the second query's answers.**

   Each successive query whittles down your results until the final set of records appears.

   This procedure lets you double-check every step of your logic, so it minimizes the chance of any errors accidentally slipping into your results. You can also use it to build on an existing query, adding more criteria and including more (or different) fields in the query — just open the previously created query and begin working on it as though it were a new query in progress.

Each OR line (each line within the query) is evaluated separately so that all the records returned by a single line will appear in the final results. If you want to combine several different criteria, make sure that each OR line represents one aspect of what you're searching.

For example, in our Pantry database, querying for events that happened before June 1, 2018 and after June 1, 2018 requires the OR condition, and using an OR condition means that the criteria go on separate lines.

Imagine, however, that you want to find only the events that happened within that range of dates but that were also of a particular type or run by a particular volunteer. For such a query to work, you need to repeat the date-range information on each OR line.

To set up this query, you need criteria on separate lines:

>> One line asks for events that happened within a range of dates (EventDate).

>> The other Criteria line shows the EventType you want to see — Fundraising or Collection this time.

Figure 14-6 shows this combination of AND and OR operators in action — a range of dates within one year, and events relative to another year, along with specific EventType values.

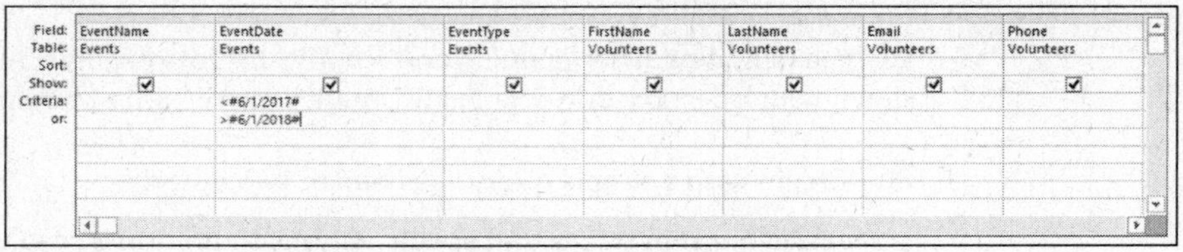

Field:	EventName	EventDate		EventType	FirstName	LastName	Email	Phone	
Table:	Events	Events		Events	Volunteers	Volunteers	Volunteers	Volunteers	
Sort:									
Show:	☑		☑	☑	☑	☑	☑	☑	
Criteria:		<#6/1/2017#							
or:		>#6/1/2018#							

FIGURE 14-6:
Any criteria placed on separate lines are seen as OR statements.

REMEMBER

When reviewing your query criteria, keep these points in mind:

» Separately, make sure each line represents a group that you want included in the final answer.

» Check to be sure that the individual lines work together to give you the answer you're seeking:

- AND criteria all go on the same line and are evaluated together.

- OR criteria go on separate lines. Each line is evaluated separately.

- Criteria that you want to use in each OR statement must be repeated on each separate line in the query grid.

Chapter **15**

Number Crunching with the Total Row

Ever need to know how many orders were placed in the past month? Or total donations for last year? How about the top ten best-selling products for the current year? If you answered yes to any of these questions (or have similar questions that need answering), then this chapter is for you. Here I discuss the fabulous Total row. The Total row does it all for your data! Well, actually, it summarizes your data via the select query. (If you don't know what a select query is or how to create one, I suggest you go back and read Chapter 13 before beginning the material in this chapter.)

Say Hello to the Total Row

In Chapter 13, I show you how simple select queries can fetch data, such as a list of volunteers who reside in California or all the details of tofu sales. The Total row takes the select query one step further and summarizes the selected data. The Total row can answer questions such as, "How many of our volunteers reside in California?" and "How much money did we make in tofu sales last month?" It can also do statistical calculations, such as standard deviations, variances, and maximum and minimum values. For a complete list of what the Total row can do for each field selected in the Field row, see Table 15-1.

To make Access perform these calculations, you must first group your records together by using the Total row's Group By function. (The Total row makes an appearance in Figure 15-1.) As you might imagine, Group By treats multiple repeated instances of information as one. It puts all the Californians together on one row so you can count the number of Californians in your database. Typically, you apply Group By to a text or ID field and the remaining functions in the Total row on numeric fields.

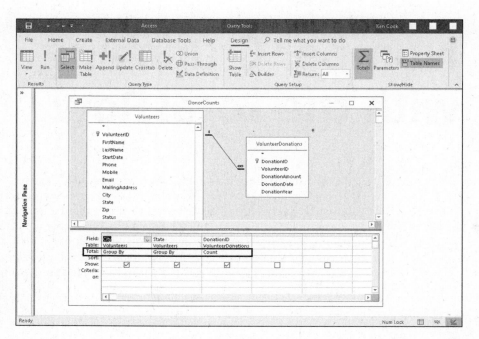

FIGURE 15-1:
The Total row appears between the Table and the Sort rows.

The most commonly used items among the Total row's offerings are Group By, Sum, Avg, Count, and the odd-sounding option Where. Later sections in this chapter go into more depth about these items — explaining what they do, how to use them, and why you really *do* care about all this stuff.

TABLE 15-1   **Total Row Functions**

Instruction	What It Does
Group By	Groups the query results by the field's values.
Sum	Totals all the values from this field in the query results.
Avg	Averages the values in this field in your query results.
Min	Tells you the lowest value found in the field.
Max	Reports the highest value found in the field.
Count	Counts the number of records that match the query criteria.
StDev	Figures the statistical standard deviation of the values in the field.
Var	Calculates the statistical variance of the values in the field.
First	Displays the first record that meets the query criteria.
Last	Displays the last record that meets the query criteria.
Expression	Tells Access that you want a calculated field. (See Chapter 16 for the different calculations Access can perform.)
Where	Uses the field for record–selection criteria, but doesn't summarize anything with it.

Adding the Total Row to Your Queries

By default, Access always assumes you want a simple select query. You must tell it specifically that you want to summarize your data; adding the Total row to your query does the trick.

Okay, enough chatter about the Total row; it's time to get busy. Make sure you're in Design view, and then follow these steps to create summary queries with the Total row:

1. **Create a new select query or open an existing select query that contains the data you want to summarize in Design view.**

   TIP

   If you're scratching your head at this point, refer to Chapter 13 for information on creating select queries.

2. **Turn on the Total row by clicking the Totals button in the Show/Hide group of the Design Ribbon's Query Tools tab.**

   The Total row appears between the Table and Sort rows on the query grid. For every field already in your query, Access automatically fills the Total row with its default entry, Group By.

The Totals button displays the Greek letter sigma (Σ). Mathematicians, engineers, and others with questionable communication skills use this symbol when they mean "give me a total."

3. **To change a field's Total entry from Group By to something else, click that field's Total row.**

   The blinking-line cursor appears in the Total row, right next to a down-arrow button.

4. **Click the down-arrow button in the field's Total row and then select the new Total entry you want from the drop-down menu that appears.**

   The new entry appears in the Total row.

5. **Make any other changes you want and then run the query.**

   By setting values in the Total row, the query results automatically include the summary (or summaries) you selected. How about that?

The following section shows how to use the most popular and useful Total row options.

Working Out the Total Row

This section focuses on the most commonly used items in the Total row's toolbox: Group By, Sum, Count, and Where. Remember, the choice made in the Total row applies to the field selected in the Field row above it.

TIP

Unless you're a statistician or scientist, the information in this chapter should suffice for all your Total row needs. Even though I don't discuss standard deviations or variances, they work the same way as Sum or Count. Check the Access Help system (press F1 on your keyboard) for more about the less popular Total row functions.

REMEMBER

Most Total row options perform well by themselves, but they also work well with others. When you run multiple queries, try using several different options together to save yourself time. It takes some practice to ensure that everything works the way you want, but the benefits (more information with less effort) make up for the investment.

Putting it together with Group By

The Group By instruction has two functions:

>> To organize your query results into groups based on the values in one or more fields.

>> To eliminate duplicate entries in your results.

When you turn on the Total row in your query grid, Access automatically puts in a Group By for every field on the grid. Group By combines like records so that the other Total row instructions (such as Sum and Count) can do their thing. So to make effective use of the Total row, your query must return one or more fields that contain duplicate information across records.

>> Putting a single Group By instruction in a query tells Access to total your results by each unique value in that field (by each volunteer or product name, for example). Each unique item appears only once in the results, on a single line with its summary info.

>> If you include more than one Group By instruction in a single query (such as the one shown in Figure 15-2), Access uses the Group By instruction to build a summary line for every unique combination of the fields. Grouping works like sorting. Access groups by the position of grouped fields from left to right in query design. It'll group by the closest field to the left first, the second closest field to the left second, and so on.

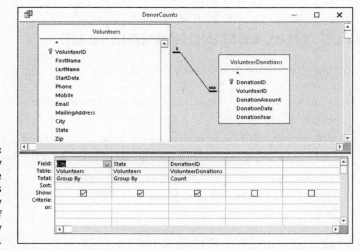

FIGURE 15-2: This query counts the donations for every combination of data in the City and State fields.

Put the Group By instruction into the field you want to summarize — the one that answers the question, "What do you want to count *by?*" or "What needs totaling?" To count California volunteers (for example), group by the State field in your table. To produce a list of total dollar donations by volunteer, you need to group by the FirstName and LastName fields.

When you use Group By, Access sorts the results automatically, in an order based on the field you specified with the Group By instruction. If you put Group By in the State field, for example, Access sorts your results alphabetically by the contents of that field. To override this behavior and choose a different sorting order, just use the Sort row in your query grid. Here's how:

1. **Choose the field that you want to sort everything by.**

2. **Put the appropriate sorting command (Ascending or Descending, depending on your needs) in that field's Sort row, as shown in Figure 15-3).**

   Access organizes the query results in the indicated order.

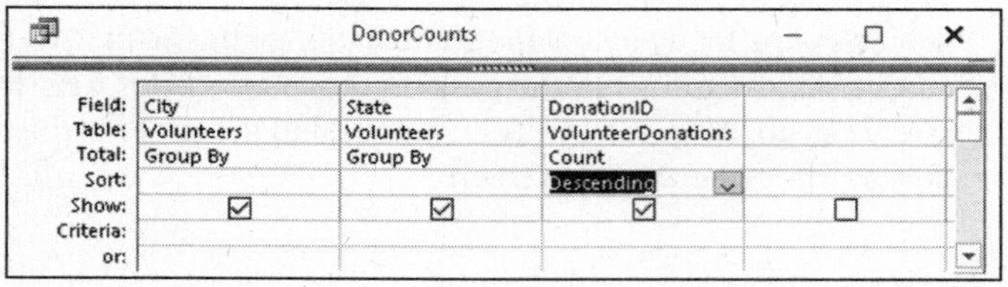

FIGURE 15-3: Make Access sort your results the way you want with a quick click in the query grid's Sort row.

Well, that certainly sums it up

Sum finds the total value of numeric fields:

» When you put the Sum instruction in a field, Access totals the values in that field.

» If you use the Sum instruction on the only field in a query grid, Access calculates a grand total of the values in that field for the entire table.

» When you pair a Sum instruction with a Group By instruction (as shown in Figure 15-4), your results display a sum for each unique entry in the Group By field.

Pair the Sum instruction with any other Total row option to get more than one summary for each line of your results. Count and Sum naturally go together, as do Sum and Avg (Average), Min (Minimum value), and Max (Maximum value).

DON'T SEE WHAT YOU EXPECT IN YOUR RESULTS?

Sometimes, when I run a summary query, a few lines are "missing." I expect to see them, but they just aren't there. That begs the question "Why?" Usually it's because of the type of join between tables in my query. The default join is called an inner join, in which a row can appear in the query only if matching records exist in both tables. So for a volunteer to show up on a donations count query that joins the Volunteers and Donations tables, that volunteer must have at least one donation in the Donations table. If I want a query to show volunteers who haven't made a donation yet, I have to change the type of join to an outer join, which will accommodate that condition.

To change join types between any two tables in a query (in my example here, the Volunteers and Donations tables), display the Join Properties dialog box by double-clicking the line that connects the two tables. You have to be good with the mouse on this one. If you miss the join line, nothing happens. This can be one of those take-a-sledge-hammer-to-your-computer moments. However, don't despair. Just point to the line once again and double-click. If the tip of the mouse pointer is on the line, the Join Properties dialog box will pop up.

Read options 2 and 3 carefully and select whichever one is appropriate for your situation. Each option will create an outer join. In the example given previously, the option that reads "2: Include ALL records from 'Volunteers' and only those records from 'Donations' where the joined fields are equal" would be correct. This option displays all volunteers, regardless of their donation situation. So I'll see an empty cell next to each volunteer who has yet to donate — plus a donation count next to those who have donated.

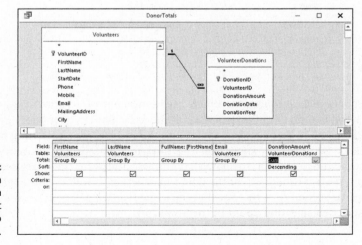

FIGURE 15-4: Put the Sum instruction in a numeric field so it has something to work with.

TIP

To limit the range of the records totaled in Sum, use the Where instruction (described later in this chapter).

Counting, the easy way

Use the Count instruction in the query when you want to know how many entries are in the group, instead of performing mathematical calculations on numeric fields for the group.

Because Count doesn't attempt any math on a field's data, it works on a field of any data type in your tables.

TIP

When used by itself in a query (as shown in Figure 15-5), Count tallies the number of entries in a particular field across every record in the entire table and then displays the answer. By using Count with one or more Group By instructions in other fields, Access counts the number of items relating to each unique entry in the Group By field.

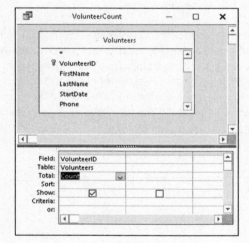

FIGURE 15-5:
Use Count on a single field to easily count the records in a table.

TIP

For a quick and accurate count of the number of records in a group, point the Group By and Count instructions at the same field in your query grid, as shown in Figure 15-6. To be part of the group, the records need matching data in a certain field. Because you *know* that the field for your Group By instruction contains something (namely, the data that defines groups for the query results), that field is a perfect candidate for the Count instruction as well. Add the field to your query grid a second time by choosing the same field name again — in a new column — and then selecting Count in the Total row.

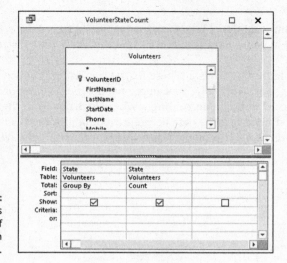

FIGURE 15-6:
This query counts the number of volunteers in each state.

TIP

Apply a calculation to a field, and Access tacks on a newfangled word such as *SumOf* or *CountOf* or *<insert calculation name here>Of* to the beginning of the field name in Datasheet view. To insert your own (more meaningful) column heading, type the heading followed by a colon (as in **StateCount:**) in front of the field name on the query grid (see Figure 15-7).

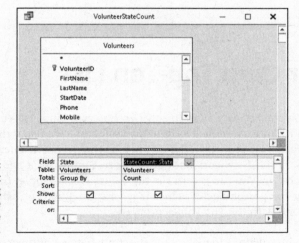

FIGURE 15-7:
The StateCount column heading is added to the count of the State field.

Narrowing the results with Where

The Where instruction works a bit differently from the other options in the Total row. The Where instruction lets you add criteria to the query (such as showing volunteers from certain states, or including orders placed only after a certain date) without including additional fields in your results. In fact, Access won't allow you to show a field in your query results that contains the Where instruction.

The query in Figure 15-8 uses a Where instruction to limit which records appear in the query results. Normally, that query would count donations by volunteer, using every record in the table. Adding a Where instruction to the `City` field tells the query that it must test the data before including it in the results. In this case, the Where instruction's criteria include records for those people living in Lancaster or Marietta.

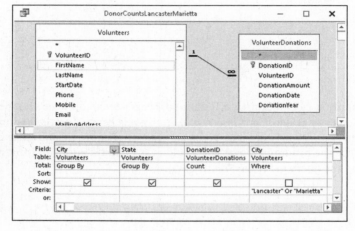

FIGURE 15-8:
The Where instruction limits records in the results to Lancaster or Marietta volunteers.

Creating Your Own Top-Ten List

Here's a problem that is a snap to solve with Access. Suppose you need a list of your top ten volunteers, ranked by donation amounts. Or a list of the top five best-selling products last year. Or a list of the top whatever. The query property Top Values takes all the dirty work out of this chore. Simply set it and forget it — the dirty work, that is! You can return the top values (for example, the top 5 out of a list of 40) or top percentage of values (say, the top 5 percent, which returns the top 2 out of 40) with the Top Values property.

Follow these instructions to make a top-ten (or whatever number you choose) list:

1. Open the query containing the data for your top-values list in Design view.

The query must contain at least one numerical field so that a set of top values can be selected. Usually, it's a summary query, such as total donation amount by volunteer. The query must be sorted on the numerical field.

2. **From the Design tab on the Ribbon, locate the Return button in the Query Setup group of buttons.**

3. **Click the drop-down list arrow next to the Return button and select a choice from the list or type your own number in the box.**

Because 10 isn't on the list, you'll have to type 10 in the box to generate a top-ten list. (See Figure 15-9.)

4. **Switch to Datasheet view.**

The list is limited to the range of top values determined by the number or percentage you entered in the box.

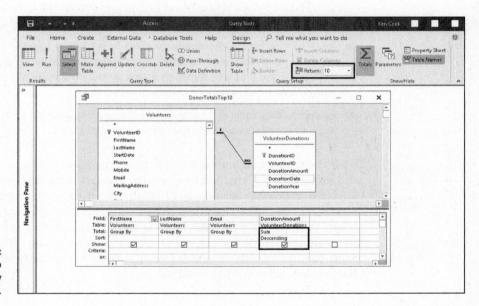

FIGURE 15-9:
Setting the Top Values property to 10.

TIP

The Top Values property returns the top values for whatever column is sorted first in the query (Access sorts first by the leftmost field that has Sort row instructions in the QBE grid). If you tell Access to show you the top ten volunteers in donation amount based on a field called DonationAmount, you won't get them unless you sort on the DonationAmount field. Choose Descending in the Sort row of the DonationAmount field to have Access order them for you from highest to lowest.

Choosing the Right Field for the Summary Instruction

Deciding which field gets a Sum, Count, or other Total row instruction *greatly* affects your query results. If you choose the wrong field, Access fails to tally things correctly.

REMEMBER

Follow these guidelines when choosing fields for your summary queries:

>> Don't apply summary functions that require numbers to calculate (such as Sum and Avg) to a text field. You'll get the ever-popular Data type mismatch error message if you do.

>> Fields with repetitive information (such as order date in an orders table or volunteer ID in a donations table) make excellent Group By fields. For example, if you group by donation date and count the VolunteerID field, you get a count of donations per day.

>> When counting records, choose a field that contains data for each record. If you don't, Access excludes the blank fields in its count.

To see the kinds of miscues that can happen, check out Figure 15-10. There you'll see a summary query that has been written to count volunteers and zip codes. The Count instruction has been applied to both the VolunteerID and Zip fields of the Volunteers table. The Zip field returns 17, whereas the VolunteerID field returns 19. Which is right? The latter is correct because each record in the table has a volunteer ID. Not every record has a zip code specified. Therefore, Access counts only the records for which a value appears in the Zip field for a customer. Choose your fields wisely to avoid this problem.

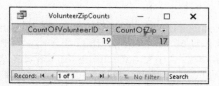

FIGURE 15-10:
The Zip and VolunteerID fields counted.

The Total row takes some getting used to. But in no time, you'll master the power of this tool in your queries. When that day comes, say goodbye to your old friend Mr. Spreadsheet forever!

Chapter 16

Express Yourself with Formulas

Efficient database design requires that tables contain only necessary fields. Too many fields can cause a table to load slowly — you won't notice the difference with a few hundred records, but you certainly will with a few hundred thousand. So what fields are often added unnecessarily to a table's design? The short answer: fields that could be generated from calculations on data stored in other fields.

For example, suppose you have a Commitment table with a DonationCommitment field and a Donation table with a DonationAmount field. You may be tempted to add an AmountOwed field to your Donation table that stores the result of subtracting DonationAmount from DonationCommitment. This is unnecessary because Access can perform these calculations on the fly — in what's called a Calculated field.

A *Calculated field* takes information from another field or fields in the database and performs some arithmetic to come up with new information. Access calls the arithmetic formula used to perform the calculation an *expression*. In fact, a Calculated field can take data from more than one field and combine information to create an entirely new field if that's what you want. You can perform simple arithmetic (such as addition and multiplication) or use Access's built-in functions, such as DSum and DAvg (average), for more difficult calculations.

In this chapter, you build all kinds of calculations into your queries. From simple sums to complex equations, the information you need is right here.

TIP

Although the examples in this chapter deal with Calculated fields in queries, the same concept applies to Calculated fields in forms and reports.

A Simple Calculation

The first step in creating a Calculated field in a query is to include the tables that contain the fields you need for your calculation. In the preceding example, the commitment amount was in the Commitment table; the donation amount was in the Donation table. Therefore, a query to calculate donation amount from commitment amount must include information from both the Commitment and Donation tables. Access can't pull the numbers out of thin air for the calculation; you must make sure the fields that contain the numbers you need are present in your query.

Access uses a special syntax for building Calculated fields. Here's how to create a Calculated field:

1. **Click an empty column in the Field row of the query Design view grid.**

The good old cursor will blink in the row. Access puts the results of the calculation in the same grid position as the calculation itself, so if the calculation sits in the third column of your query grid, the calculation's result will be in the third column, too.

2. **Enter a name for your calculation followed by a colon (:).**

Access will refer to this calculation from now on by whatever name you enter before the colon (known as an alias). Keep it short and sweet (say, **AmountOwed** or **Tax**) so it's easier to refer to later on. If you don't name your calculation, Access will put the generic Expr (followed by a number) as its name. It has to be called something, so why not Expr1 or Expr2, right?

3. **Enter your calculation, substituting field names for the actual numbers where necessary.**

My AmountOwed Calculated field would look something like (well, *exactly* like) the calculation in Figure 16-1.

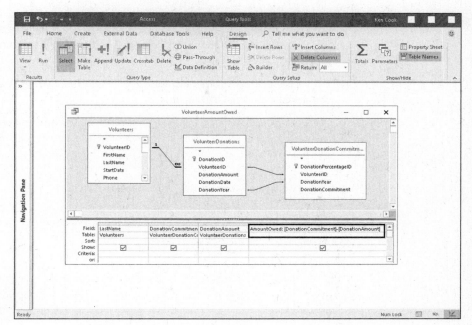

FIGURE 16-1:
The AmountOwed
calculation.

You don't have to use only field names in your calculations. You can also enter formulas with numbers, like this:

```
NewCommitment: DonationCommitment *1.05
```

TIP

If a field name contains more than one word, put square brackets around it. Access treats anything else it finds in the calculation as a constant (which is the math term for *it is what it is and it never changes*). If the field name contains no spaces, Access will put the square brackets in for you after you enter the field name. That's why I always use one-word field names — so I don't have to type those irritating square brackets.

TIP

When you create formulas, keep these general guidelines in mind:

>> **You must type the field names and constants into your formula.** You can't just drag and drop stuff from the table list.

>> **Don't worry if your calculation grows past the edge of the Field box.** Access still remembers everything in your formula, even if it doesn't appear onscreen.

TIP

To make the query column wider, aim the mouse pointer at the line on the right side of the thin bar above the calculation entry. Keep trying until you see a vertical line with a horizontal double arrow through it. When that happens, click and drag the mouse to the right. As you do, the column expands according to your movements. To fit the width to just the right size, position the mouse to size the column as described earlier — and then double-click! Isn't Access a gem?

>> **If it's a super-duper long calculation, press Shift+F2 while the cursor is somewhere on the calculation.**

This opens the Zoom dialog box so you can easily see and edit everything in a pop-up window. You can even change the font and size in Zoom for easier viewing. Wow!

When you run a query containing a calculation, Access:

>> Produces a datasheet showing the fields you specified.

>> Adds a new column for each Calculated field.

In Figure 16-2, the datasheet shows the VolunteerID, FirstName, LastName, DonationCommitment, DonationAmount, and the Calculated field AmountOwed for each volunteer.

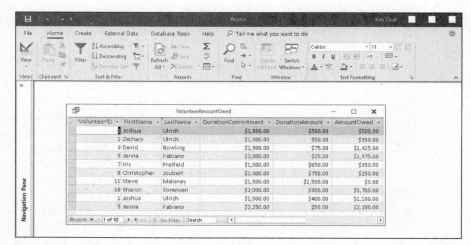

FIGURE 16-2:
The results of the amount owed calculation in Datasheet view.

Complex Calculations

After getting the hang of simple calculations, you can easily expand your repertoire into more powerful operations, such as using multiple calculations and building expressions that use values from other calculations in the same query. This stuff really adds to the flexibility and power of queries.

Calculate 'til you drop!

Access makes it easy to put multiple separate calculations into a single query. After building the first calculation, just repeat the process in the next empty Field box. Keep inserting calculations across the query grid until you've calculated everything you need.

TIP

You can use the same field in several calculations. Access doesn't mind at all.

Using one calculation in another

One of the most powerful Calculated-field tricks involves using the solution from one Calculated field as part of another calculation *in the same query*. This is sometimes called a *nested* calculation, and it can do two useful tricks:

>> It creates a field in the query results.

>> It supplies data to other calculations in the same query, just as if it were a real field in the table.

Figure 16-3 shows an example of a nested calculation in Design view.

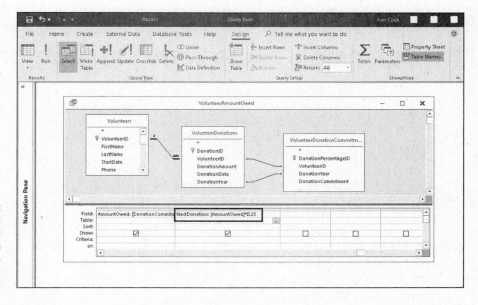

FIGURE 16-3:
The AmountOwed Calculated column is referred to in the NextDonation column.

Figure 16-4 shows the actual results of the calculations.

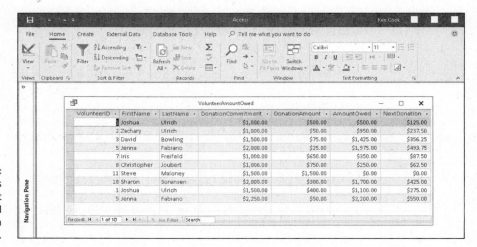

FIGURE 16-4:
The results
of the Amount
Owed and
NextDonation
columns.

WARNING

Although this technique seems simple, be careful. A small error in one calculation can quickly trickle down to other calculations that are based on it, compounding a simple error into a huge mistake. Yikes!

To use the results from one calculation as part of another, just use the name of the first calculation as if it were a field name. In short, treat the first calculation like a field in your table.

ORDER, ORDER IN THE CALCULATION!

You've written your formula and don't see the answer you expect to see. You double-check the formula, and it seems correct. How can the formula be correct yet the result wrong? If you have more than one mathematical operation in a calculated expression, Access will follow these rules (called the *order of operations*) when determining the results of your expression.

- All operations in parentheses are calculated first.

- Exponents (^) are calculated second.

- Multiplication (*) and division (/) are calculated third.

- Addition (+) and subtraction (−) are calculated fourth.

For example, you might expect the formula 2+3*6 to equal 30. However, due to the order of operations (multiplication before addition), Access will return 20. To make Access generate the expected result, the formula must be entered as (2+3)*6.

Using parameter queries to ask for help

At times, you may want to include a value in a formula that doesn't exist anywhere in your database (for example, the number .25 for a 25-percent next donation rate in the calculation example earlier in this chapter). If you know the value, you can type it directly into the formula.

But what if the number changes all the time? You don't want to constantly alter a query; that's a big waste of time and effort. Instead of building the ever-changing number into your formula, why not make Access *ask* you for the number (called a *parameter*) when you run the query? This is an easy one:

1. **Think of an appropriate name for the value (such as Tax Rate, Last Price, or Next Donation Percentage).**

When choosing a name for your parameter, don't use the name of an existing field in your table — Access will ignore the parameter if you do. Instead, go with something that describes the number or value itself. As you can see in the query grid shown in Figure 16-5, entering something like [Enter next donation percentage as decimal] makes it very clear what is required from the user. When you look at this query months (or even years) from now, you can easily recognize that something called [Enter next donation percentage as decimal] probably is a value that Access asks for when the query runs, not a normal field.

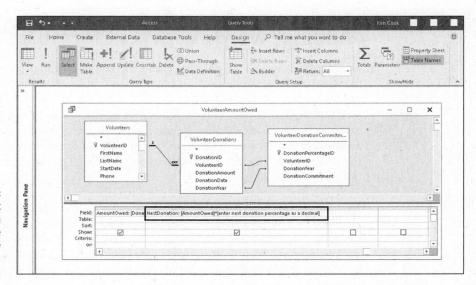

FIGURE 16-5:
The next donation percentage parameter in the NextDonation Calculated field.

2. **Use the name in your formula as if it were a regular field.**

Put square brackets around it and place it into your calculation, just as you did with the other fields.

3. **Run the query.**

Access displays a dialog box like the one shown in Figure 16-6.

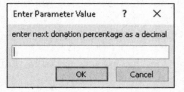

FIGURE 16-6:
Access asks for a
next donation
percentage.

4. **Enter the prompted information.**

For this example, just enter the value of your next donation percentage (as a decimal value). Access does the rest.

TIP

This option means you can use the same query with different values to see how changing that value affects your results. Each time you run the query, you'll be prompted for a value and the query will return results based on the value you enter.

"Adding" words with text formulas

Number fields aren't the only fields you can use in formulas. Access can also use the *words stored in text fields*.

TIP

A classic formula comes from working with names. If you have a Volunteers table with FirstName and LastName fields, you will at some point want to string those names together on a form or report. A text formula can do this for you. It can add the first name to the last name with a space in between; the result is the person's full name in one column.

The syntax for text-field formulas is similar to the syntax for number-field formulas — the field name is still surrounded by square brackets and must be carefully entered by hand (unless you use Expression Builder, which I discuss in the next section). Include literal text in the formula (such as spaces or punctuation) by surrounding it with quotation marks (for example, you'd type " , " to insert a comma).

You connect text fields with the ampersand character (&). Microsoft calls the ampersand the *concatenation operator*, which is a fancy way to say that it connects all things text.

Figure 16-7 shows a text-field formula. This example solves the problem I describe earlier in this section: making one name out of the pieces in two separate fields. The formula shown in the figure combines the FirstName and LastName fields into a single full name, ready to appear on a mailing label, report, or some other useful purpose you dream up.

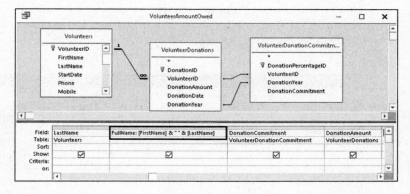

FIGURE 16-7: Turning two names into a single Calculated field.

This formula consists of the FirstName field, an ampersand (&), a single space inside quotation marks, followed by another ampersand, and then the LastName field. Here's what it looks like:

```
[FirstName]&" "&[LastName]
```

When you run this query, Access takes the information from the two fields and puts them together, inserting the space between them so they don't run straight into each other. Figure 16-8 shows the results of this query.

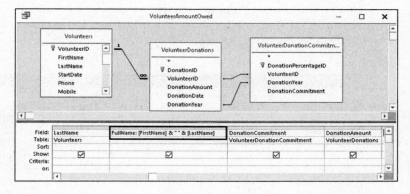

FIGURE 16-8: First and last names are combined to the single field, FullName.

Hooray for Expression Builder

Creating Calculated fields presents you with two basic challenges:

» Figuring out what the formula should say

» Entering the formula in a way that Access recognizes

Although Access can't help you with the first problem, it tries hard to offer some assistance with the second. When all else fails, and you just can't assemble a Calculated field in query design exactly the way Access wants it, click the Builder button in the Query Setup group of the Ribbon's Design tab to open Expression Builder (see Figure 16-9).

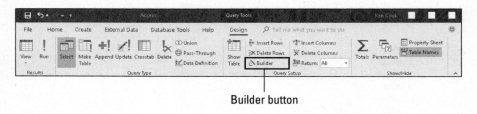

FIGURE 16-9:
The Builder button launches Expression Builder.

Builder button

WARNING

DON'T RELY ON EXPRESSION BUILDER

In theory, Expression Builder walks you through the frustrating syntax of building a calculation (what Access calls an *expression*) that meets all the nitpicky requirements Access puts in place. Although it does present you with the tools to build the formula, you have to wade through lists of every object, field, control, and function in the database to find what you need. You must also have some idea of how to build the formula to have success with Expression Builder. I find Expression Builder helpful for locating a list of built-in Access functions, for referring to a field properly in an expression, or for building a really long expression — but beyond that, it isn't much help. For me, it's faster to type my numerical operators instead of clicking those operators from a list in Expression Builder.

Before resorting to Expression Builder, try a little troubleshooting on your own. If your formulas don't work the way you think they should, double-check the spelling of every field, punctuation, and spacing. Most problems come from simple field-name spelling errors, a missing quotation mark, or a missing space. If all else fails and you're feeling adventurous, give Expression Builder a try. With any luck, it might actually solve your problem.

Expression Builder has several parts, as shown in Figure 16-10.

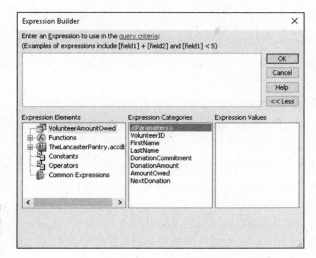

TIP

>> You create the expression in the large text box at the top of the dialog box.

>> The lower half of the dialog box contains three lists that work as a team:

- The Expression Elements list provides a navigational tree containing all the items that are at your disposal to build an expression such as tables, queries, forms, reports, constants, functions, and operators.

  You'll find the tables, queries, forms, and report objects within your database under an Expression Element with the same name as the name of your database. For example, if you want to select a Volunteers table field and you're in a database named Access 2019 Dummies.accdb, you'll see an item with that name on the Expression Elements list. Expand that item by clicking the plus sign (+) next to it to see the Tables item. Expand the Tables item to see the list of tables. Click the Volunteers table to see the fields in the Expression Categories list. Double-click the desired field to add it to the expression.

- When you click something in the Expression Elements list (such as Operators), the Expression Categories list populates with the categories within the selected element.

- When you click a category in the Expression Categories list (such as Comparison), the Expression Values list populates with the items within the selected category that finally (whew!) you can use in your expression.

>> Near the bottom of the Expression Elements list, Access also includes a few items for the Truly Technical Person — including these:

- Constants (values that never change, such as *true* and *false*).

- Operators that are available for comparisons and formulas:

    The Arithmetic category contains operators for addition, subtraction, division, and multiplication.

    The Comparison category contains operators such as =, >, <, <>

TIP

    Use comparisons to develop expressions for the Criteria section of your queries, when you need a response of *true* or *false*.

    The Logical category contains logical operators such as and, or, and not.

    The String category contains the Ampersand (&) operator that is used to combine two text fields.

- A folder called Common Expressions that contains stuff that's common only if you're creating reports or working with dates.

Expression Builder works like a big calculator crossed with a word processor:

>> At the bottom, double-click items in the Expression Categories or the Expression Values list (depending on the situation) to include them in your expression at the top.

>> Click anywhere in the big pane on top; then type whatever you need to type.

TIP

Expression Builder can refer to controls on a form in your query so you can easily control the criteria used to run the query. Figure 16-11, for example, shows a simple form called Donation Report with one combo box called Volunteer that lists all volunteers in the Volunteers table.

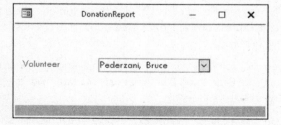

FIGURE 16-11:
The Donation
Report form with
the Volunteer
combo box.

Figure 16-12 shows how Expression Builder finds and uses the combo box on the form.

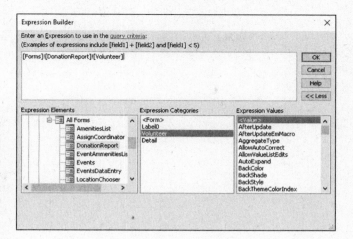

FIGURE 16-12:
Expression Builder is used to select the Volunteer combo box from the Donation Report form.

Finally, Figure 16-13 shows the expression in the Criteria row of the Donor Totals Report query. So how does all this work? Open the form and select a volunteer. Run the query, and the query will be limited to just the donations for the volunteer selected on the form. Cool, huh?

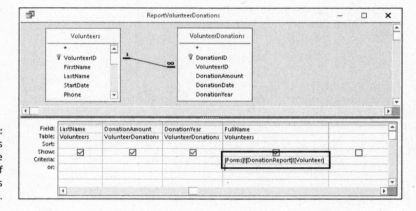

FIGURE 16-13:
The expression as it appears in the Criteria row of the Donor Totals Report query.

Chapter **17**

Take Charge with Action Queries

Ever have to update multiple records in a table with the same information? How about copying data from a linked spreadsheet into an existing Access table? What about deleting a certain group of records from a table? If you answered yes to any of these questions, then you've come to the right place. *Action queries* perform a specific task on a group of records in a table, all in one fell swoop, so you don't have to add or update each record manually. (Now, try to control your excitement! If you ever get into the situation where an action query is needed, I know you'll thank me for writing this.)

The three most common action queries are:

» **Update:** This query updates the value in a field for the records you select via the Criteria row. For example, if an employee keys in the wrong order date of 11/2/2019 on 25 orders, an update query would allow you to easily update all 25 order dates to the correct date of 11/3/2019.

» **Append:** Use this query type to add records from one table to another. For example, your credit card company gives you monthly expense transactions in an Excel spreadsheet, and you need to input the expenses into your Access database Expense table. You can link or import (see Chapter 9 for details) the spreadsheet into your Access database and then use an append query to add the records to your Expense table. An append query gives you control over what records you add from the spreadsheet to the Expense table. Importing directly to the Expense table will import every record from the spreadsheet.

>> **Delete:** If you're in a destructive mood, use this query to delete groups of records from a table. Suppose you work for a company that has discontinued a product as of 12/1/2018 — and customers have been notified that any order dated after 12/1 for delivery of the discontinued product will be deleted. Okay, they were warned; you can use a Delete query to eliminate all orders for the discontinued product that have delivery dates after 12/1/2018.

WARNING

The action queries described in this chapter will alter data in your database PERMANENTLY. Although they're beneficial when used correctly, they can wreak havoc if used incorrectly. The results of running an action query cannot be undone. Therefore, it's wise to back up your database file before you run *any* action query!

Easy Update

The *Update query* can replace the value in a field in a group of records with another value. To create an Update query, first you need to determine the table (and the field within it) in need of updating — and decide how you want to update that field. When you've figured that out, do this:

1. **Click the Create tab on the Ribbon.**

The Create buttons appear onscreen. Notice the Queries group toward the left side of the Ribbon.

2. **Click the Query Design button from the Queries group on the Ribbon (see Figure 17-1).**

A new query opens in Design view, and the Show Table dialog box pops up.

3. **Select the table that contains the field you'd like to update; then click the Add button.**

The selected table is added to the top half of the Query Design window, as Figure 17-2 illustrates.

4. **Click the Close button in the Show Table window.**

The Show Table window closes.

5. **From the Table field list, double-click the field name that the query will update along with any fields you'll need to write criteria.**

The fields are added to the bottom half of the Query Design window (see Figure 17-3).

Query Design button

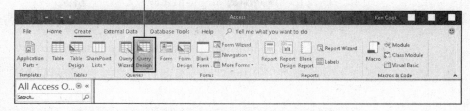

FIGURE 17-1:
Click the Query Design button on the Ribbon.

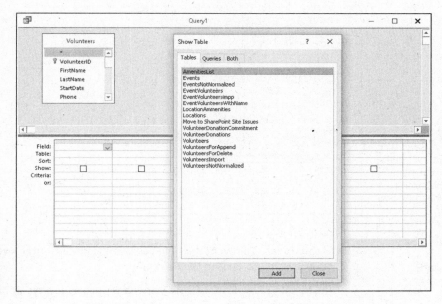

FIGURE 17-2:
The Volunteers table added to the query.

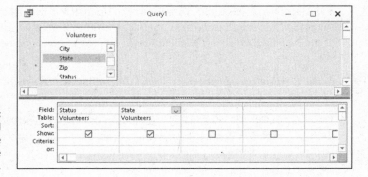

FIGURE 17-3:
The Status and State fields are added to the query.

6. **Click the Design tab on the Ribbon.**

The Ribbon displays the design commands, including the Query Type group.

7. **Select the Update button from the Query Type group.**

The Update To row appears on the query grid, as Figure 17-4 illustrates.

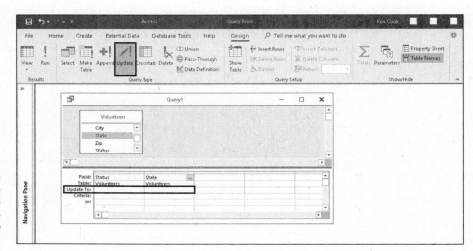

FIGURE 17-4:
Select the Update
button on the
Ribbon, and the
Update To row
appears.

8. **In the Update To row of the field you want updated, enter a value or expression to update the field.**

The Update To row can contain a static value such as a status (Active), an expression such as Date()+10, or the name of a field such as [RequiredDate].

TIP

If you're not sure what you can enter in the Update To row, make sure the cursor is in the row and click the Builder button from the Design tab of the Ribbon. Expression Builder shows you your options and helps with syntax.

9. **In the Criteria row, enter the criteria that will select the records you want updated.**

The query in Figure 17-5 updates the status in the Status field to Active for those volunteers in Pennsylvania with a current status of Prospective.

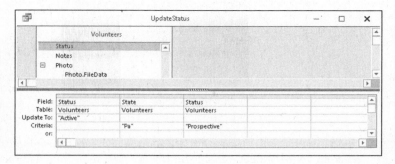

FIGURE 17-5:
This query will update the Status field to Active for volunteers from Pennsylvania that are currently Prospective.

10. **Click the Run button from the Ribbon's Results group to run the query and update the records.**

A message box (see Figure 17-6) appears, telling you how many records will be updated.

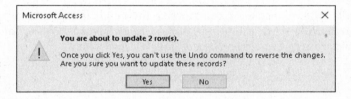

FIGURE 17-6:
Click Yes to update your data.

TIP

If you're not sure what records you'll update, change the query type to a Select query and run it. If the resulting records are correct, switch back to an Update query and you'll run the update with confidence knowing what records you're updating. Switch query type using the Query Type group on the Ribbon's Design tab.

11. **Click Yes in the message box window to run the query and update your data.**

Figure 17-7 shows the state of things before you run an update, and Figure 17-8 shows what changes an update has produced.

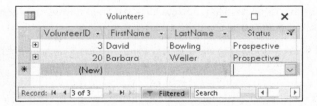

FIGURE 17-7:
The Status field *before* running the Update query.

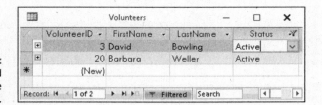

FIGURE 17-8:
The Status field
after running the
Update query.

WARNING

Update queries will update the data you specify — but the update can't be undone. Back up your data before you run Update queries — and use them with caution! Don't say I didn't warn you!

Add Records in a Flash

Append queries add records from one table (called the *source table*) to another table (called the *destination*). A common use for an Append query is to add data from an external file (such as an imported or linked spreadsheet) to an existing Access table. To create an Append query, follow these steps:

1. **Click the Create tab on the Ribbon.**

   The Create buttons appear onscreen. Notice the Queries group toward the left side of the Ribbon.

2. **Click the Query Design button from the Queries group (as shown earlier in Figure 17-1).**

   A new query opens in Design view, and the Show Table dialog box pops up.

3. **Select the table that contains the source data to be appended, and then click the Add button.**

   The selected table is added to the top half of the Query Design window.

4. **Click the Close button in the Show Table dialog box.**

   The Show Table dialog box closes.

5. **From the Table field list, double-click the field names that contain the data to be added to the destination table.**

   The fields are added to the bottom half of the Query Design window (see Figure 17-9).

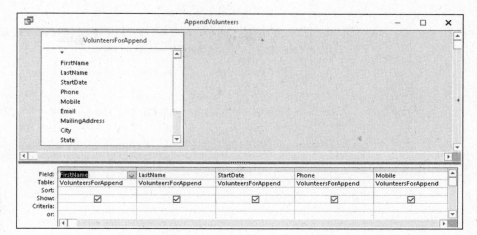

FIGURE 17-9:
Selected fields for
an Append query.

6. **Click the Design tab on the Ribbon.**

   The Ribbon displays the Design buttons, including the buttons in the Query Type group.

7. **Select the Append button from the Query Type group.**

   The Append dialog box appears, as Figure 17-10 illustrates.

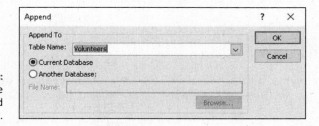

FIGURE 17-10:
Say hello to the
Append
dialog box.

8. **Select the destination table from the Table Name drop-down list, and then click OK to close the Append dialog box.**

   The Append To row appears in the query just above the Criteria row. If a source field name matches exactly a destination field name, the Append To row will pre-populate with each matching field name from the destination table.

TIP

If the source and destination field names do not match for a specific field, the Append To row will not pre-populate with a field name from the destination table. To fix this, click in the Append To row with a missing destination field name. A drop-down arrow appears to the right. Select the matching destination field from the drop-down list.

9. **Add criteria to the Criteria row in Query Design if necessary, to select just those records you want from the source table.**

See Figure 17-11 for the completed Append query.

In most cases, the source and destination fields must be of the same data type. For example, you cannot append data from a text field to a number field.

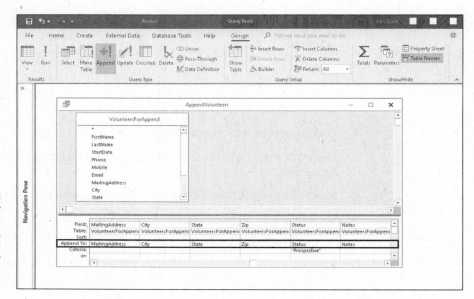

FIGURE 17-11: This query appends all records that equal "Prospective" in the Status field.

10. **Click the Run button from the Ribbon's Results group to run the query and append the records from the source table to the destination table.**

A message box appears, telling you how many records will be added.

When Append queries add records to the destination table, you cannot undo the results. Be sure to back up your database file before you run an Append query.

11. **Click Yes in the message box to run the query and add the records.**

If you run an Append query in error, you can take one of two actions:

>> Delete the appended records from the destination table manually (they will be near the bottom) or via a Delete query (see next section).

>> Revert to your backup file, correct the problem, and try again.

Quick Cleanup

The Delete query can clean up unwanted records in a hurry. Of the three action queries that have been discussed in this chapter, the Delete query is the most dangerous: It can wipe out all the data in your table in an instant. Pay special attention to the selection criteria you write for a Delete query so you're sure you'll delete only the correct records. To build a Delete query, follow these steps:

1. **Click the Create tab on the Ribbon.**

   The Create buttons appear onscreen. Notice the Queries group toward the left side of the Ribbon.

2. **Click the Query Design button from the Queries group (as shown previously in Figure 17-1).**

   A new query opens in Design view and the Show Table dialog box pops up.

3. **Select the table that contains the data to be deleted, and then click the Add button.**

   The selected table is added to the top half of the Query Design window.

4. **Click the Close button in the Show Table dialog box.**

   The Show Table dialog box closes.

5. **From the Table field list, double-click the asterisk (*) at the top of the list and any individual field names you intend to use for criteria.**

   The fields will be added to the bottom half of the Query Design window. The word *From* is added to the Delete row in Query Design under the asterisk to indicate you're deleting all records that match criteria written in the Criteria row from the selected table.

6. **Click the Design tab on the Ribbon.**

   The Ribbon displays the Design buttons, including the Query Type group.

7. **Select the Delete button from the Query Type group.**

   The Delete row appears in the query grid, as pictured in Figure 17-12.

8. **Add criteria to the Criteria row in Query Design if necessary, to select just those records you want to delete from the table.**

   See Figure 17-13 for the completed Delete query.

WARNING

If you don't write any criteria, every record in the selected table will be deleted! It is very unlikely you'll want to delete every record in a table, so write your criteria carefully and check it thoroughly!

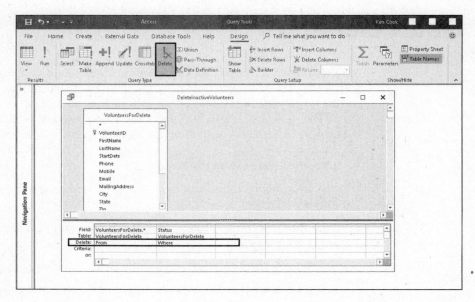

FIGURE 17-12:
The Delete query designed.

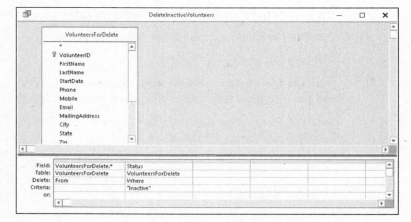

FIGURE 17-13:
This query deletes all records where status is Inactive.

TIP

After you've written your criteria, change the query back to a Select query using the Query Type group on the Ribbon's Design tab to see which records will be deleted. If the Select query returns the records you wanted to delete, change the query back to a Delete query, run it, and you'll know you deleted the correct records. What a relief!

9. Click the Run button from the Ribbon's Results group to run the query and delete the records from the selected table.

A message box will appear, telling you how many records will be deleted.

WARNING

A Delete query deletes records permanently from the selected table. You cannot undo the result of running this query type. Back up your database file before running a Delete query!

10. Click Yes in the message box to run the query and delete the records.

5

Simple and Snazzy Reporting

Contents at a Glance

Chapter **18**

Fast and Furious Automatic Reporting

The fact that you're reading this chapter right now tells me that either you've already been asked to create a report or you're afraid that might happen. Yes, if you're like the rest of us, *afraid* applies now and then — the idea of reporting on a database seems daunting to many users. You might be wondering if you have to learn any complex programming language or master a word processor or desktop publishing application in order to create a professional-looking report.

The answer? Nope. You don't have to learn anything other than a couple of quick mouse clicks in the Access workspace in order to whip up a snazzy report on the currently open or selected table, in just seconds. And you don't have to master Word or any other word-processing program to dress up your report and make it look serious and important. No, you have all you need to make a quick, simple, yet professional-looking report, right here in Access 2019.

"But what if I have to report on more than one table?" you're asking. What if your boss/customer/partner needs a report on data from Table A and Table B, and you know he or she does *not* want to see certain pieces of data from those tables anywhere on the report? In situations such as these, the Report Wizard comes in handy; using it, you can choose multiple tables as the sources for your report — and even pick and choose which fields to include from those tables.

TIP

Knowing that there are two very simple paths to follow, depending on the report you're looking for (or that someone else is hounding you for), it's time to take a look at the two paths and figure out which one is right for you.

Chances are you'll need both of Access's simple reporting tools (the Access Report and the Report Wizard buttons) over time — so it's worth checking them both out now. I start with an analysis of both of them and then get into the procedural specifics of the simplest one first.

Quick and Not-S0-Dirty Automatic Reporting

The Access Report and Report Wizard tools make reporting on your database extremely simple. If you use the Access Report tool, Access uses your table (the open or selected one at the time you click the tool's Report button) to generate a report instantly. You can then go in and tweak margins, fonts, and other formatting so the result looks more like what you'd imagined and/or fits on the number of pages you prefer.

If you use the Report Wizard, you're taken step by step through the process of choosing which fields (and which tables) to include in your report, how the report will look, and how the content will flow over one or more pages.

Each method has its merits in different situations:

>> **If you want every field in your single table included in your report,** and you don't mind if your report looks a lot like a worksheet or the way your table looks onscreen while you're in Datasheet view, then the Report tool is for you. It's quick, and it gives you a report without any formatting or other fanfare required.

>> **If you want to choose which fields to include in your report,** and maybe want your report to include fields from more than one table, the Report Wizard is for you. It takes a little longer than the Report tool, but the flexibility and ability to customize the report's appearance through a series of dialog boxes (instead of using multiple tabs and buttons) is a real plus.

Creating a quick, one-table report

To generate a report on an open table, all you really have to do is click your mouse twice:

1. **Click once on the name of the table you want to report on — you don't need to open the table — in the left-hand All Access Objects panel.**

2. **Click the Create tab on the Ribbon, and then click the Report button. An instant report appears, as shown in Figure 18-1.**

   The table is now a report, laid out exactly as it appeared in Table view — as a series of rows and columns. It has a heading and a small graphic in the upper left corner, and some color has been added — using a default template — to the field names and the report's title (which is the same as the table name).

   If the Property Sheet panel opened along with your report, you can close it at this point. If you want to use the panel at some point in the future, however — perhaps when making design changes to the report — press the F4 key to redisplay it, or you can click the Property Sheet button on the Design tab while in Design view of the report. Once the Property Sheet is open, you can make changes to the settings for your report, and you learn more about how to do that in Chapter 19.

   TIP

3. **Use the File tab to access the Print command (or press Ctrl+P) if you want to print the report you see onscreen.**

   You can also display the report onscreen, now and in the future; there's no requirement that you print the report immediately.

   To save the report, press Ctrl+S or click the Save button on the Quick Access Toolbar. The Save As dialog box appears, as shown in Figure 18-2, and I suggest adding the word "Report" to the default name (which is the same as the table name). It helps later on when you're making quick selections from the All Access Objects panel to not have two items (the table and the report) with the exact same name.

   TIP

Report button

FIGURE 18-1: You can find the Report button on the Create tab.

FIGURE 18-2:
Save your report
to make it a
permanent part
of the database.

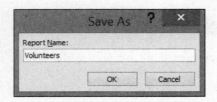

Your instant report formatting options

Although the Report tool works with only one table or query at a time, it still offers some choices for the way the report looks and how the fields appear in the report.

TIP

Did I say something about reporting on queries? Yes, I did! Check out Chapters 13, 14, and 15 for all the basics — and then some — on queries. When you have your own queries put together and run, you can use the Report button to document them!

In the Report Layout Tools section of the Ribbon (the section is displayed after you use the Create tab to generate the quick, one-table report), you can choose from a variety of options for the tabular layout of your report. You can have each record listed on its own row, as a series of columns, or you can stack your fields with the Tabular button in the Table section of the Ribbon's Arrange tab. The results of clicking the Stacked button are shown in Figure 18-3.

FIGURE 18-3:
Change your
report layout
with a quick
click of the
Stacked or
Tabular
button on the
Arrange tab.

Stacked button

Tabular button

Hey, where is it, you say? If you can't find the buttons to change your report's tabular settings, click the Arrange tab, and look at the Tables section (far left), also shown in Figure 18-3. There are several choices available, and my advice is that you experiment with different layouts, and when you like what you see onscreen, print. If you hate what you've done, just keep clicking the Undo button (up on the Quick Access Toolbar) until the report is back at its pre–I Don't Like That state.

If you hate the report entirely, just right-click it in the left panel that lists the components of your database and choose Delete from the resulting pop-up menu. When a prompt appears, asking whether you really want to delete the report, just click Yes. Remember, all you had to do was click the Create tab and then click Report to make this thing — so how bad would it be to start over?

Rearranging columns

Not only can you pair up your report's fields vertically, stacking them to keep relevant fields together, but also you can rearrange your columns so that (a) your report's readers see what they want to see first (assuming they read from left to right), and (b) you can horizontally pair up things that relate to each other. As shown in Figure 18-4, all you have to do to rearrange columns is click on the heading for the column you want to move, and then Shift+click on any data in that column to select the data as well. You can also click the column heading and then click the Select Column button on the Arrange tab.

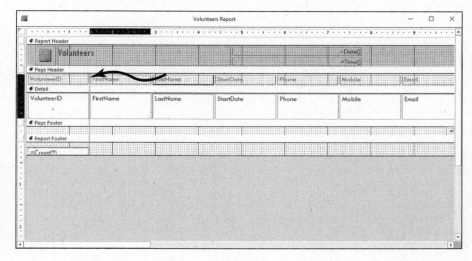

With your column selected, drag the heading and all the data that comes with it. When you release your mouse, the fields — the headings and then the data — are rearranged.

Sizing columns to fit the data

One thing that can be very appealing about a quick report on a single table is the ability to put the entire report on a single page (if you have only 20 or 30 records) or on a series of pages that includes all the table's fields on each page (for large databases with hundreds or thousands of records, but not a whole lot of fields per record). This can be difficult on a report that has a lot of fields or uses all the fields in a table because rarely do they fit across an $8\frac{1}{2}$-x-11-inch sheet of paper. Sometimes you can fit them all across a sheet of paper — if you resize the fields, narrowing them so they're no wider than they have to be to display the widest entry in the column.

The easiest way to do this is to narrow the columns manually. You can widen all the columns in one fell swoop, but that requires working in Design view, which is discussed way over in Chapter 19. This way is quicker for now.

To adjust columns manually — the one column that's taking up too much room or each of them, one at a time — simply click the column's heading and then use the two-headed arrow that appears when you mouse over the column's right seam to move the seam to the left to make the column narrower. The adjustment applies to the entire column by default. The dragging process is shown in Figure 18-5, where I narrow the LastName column, the first of several adjustments intended to help all the columns fit without the content being cut off.

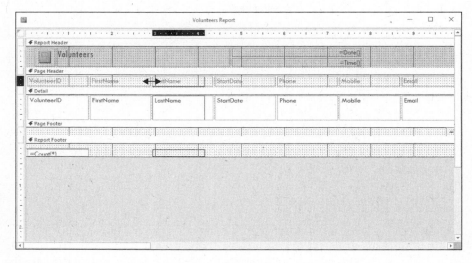

FIGURE 18-5:
Click and drag to widen or narrow your report's columns, one at a time.

THE QUERY ADVANTAGE

TIP

The fact that Access lets you base a report on a query is wonderful. When you build a report on a table, you get a report containing each and every record in the table. But what if you want only a few of the records? Access makes it easy to create a query and then base the report upon that query. (Chapter 13 shows how to make a query.)

The advantages don't stop there. If you create a query based on multiple tables, Access neatly organizes your results into a single datasheet. This allows you to use the quick, one-click Report tool to report on multiple tables — essentially duping Access into giving you a quick report on more than one table because the tables are part of a single query, and that single query is your Report source. (If you're unclear on the process of creating a query on multiple tables, take a look at Chapter 14.)

Starting the Report Wizard

So you've decided to take things step by step, perhaps because you want to include multiple tables and/or queries in your report. Or maybe you're still deciding what the best path is, and want to see what's involved in the process.

The Report Wizard is simple. It requires a few more steps and decisions from you than the Report tool does, but it's much more flexible than the instant Report tool. Here goes:

1. **In your database window, click the Ribbon's Create tab and then click the Report Wizard button. (It's right there in the tab's Reports section.)**

   The Report Wizard dialog box appears, listing all the fields in the active table. As shown in Figure 18-6, the dialog box offers

   - A drop-down list from which you can choose other tables and queries

   - Two columns, the Selected Fields and Available Fields, which you use to determine which fields from the selected table(s) will be used in your report

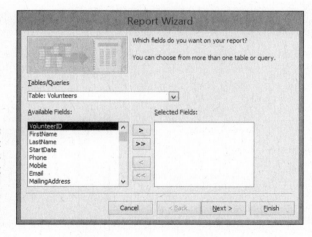

FIGURE 18-6: The Report Wizard starts by offering you tables and the fields within them to use in your report.

2. **Use the Tables/Queries drop-down list to choose the table you want to start with.**

   The fields from the table you select appear in the Available Fields box.

3. **Add fields to your report by double-clicking them in the Available Fields box.**

   By double-clicking, you add the fields to the Selected Fields box, and they become part of the report. You can also click a field once and then click the button with a > symbol on it, as shown in Figure 18-7.

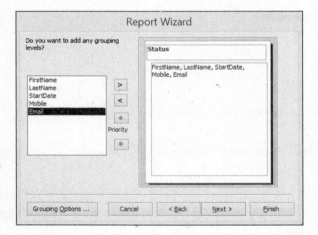

FIGURE 18-7:
Add fields by double-clicking them or by using the buttons between the Available and Selected Fields boxes.

4. **Repeat Steps 2 and 3 for each table and/or query in the database that you want to include in the report.**

TIP

If, at any point, you want to add all the fields in a given table or query, just click the >> button to add all the Available Fields to the Selected Fields list.

5. **Click Next to move on to the next page of the Report Wizard (see Figure 18-8).**

You can also click Next twice, which bypasses grouping issues, which, for a simple report, are often unnecessary. To explore this step of the Report Wizard in greater detail, check out Chapter 20.

FIGURE 18-8:
Your list of volunteers will be grouped by their Status field value.

6. **Choose a sort order for your report — typically sorting on the field people will use to look up information in the report — as shown in Figure 18-9.**

For example, if your report documents a list of employees, Last Name might be a good choice. A report on product sales would be useful in Product Number or Product Name order. You can sort by more than one field, choosing up to four fields to sort by and either Ascending or Descending for the sort order on each field. Figure 18-9 shows the LastName field chosen for sorting in Ascending order, adding to the value of having grouped by Status, so that each status group is in alphabetical order by the volunteer's LastName value.

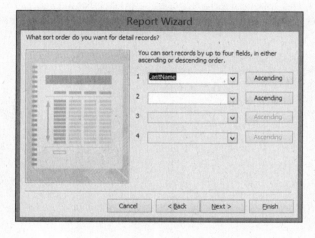

FIGURE 18-9:
Sort by the most important field in the table, or the one that will make the most sense to your report's readers.

TIP

Sorting is best done on fields that have either very few entries or a lot of duplicate entries:

- In a name and address list, sorting by Last Name (which may have very few duplicates) will put the list in an order for which there's very little opportunity for subsequent sorting — because the unique records in Last Name don't create any groups that can be sorted further.

- If you sort that name and address list by City or State (which may have lots of duplicate entries), a subsequent sort can be done on Last Name, putting each group of people living in the same city or state in last-name order.

- To choose between Ascending (the default) and Descending sort order, you'll either leave the Ascending button alone (for A–Z sorting) or click it to change it to Descending (for Z–A sorting).

7. **Click Next to display your options for Layout and Orientation.**

8. **Choose a Layout and an Orientation from the two sets of radio buttons and click Next.**

- Layout options (Tabular or Columnar) are simple — you either want to see your report as a list (Tabular) or in sections (Columnar), in which each record appears in a section on its own. Justified is similar to Tabular, but groups the fields in a sort of stacked jumble.

- Orientation decisions (Portrait or Landscape) are generally easier if you envision the report in your head — are there more fields than will fit across a sheet of 8½-inch-wide paper? If so, choose Landscape to give yourself 11 inches of paper (or 10 inches, to allow for the smallest margin possible) across which your fields will appear.

Figure 18-10 shows a format chosen at this stage of the Report Wizard and allows the user to set up the layout and orientation for that report.

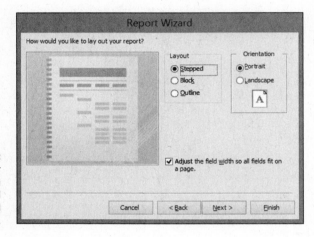

FIGURE 18-10:
Choose your report's layout in terms of field structure and orientation.

TIP

You probably don't want to use Justified unless your report has very few fields per record.

WARNING

If you leave the Adjust the Field Width So All Fields Fit on a Page option checked, you run the risk of data being chopped off in the report and rendering the report unusable. If you have more than four or five fields, and if any of your fields have very long entries, turn this option off.

9. **Click Next.**

A default name for your report now appears in this next step in the wizard, as shown in Figure 18-11.

10. **Give your report a name.**

Type a name in the long box at the top of the dialog box. At this point, you also need to decide how to finish things up — with a Preview of the report, or by leaping right into Design view to make more changes to your report's appearance and content. (This part of the process is covered in Chapter 19.) For now, choose to Preview the Report, which is the default.

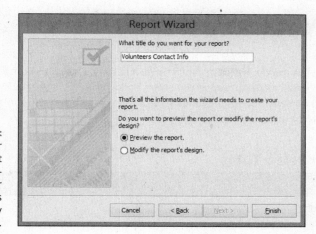

FIGURE 18-11: Name your report, or accept the table-name-based moniker that Access applies by default.

11. Click Finish.

The report appears on a Preview tab, at which point, you can print it or close it. To close it, right-click the report's tab and choose Close from the pop-up menu. If you make additional changes and haven't chosen to save, you'll be asked if you want to close without saving.

Figure 18-12 shows a preview of a report that lists the organization's volunteers, in LastName order, grouped by Status, and including their contact information.

Volunteers Contact Info

Status	LastName	FirstName	StartDate	Mobile	Email
Active					
	Burrell	Eugenia	4/1/2013	717-444-4324	eburrell@domain.com
	Fabiano	Jenna	5/1/2014	717-444-4325	jfabiano@domain.com
	Frankenfield	Daniel	6/1/2015	717-444-4326	dfrankenfield@domain.com
	Freifeld	Iris	7/1/2014	717-444-4327	ifreifeld@domain.com
	Joubert	Christopher	8/1/2015	717-444-4328	cjoubert@domain.com
	Kline	Linda	9/1/2013	717-444-4329	lkline@domain.com
	Maloney	Steve	2/15/2000	717-444-4331	smaloney@domain.com
	Mermelstein	David	6/5/2010	717-444-4332	dmermelstein@domain.com
	Myers	George	7/25/2009	717-444-4333	gmyers@domain.com
	O'Neill	Karen	2/1/2003	717-444-4334	koneill@domain.com
	Patrick	Kyle	6/5/2010	717-444-4335	kpatrick@domain.com
	Shapiro	Mimi	7/5/2008	717-444-4337	mshapiro@domain.com
	Sorensen	Sharon	6/9/1999	717-444-4338	ssorensen@domain.com
	Talbot	Ann	7/1/1989	717-444-4339	atalbot@domain.com

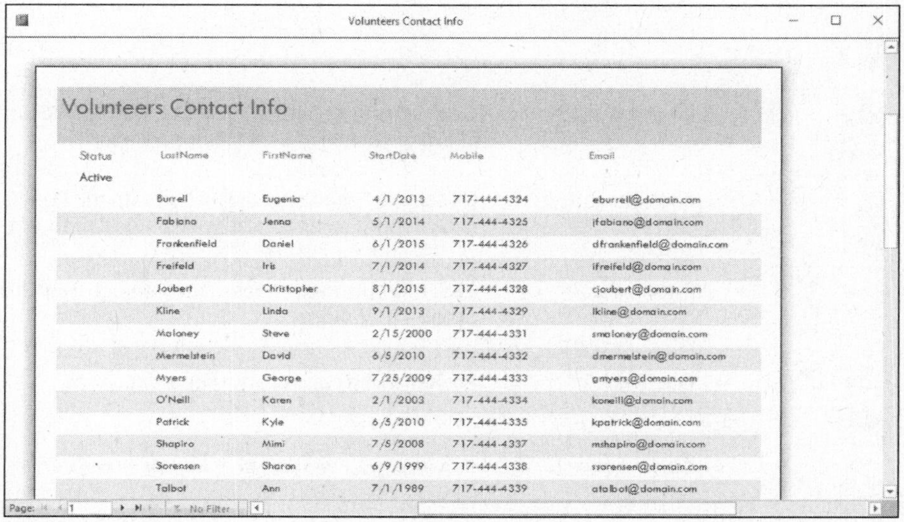

FIGURE 18-12: Even a simple report with few fields can look important.

Previewing Your Report

Print Preview mode (which results from clicking Finish to complete the Report Wizard process, as described in the steps in this chapter's previous section) shows exactly what your document looks like. Table 18-1 shows the tools Print Preview provides to help with your inspection.

TABLE 18-1   **Print Preview Tools**

Tool	What It Is	What It Does
Print	Print button	Opens the Print dialog box.
Size	Size button	Allows you to choose a paper size for your report.
Margins	Margins button	Allows you to set Normal, Wide, or Narrow Margins for your report.
Show Margins	Show Margins	Click the check box to display or hide the margins.
Print Data Only	Print Data Only	Click the check box to include only your data in the report.
Portrait	Portrait button	Converts your report to Portrait mode.
Landscape	Landscape button	Converts your report to Landscape mode.
Columns	Columns button	Opens the Page Setup dialog box with the Columns tab chosen, allowing you to set up a columnar report.
Page Setup	Page Setup button	Opens the Page Setup dialog box with the Print Options tab chosen, allowing you to customize your printed output.
Zoom	Zoom button	Click this button to choose a percentage view (from 10% to 1000%) or to Fit to Window.
One Page	One Page	Previews one page of your report at a time.
Two Pages	Two Pages	Previews your report two pages at a time.

Tool	What It Is	What It Does
More Pages	More Pages	Click this to choose to preview four, eight, or twelve pages at a time.
Refresh All	Refresh All	Refreshes the report to display the latest data in the table(s) included in the report.
Text File, PDF or XPS, Email, More — Data	Data buttons	Exports your report to any of the following: Excel, a text file, a PDF or XPS file, or an email message; click the More button to choose Word or other options.
Close Print Preview	Close Print Preview	As you might have guessed, this closes the Preview window.

TIP

Another way to see a Print Preview — say, for a report you created a while ago and you don't remember what it looks like on paper — is to open the report (double-click it in the left panel to open it) and then click the File tab. From there, click the Print command, and choose Print Preview from the resulting choices.

Zooming in and out and all around

In Figure 18-12, you see the report. In your preview (assuming you're working along with me here or have tried this on your own), you may be able to see the entire page of your report. The parts you can see look okay, but how can you commit to printing if you don't know how the whole page looks? In Figure 18-13, you can click your mouse when the pointer turns to a magnifying glass — as it will when you mouse-over the page. You can also use the Zoom tool to choose a lower zoom percentage.

TIP

When you move your mouse pointer over the preview of your report, your pointer changes into a magnifying glass. Use this magnifying glass to zoom in to the report and check individual sections:

>> Just click what you want to see, and Access swoops down, enlarging that portion of the report so you can see it clearly.

>> Click again, and your view changes back to the previous setting.

Clicking any of the page-number buttons (One Page, Two Pages, More Pages) sets the Zoom view to the Fit View setting. When you have two pages showing, the odd-numbered page is always on the left, unlike book publishing, which puts the odd-numbered page on the right (unless the typesetting department is having a very bad day).

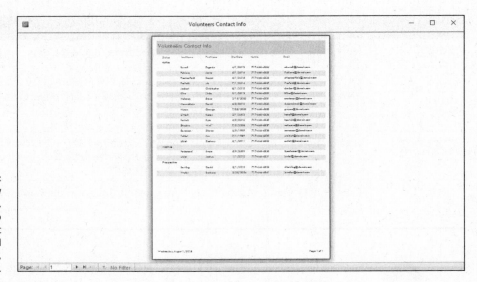

FIGURE 18-13:
When you view
the whole page,
the report is too
tiny to read, yet
you can't see all
the content,
either.

If you use the Zoom section of the Ribbon's Print Preview tab rather than one of the page-number buttons, Access offers quite the selection of Page View options, as you see in Figure 18-14. Set your system to show 1 page or 2 pages — or click the More Pages button's drop-down list to choose up to 12 pages per screen (of course, you won't be able to read anything at this setting, but at least you can see how the whole report lays out).

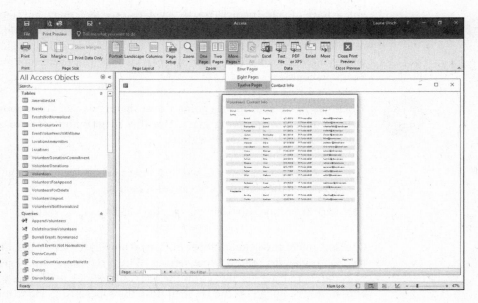

FIGURE 18-14:
Preview up to
12 pages of your
report at a time.

Pop goes the menu

You can right-click anywhere on the Print Preview screen to see a pop-up menu that gives you the choice of switching the zoom or viewing a specific number of pages, as shown in Figure 18-15. When you click the Zoom button drop-down list in the Zoom section of the Print Preview tab, you get a similar pop-up menu offering various zoom percentages, from 10% to 1000%.

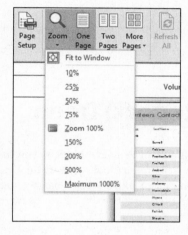

FIGURE 18-15:
Choose the view you want to use or how many pages you want to see simultaneously.

Other than the Zoom submenu, the following useful commands are available when you right-click the Print Preview screen:

>> **Report View, Layout View, Design View, and Print Preview:** These four options appear at the top of the pop-up menu and give you lots of ways to look at your report.

>> **Zoom:** Enter or choose a zoom percentage.

>> **One Page and Multiple Pages:** If you choose to see Multiple Pages, you must tell Access exactly how many pages by using the submenu that appears when you make that pop-up menu selection. Drag through the grid (it appears as six blocks to start with), and the grid expands as you drag. Release your mouse button when the grid shows the number of pages you want displayed.

>> **Page Setup:** This opens the handy Page Setup dialog box.

>> **Print:** This opens — yep, you guessed it — the Print dialog box.

>> **Save As:** Choose this command to save your report with a new name and choose what type of object to save it as — Report is the default.

>> **Export:** Choose this command to save your Access report in a format used by another program. Your choices include exporting as a Word document, PDF (Portable Document Format) file, text file, XML document, or HTML document.

>> **Send To:** Choose this command and then select an email recipient to send the report to.

>> **Close:** This closes Print Preview and prompts you to save your changes, if any, to the report's design.

Beauty Is Only Skin (Report) Deep

After looking at your report in the Print Preview window, you have a decision to make. If you're happy with how your report looks, great! Go ahead and print the document. However, a few minutes of extra work does wonders for even the simplest of reports.

Start with the basics in the Page Setup dialog box. To get there, right-click anywhere on the report and choose Page Setup from the pop-up menu. (This command and others hidden away in the pop-up menu are briefly explained in the preceding section of this chapter.)

Use the Page Setup dialog box to fine-tune your report in terms of its Print Options, Page, and Columns settings. You can adjust margins, change orientation, and control how many vertical columns your report content is divided into — all from within this handy dialog box.

The Print Options tab

The Print Options tab of the Page Setup dialog box controls the width of the margins in your report — no surprises here.

Figure 18-16 shows your margin options. The page has four margins, so the dialog box includes a setting for each one (Top, Bottom, Left, and Right).

FIGURE 18-16:
Adjusting margins to specify how much white space surrounds your report.

Here is how you set or change margins:

1. **Double-click in the appropriate box (Top, Bottom, Left, or Right) and type a new setting.**

   When you double-click the box, the current entry is selected. Access automatically uses whatever Windows thinks is your local unit of measurement (inches, centimeters, or whatever else you measure with). On the right side of the dialog box, Access displays a sample image, which shows you how your current margin settings work on a page. After editing one margin, you can press Tab to move through the remaining fields (Bottom, Left, and Right, if you started out in Top), and you can adjust each one.

2. **Make all the changes you want to your report's layout, and then click OK.**

3. **Look at your report in Print Preview to check your adjustments.**

   If you need to tweak the report, simply go back to Page Setup and play with the options until everything looks just right.

TECHNICAL STUFF

Also found on the Print Options tab is the Print Data Only check box. (Maybe the programmers couldn't think of anywhere else to put this box because it has nothing to do with margin settings.) If you select this option by checking its box, Access prints only the data in your records; field headings won't appear on the printed document. Use Print Data Only if you plan to use preprinted forms. Otherwise, leave it alone because your report looks pretty odd without any field labels.

The Page tab

The Page tab of the Page Setup dialog box tells Access about the sheet of paper on which you plan to print your report — including its size and layout — as well as what printer you keep the paper in. You make some of the most fundamental decisions about how your report looks from the Page tab of the Page Setup dialog box. (See Figure 18-17.)

FIGURE 18-17:
Use the Page tab
to choose a
printer, page size,
and more.

The Orientation box sets the direction that your report prints on paper:

>> Portrait (the way that this book and most magazines appear) is the default choice.

>> Landscape pages lie on one side, giving you more horizontal room (width) but less vertical space (height).

TIP

Deciding whether to use Portrait or Landscape is more important than you might think:

>> For tabular reports, landscape orientation displays more information for each field, thanks to the wider columns. Unfortunately, the number of records you can view per page decreases in the process. (After all, that piece of paper is only so big.)

>> Columnar reports don't do very well in a landscape orientation because they usually need more vertical space than horizontal space.

Your other choices for the Page tab are determined by your printing capabilities:

>> The Size drop-down list in the Paper section of the tab enables you to choose the size of the paper you want to use. (Refer to Figure 18-17.)

>> The Source drop-down list gives you the option to

- Use your regular paper feed (the Automatic choice).

- Use another automatic source, should your printer be equipped with multiple trays.

- Feed your paper manually into the printer.

>> The last part of the Page tab lets you choose a specific printer for this report.

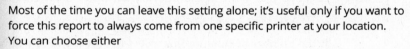

Most of the time you can leave this setting alone; it's useful only if you want to force this report to always come from one specific printer at your location. You can choose either

- **The Default Printer option:** Access uses whatever printer Windows says to use.

- **The Use Specific Printer option: You choose the printer yourself.**

- If you click the Use Specific Printer option, the Printer button comes to life. Click this button to choose from among your available printers.

The Columns tab

You get to make more decisions about your report's size and layout on the Columns tab, as shown in Figure 18-18.

FIGURE 18-18:
The Column Layout area of the Columns tab enables you to format a report with vertical columns.

The Columns tab of the Page Setup dialog box is divided into three sections:

>> **Grid Settings:** Controls how many columns your report uses and how far apart the different elements are from each other

>> **Column Size:** Adjusts the height and width of your columns

>> **Column Layout:** Defines the way Access places your data in columns (and uses an easy-to-understand graphic to show you as well)

REMEMBER

The default number of columns is one column to a page, but you can easily change the setting to suit your particular report. Just keep in mind that with more columns, your report may show less information for each record. If you use so many columns that some of the information won't fit, Access conveniently displays a warning.

If the number of columns you select fits (or if you're willing to lose your view of the information in some of your fields), click OK to see a view of how your document looks with multiple columns.

The Grid Settings section of the Columns tab also adjusts:

>> **Row Spacing:** Adjusts the space (measured in your local unit of distance) between the horizontal rows. Simply click the Row Spacing box and enter the amount of space that you want to appear between rows. Again, this setting is a matter of personal preference.

>> **Column Spacing:** Adjusts the width of your columns. If you narrow this width, you make more room, but your entries are more difficult to read.

The bottom section of the Columns tab, called Column Layout, controls how your columns are organized on the page. You have two options here:

>> **Down, then Across:** Access starts a new record in the same column (if the preceding record has not filled up the page). For example, Record 13 starts below Record 12 on the page (provided there's enough room), and then Records 14 and 15 appear in the second column.

>> **Across, then Down:** Access starts Record 13 across from Record 12, and then puts Record 14 below Record 12, and Record 15 below Record 13, and so on.

TIP

If your columns don't look exactly right the first time, keep trying. Small adjustments to the row and column spacing produce big changes throughout a long report. The onscreen preview gives you an easy way to check how the report looks — and prevents you from killing multiple trees in the quest for perfection.

Chapter **19**

Professionally Designed Reports Made Easy

The Report Wizard does most of the dirty work of report creation. However, it has its shortcomings. Most of the Report Wizard's shortcomings have to do with text — sometimes the text is cut off, it's not aligned properly, it's too small, it's too big — you get the idea.

Along the way, you may not like the Report Wizard's color choices or design elements either. Don't despair. (Hopefully, you're never at a point in your life where you'll despair over an Access report, but I have to throw some drama in here somewhere.) Design and Layout views hold the key to unlocking the report of your dreams. (I know — who *isn't* dreaming about Access reports?)

In this chapter, I discuss some of the most popular report Design and Layout view tasks. With this knowledge, you can create professional-quality reports and be the envy of the office.

Report Repairs

Design and Layout views are the places to be for tweaking reports — but which view to use and when? Usually your best options are as follows:

>> **Design view:** Great for those situations where you want to add new elements (stuff like lines, titles, and subtitles) to the report.

Figure 19-1 shows a report in Design view.

>> **Layout view:** A better choice for when you want to format existing elements. (Layout view shows you actual data as it will appear on the printed page.)

Figure 19-2 shows the same report in Layout view.

TIP

You have many ways to change report views. Here are some of the most common:

>> **After you create a report with the Report Wizard, the wizard asks whether you want to**

- *Preview* the report.

- *Modify* the report's design.

  Click the Modify the Report's Design option to send the wizard's creation straight into Design view.

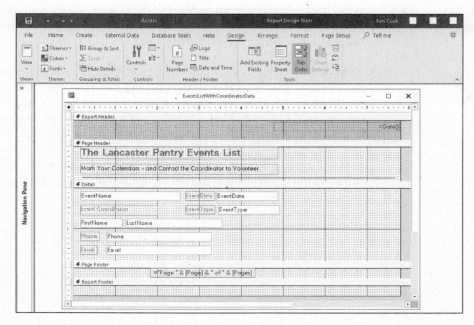

FIGURE 19-1:
Design view is best for adding new design elements to your report.

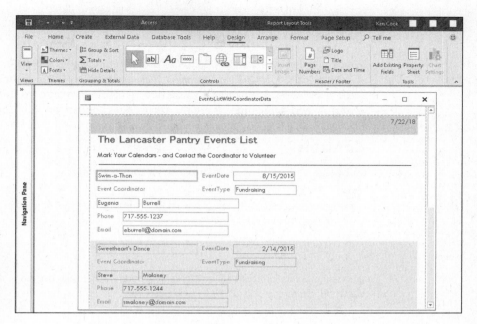

FIGURE 19-2:
Layout view is best for modifying existing report elements.

>> **While a report is print previewed on the screen, use the row of View buttons on the lower right corner of your screen:**

- *Design view* is the last button from the right.
- *Layout view* is the second-to-last button from the right.

>> **To open a report in Design or Layout view from the Navigation pane, follow these steps:**

1. *Right-click the report you want to work on.*

   A shortcut menu pops up.

2. *Select Design View or Layout View from the shortcut menu.*

Report Organization

Access provides the following design tools to control the *layout* of your report — where the report data appears on the printed page and where the pages break.

Structural devices

When you look at a report in Design or Layout view, Access displays a ton of markers (called *controls* by Access) that are grouped into several areas (called *sections* by Access). Together, these design elements make up the layout of your report — and determine where the report data appears on the printed page.

Controls

In Design or Layout view, *controls* show the following:

>> Where Access plans to put the report elements (such as text, lines, or logos) on the printed page.

>> How the program plans to format each element.

Access uses three kinds of controls for text, depending on what information the report includes:

>> **Text boxes:** Boxes that display a particular field's data in the report.

Most fields you want to include in the final report are represented as a text box in Design view. (The exception is a Lookup field, which is represented on the report as a combo box.)

>> **Combo boxes:** Report combo boxes do not act the same way as form combo boxes. On a report, you'll see the value of the combo box but will not see the drop-down arrow toward the right end of the combo box.

>> **Labels:** Plain, simple text markers that display a text message on the report.

Sometimes labels stand alone (for example, "The Lancaster Pantry — Volunteer Donations"). Often they accompany a text box to show people who read the report what data they're looking at ("Volunteer ID," or "Event," for example).

Sections

The *sections* (report headers, for example) determine *where* and *how often* the elements will print.

The report design in Figure 19-3 displays the most common sections (in the order of their appearance on the page).

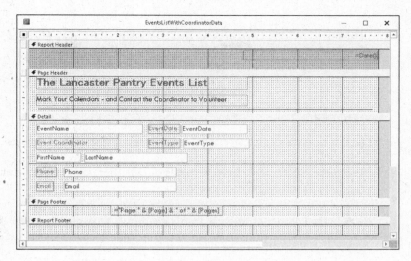

FIGURE 19-3:
Common report
sections.

TIP

Chapter 20 shows how to slice and dice your sections. The following information is a summary of the report sections.

HEADERS

Access provides a pair of header sections for the top of reports.

The header section you use depends on whether you need to print information at the *beginning* of the report or on *every page*:

>> **Report Header:** Anything in the report header prints just once at the very start of the report — the top of the first page.

   Typically, a report title appears in the report header.

>> **Page Header:** Information in the page header prints at the top of every page.

   On the report's first page, the page header appears *below* the report header.

   Typically, the page header contains column heading labels. You can also add design elements such as lines or shaded rectangles to the page header to separate the data rows from the column headings. You may want the report title to appear on every page. If so, place it in the page header and it will!

DETAIL

The Detail section displays the essence of the report — the actual database records. The Detail section appears only once in Design view. However, the Detail section is *repeated* for every record in the actual report as seen in Layout view.

The report automatically fits as many Detail sections (records) as possible between the header and footer sections on each page of your report.

The data in the Detail section usually fills the majority of each report page.

FOOTERS

Access provides a pair of footer sections for the bottom of reports.

The footer section you need depends on whether you need to print information at the *end* of the report or on *every page:*

>> **Page Footer:** When each page is nearly full, Access finishes it off by printing the page footer at the bottom.

   Common page footer elements are the date and page number.

>> **Report Footer:** At the bottom of the *last* page, immediately following the page footer, the report footer is the last thing that prints on the report. This information prints only once.

   Typically, the report footer contains summary formulas that calculate grand totals for numeric columns (such as total donations).

Page breaks

By default, Access fills each report page automatically with as many records as possible and then starts another page. But Access does provide a couple of ways that *you* can control how reports start new pages:

>> **Grouping:** Places like records together

   For example, you're printing a donation report by month and you want each month to start at the top of a page. If you group the report by month and add a group footer, you can tell Access to start a new page after each month's footer prints.

   For more about putting records into groups, see Chapter 20.

>> **Page Break control:** Starts a new page from the point where the control is placed in the Report layout

   The following sections show how to add and remove page breaks.

TIP

Grouping is much more efficient in controlling page breaks than the Page Break control. Only use the Page Break control if you can't get the pages to break the way you want with grouping.

Inserting a page break

Here's how to add a page break in Design view:

1. **On the Design tab of the Ribbon, click the More button in the lower right corner of the Controls gallery in the Controls group and then select the Insert Page Break button. (See the Ribbon in Figure 19-4.)**

    The mouse pointer changes to a crosshairs with a page next to it.

2. **Position the crosshairs wherever you want the page break and then click.**

    A small horizontal line appears on the left side of the report. What you are seeing is actually the *selected* Page Break control. Click somewhere away from the line, and that line will become a series of dots, as shown in Figure 19-4. From now on, a new page always begins at the spot of the marker.

Page Break control   Page Break tool

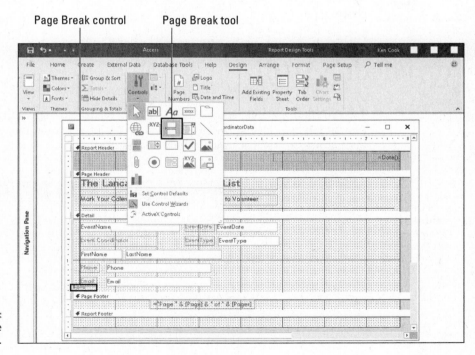

FIGURE 19-4:
The Page
Break control.

Removing a page break (or any other control, for that matter)

If you want to remove a page break, just follow these steps:

1. **With the report in Design view, click the Page Break marker — those series of dots you can see in the preceding Figure 19-4.**

Selection markers appear around the Page Break control.

TIP

If you're having trouble selecting the Page Break control, roll the mouse just under or over the control and away from other controls. Click and drag up over the Page Break control. Let go of the mouse button and you have a selected Page Break control. I know, magical, isn't it? This tip works for any control on a form or report.

2. **Press the Delete key on the keyboard.**

Goodbye, Mister Page Break!

TECHNICAL STUFF

This will not remove any page breaks that are *automatic* or created with *grouping*. Manual deletion will get rid of only page breaks created using the Page Break control.

Formatting Stuff

You can change almost any existing item in a report's design with the help of the Format tab, which is shown in Figure 19-5. With the Format tab, you can change item properties such as fonts, colors, and borders.

FIGURE 19-5:
The Format tab on the Ribbon.

The Format tab is visible only while a report is in either Layout or Design view. Because you can see the results of formatting changes better in Layout view, the upcoming steps use that view.

To adjust items in your report with the buttons on the Format tab, follow these steps:

1. **From the Navigation pane, right-click the report you want to change and select Layout View from the shortcut menu.**

The report displays in Layout view, and the Format tab appears on the Ribbon.

2. **Click the Format tab to select it.**

The Format buttons appear on the Ribbon.

3. **Click the item you want to format.**

A thick border appears around the item, as in Figure 19-6.

4. **Click the button for the formatting effect you want.**

The appropriate buttons enable for the item you've selected. There are three kinds of buttons:

- **Toggle buttons** (like *Bold*): They are either on or off.
- **Pull-down arrows** (like *Font*): Offer many available choices on a list.
- **Gallery buttons** (like *Shape Fill*): Offer many available choices on a palette or list.

I cover these options in detail later in the chapter.

Repeat Steps 3 and 4 for all the items you want to modify.

If you make a mistake while formatting, click the Undo button on the Quick Access Toolbar or press Ctrl+Z. Your mistake will be sent away never to return. Be default, Office applications save the last 100 undoable actions.

TIP

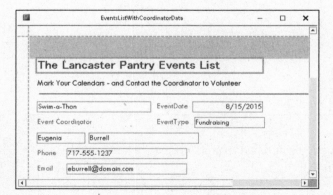

FIGURE 19-6: The report title is selected.

**TECHNICAL
STUFF**

TAKING CONTROL OF YOUR REPORT

In addition to Label, Text, and Combo Box controls, more controls are available in Design view by using the tools from the Controls group of the Ribbon's Design tab.

Some controls work with specific types of fields. For example, a check box can graphically display the value of a Yes/No field.

Some of these controls can be a bit complicated to set up. However, Access includes several control wizards to take the pain out of the process. These wizards walk you through the steps for building your controls in the usual wizardly step-by-step process. Just answer the questions, and the wizard does the rest.

A control's wizard usually pops onscreen automatically after you place the control in the report. If you create a new control but the control's wizard doesn't show up to help, be sure that the Use Control Wizards button is turned on. Click the More button in the lower right corner of the Control gallery (pictured in the following figure in Layout view) to see the Use Control Wizards button. If it's on, the Use Control Wizards button will have a colored border around it (pictured in the figure below).

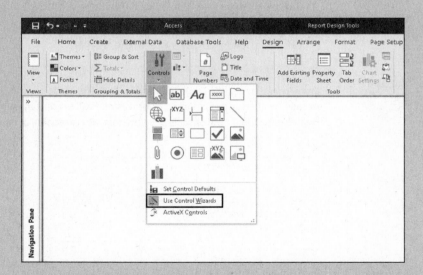

Here is a list of the report controls covered in this book and where you can find information on them:

- The Line, Rectangle, Page Break, and Image controls are covered elsewhere in this chapter.

- Using controls to create summaries in your report is covered in Chapter 20.

The following sections step through some of the most common formatting tasks. Just follow the instructions, and your report will look like a million bucks in no time. (Now if you could only *sell* it for a million bucks!)

Adding color

A little color can help keep report readers awake as they browse through 300 pages of data.

These buttons change the color of labels and text boxes in your report:

>> **Font Color:** Changes the color of text in a text box or label marker

>> **Background Color:** Changes the control's background color, but not the text

These buttons are located in both Layout and Design view on two different Ribbon tabs. You can find them in the Font group on the Format tab or the Text Formatting group on the Home tab.

TIP

You might find these buttons are easier to work with in Layout view.

When a text control is selected, the buttons will show you the current font and background colors for the control. To change colors, follow these steps:

1. **Click the control to select it.**

The control has a thick border around it.

2. **Click the arrow to the right of the Font Color or Background Color button.**

The menu of colors appears.

3. **Click the color you want to use.**

TECHNICAL
STUFF

The colors are divided into sections:

● *Theme:* Colors that the experts at Microsoft have determined work well together.

● *Standard:* All colors that have been created for you.

● *Recent:* All colors that have been used in the current Access session on the report. Recent will not display until you've used at least one color.

WARNING

If you make the text and background colors the same, the text seems to disappear! If this happens, just click the Undo button on the Quick Access Toolbar to bring back the original color setting.

Relocation, relocation, relocation

Don't like that column where it is? The position of your report title got you down? Your line won't stay in line? You can easily move just about any element (text box, label, line, and such) in a report.

>> Most elements can be moved in Layout view. You see your data in Layout view, so I recommend that you start there.

>> If you have trouble in Layout view, switch to Design view. For example, I find lines are easier to work with in Design view.

REMEMBER

The amount of space between the controls determines the space between items when you print the report:

>> Increasing spacing gives your report a less crowded look.

This is appropriate if you have only a few columns on your report and you want to spread them out to fill up the width of the page. For example, a report that shows annual donations by volunteer might have a column for the volunteer name and a column for donation amount. Spread out the controls to fill up the page width.

>> Decreasing the space enables you to fit more information on the page.

This is appropriate when you have many columns on your report and you want to fit them all on the width of one page. For example, a report that shows donations by month may have 14 columns — 1 for the volunteer name, 12 for the months, and a Total column. Crowd the 14 controls together to fit the page width.

Moving a single control

To move a line, box, label, or text box, follow these steps:

1. **Point the tip of the mouse pointer to the item you want to move. Make sure the item is deselected (click off of it first) before you point.**

2. **Press the left mouse button.**

   The mouse pointer changes to a four-headed arrow.

3. **Drag your item to a new position.**

   As you move the mouse, the four-headed arrow drags an outline of whatever object you selected.

4. **Release the mouse button when the item is in the right place.**

TIP

   If you make a mistake while moving, click the Undo button on the Quick Access Toolbar or press Ctrl+Z. This will put the item back where it started.

To move multiple controls at one time, follow these steps:

1. **Click the first control to select it.**

   The border thickens around the control, indicating that it's been selected.

2. **Press and hold the Ctrl key, and then click the next control.**

   The border thickens around each control, indicating that they're both selected.

   Follow Steps 2 through 4 in the previous procedure to move both controls.

Moving a group of controls

In a columnar report, you can move an entire group of controls in the Detail section. Here's how:

1. **Click one of the controls in the Detail section.**

   A thick border appears around the item and a Select All box (the little guy containing a four-headed arrow) appears toward the upper left corner of the group of controls. (See Figure 19-7.)

2. **Roll the mouse over the box icon containing the four-headed arrow.**

   The mouse will change to a four-headed arrow.

3. **Drag the group of controls to a new position.**

   All the controls in the group will move at one time. Everything stays in alignment.

Click here to select all controls in the group.

![Access Report Layout Tools screenshot showing the Page Setup ribbon and a report titled "Volunteer Donations" in Layout View with a table of volunteer donation records.]

VolunteerID	FirstName	LastName	DonationAm...
1	Joshua	Ulrich	$500.0
2	Zachary	Ulrich	$50.0
3	David	Bowling	$75.0
4	Eugenia	Burrell	$150.0
5	Jenna	Fabiano	$25.0
6	Daniel	Frankenfield	$1,000.0
7	Iris	Freifeld	$650.0
8	Christopher	Joubert	$750.0
9	Linda	Kline	$50.0
11	Steve	Maloney	$1,500.0
12	David	Mermelstein	$2,000.0
13	George	Myers	$250.0
14	Karen	O'Neill	$50.0
15	Kyle	Patrick	$75.0

FIGURE 19-7:
Use the Select All box with the four-headed arrow to move a group of controls.

One size does not fit all

The Report Wizard as well as the basic Report button do their best to size your report items properly. Very often, however, neither gets it right. A column will be too narrow or too wide, using the space on the page inefficiently. Do you throw your hands in the air and curse at the cyber gods? Of course not. You can size any control to your exact needs.

TIP

I find that sizing works best in Layout view; you can see the data in the controls as you're sizing them. You can also size your controls in Design view.

Follow these steps to size a control:

1. **Select the item you want to size by clicking it.**

   The item will have a thick border around it.

2. **Roll the mouse pointer to the edge of the selected item.**

   The mouse cursor changes to a two-headed arrow. See Figure 19-8 for a picture.

3. **Drag your item to its new size.**

   As you drag with the mouse, the two-headed arrow drags an outline of whatever object you selected to show you its new size.

4. Release the mouse button when the item is the right size.

The item stretches or shrinks to its new size.

Labels can be scaled to the exact size required to display all the text. To do this, follow Steps 1 and 2 in the previous steps and then double-click rather than drag. Like magic, Access figures out the correct size for the item and sizes it accordingly.

Two headed arrow mouse shape for sizing controls

	VolunteerDonations:NoParameter			— □ ✕
Volunteer Donations				Sunday, July 22,
VolunteerID	FirstName	LastName	DonationAmount	DonationYear
1	Joshua	Ulrich	$500.00	2015
2	Zachary	Ulrich	$50.00	2015
3	David	Bowling	$75.00	2015
4	Eugenia	Burrell	$150.00	2016
5	Jenna	Fabiano	$25.00	2015
6	Daniel	Frankenfield	$1,000.00	2016
7	Iris	Freifeld	$650.00	2015
8	Christopher	Joubert	$750.00	2015
9	Linda	Kline	$50.00	2016
11	Steve	Maloney	$1,500.00	2015

FIGURE 19-8:
Two-headed mouse arrow at the edge of the DonationYear label control.

Spaced-out controls

The spacing of columns is a common problem in tabular reports. The Report Wizard creates a control group in the Detail section and tends to butt columns up against each other, sometimes making data difficult to read. If this is the case for you, you can use the Control Padding button located on the Arrange tab of the Ribbon to space everything out a bit.

This adjustment can be done in either Layout or Design view, but I think you'll find Layout view is easier.

Follow these steps to add space between your columns in Layout view:

1. Click one of the controls in the group and then click the Select All box that appears. (Refer to Figure 19-7.)

The labels and text boxes for all the columns are selected.

2. Switch to the Arrange tab on the Ribbon, if necessary, by clicking it.

The Arrange buttons appear, including the Control Padding button located in the Position group. (See Figure 19-9.)

3. **Click the Control Padding button.**

Four padding choices drop down.

4. **Select one of the last three choices to add spacing between the columns and rows.**

The first choice (None) will butt all the controls up against each other, so if your goal is to add padding, you'll want to avoid that one.

Check your changes in Print Preview (see "Sneaking a Peek," later in this chapter). Sometimes adding too much space between columns pushes one or more of them off the page. If this happens, experiment with the different choices on the Control Padding button until everything fits correctly.

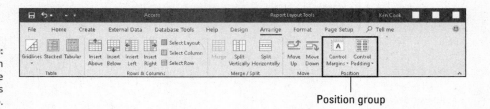

FIGURE 19-9:
The Position group in the Ribbon's Arrange tab.

Borderline beauty

Organizationally speaking, lines and borders are great accents to:

>> Draw your readers' eyes to parts of the page.

>> Highlight or divide sections of the report.

>> Add some style.

The Format tab on the Ribbon contains three commands that work with lines:

>> Shape Outline

>> Line Type

>> Line Thickness

You can use these commands on a line control to change the appearance of the line or on label and text box controls to add a border to the control. The three buttons are within the Shape Outline button in the Control Formatting group on the Format tab.

Coloring

The Shape Outline button changes the color of lines that mark a text box's border and lines you draw on your report by using the Line button.

To change the color of a line or other control border, follow these steps:

1. Click the item to select it.

The item has a thick border around it.

2. Click the Shape Outline button.

A drop-down palette of color choices appears, as shown in Figure 19-10. The colors are divided into sections:

- *Theme:* Colors that the experts at Microsoft have determined work well together.

- *Standard:* All colors that have been created for you.

- *Recent:* All colors that have been used in the current Access session on the report. Recent will not display until you've used at least one color.

- *Transparent:* No color applied to the object's outline.

Note: The Shape Outline button hangs out in the Control Formatting group of the Ribbon's Format tab.

3. Click your color choice from the many options.

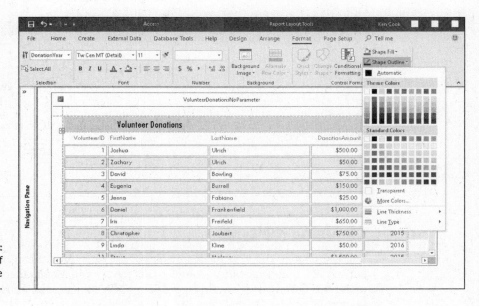

FIGURE 19-10: The palette of Shape Outline colors.

Thickness

In addition to colorizing lines and control borders, you can also adjust their thickness:

1. **Click a line or other control to select it.**

2. **Click the Shape Outline button to reveal its choices.**

   Near the bottom of the Shape Outline drop-down list is the Line Thickness button.

3. **Click Line Thickness to reveal a submenu of options, as shown in Figure 19-11.**

4. **Click the thickness option you want.**

   Mystically, your line or border thickness changes.

TIP

You've heard this tip before but it's such a good one, I've got to say it again. All together now! If you make a mistake, click the Undo button on the Quick Access Toolbar or press Ctrl+Z to undo your mistake. You can undo the last 100 undoable actions, so Ctrl+Z to your heart's content!

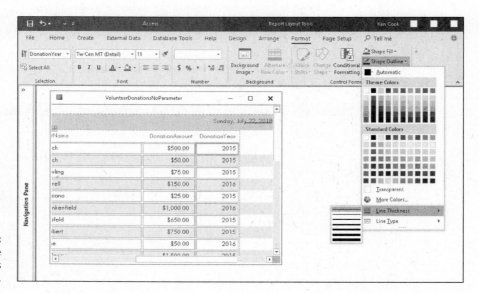

FIGURE 19-11:
The seven Line Thickness options.

Changing the type

You can change the type of line displayed by your line control or other control border. The Line Type button handles that job for you. Eight choices are available under this button, as shown in Figure 19-12. Don't know what I mean by line type? Well, think dotted, dashed, or solid.

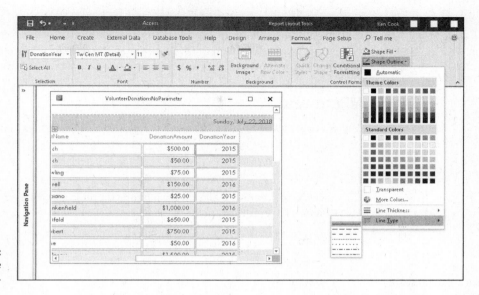

FIGURE 19-12:
The eight Line
Type options.

To change the line type of a control, follow these steps:

1. **Click the control whose line type you want to change.**

2. **Click the drop-down arrow next to the Shape Outline button to display its options.**

3. **Click Line Type (the very last choice) to reveal a submenu of line types.**

4. **Click the line type you want.**

Tweaking your text

REMEMBER

You must select the text you want to tweak before using any of the formatting tools. With Access labels, all the text in the label must be formatted the same way. You cannot format one word differently from another. The same is true with the contents of a text box — unless the text box is tied to a Long Text field with its Text Format property set to Rich Text (see Chapter 3 for details).

Fonts

You can change the font or the font size as follows:

1. **Select the text you want to change.**

2. **Click the drop-down arrow to the right of the Font or Font Size list box.**

   Both list boxes are found in the Font group of the Ribbon's Format tab.

3. **Make a selection from the drop-down list that appears.**

TIP

To turn on or off bold, italic, or underline characteristics, select a control and click the appropriate button from the Font group on the Ribbon's Format tab. The characteristic *toggles* (switches) between on and off each time you click the button.

Alignment

You can control the alignment of the text within labels and text boxes. To change the alignment of the text for a label or text box, follow these steps:

1. **Select the control.**

2. **Click one of the three alignment buttons found in the Font group of the Ribbon's Format tab.**

Figure 19-13 shows the alignment buttons. Pictured from left to right:

- ● Align Left

- ● Center

- ● Align Right

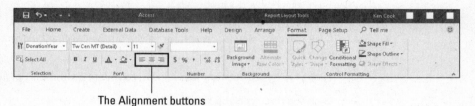

FIGURE 19-13:
The three
alignment
buttons.

The Alignment buttons

TIP

Make sure your reports follow these simple rules for your reader's pleasure:

>> Align numeric data and dates to the right so the numbers line up correctly. Use the Number group of buttons on the Ribbon's Format tab to help keep your numbers orderly.

>> Align text to the left.

>> Align your column headings to the data in the column:

- ● Text column headings should align left.

- ● Number column headings should align right.

Sneaking a Peek

Neither Layout view nor Design view give you a perspective on how the report will look on the printed page. So where can you go to see how the report will print?

Access provides a command called Print Preview that does the trick. To preview your report, click the Print Preview button from the set of four View buttons on the lower right part of your screen. (The Print Preview button is the second from the left with the magnifying glass on it.)

Figure 19-14 displays a report in Print Preview. Here's how to navigate it:

TIP

>> **Zoom:** Click anywhere on the report to zoom in or zoom out.

To zoom to a specific percentage of actual size, click the drop-down arrow on the Zoom button in the Zoom group on the Ribbon's Print Preview tab and then select your size. To fit the entire report on screen, choose Fit to Window from the Zoom button.

>> **Page buttons:** Find these on the lower left part of the Print Preview screen.

- The right arrows move to the next or last pages.

- The left arrows move to the first or previous pages.

- Type a page number in the Current Page box (the one with the number in it), tap Enter, and Access will take you to that page.

>> **Page Size group (on the Ribbon):** The buttons change page margins and paper size.

>> **Page Layout group (on the Ribbon):** The buttons change page orientation.

>> **Zoom group (on the Ribbon):** The buttons change the number of pages that appear in Print Preview and the magnification of the page.

>> **Close Print Preview button (on the Ribbon):** Exits Print Preview.

For details on setting margins, paper size, and page orientation, see Chapter 18.

TIP

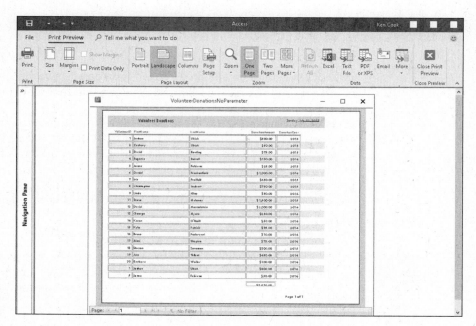

FIGURE 19-14: A report in Print Preview.

Getting a Themes Makeover

When you want to change the look of the entire report in a few easy clicks, check out the Themes button. When you click this button, Access offers several different format packages that reset everything from the headline font to the color of lines that split up items in the report.

The Themes button is available in either Layout or Design view on the Design tab of the Ribbon. Since it does change fonts, Layout view is recommended so you can see the effect of the font changes on report text.

Follow these steps to apply a theme to your report:

1. Open the report in Design or Layout view.

Right-click on the report in the Navigation pane and choose Design or Layout View from the shortcut menu.

2. Select the Design tab on the Ribbon, if necessary.

The Design buttons appear, including the Themes group.

3. Click the Themes button.

A palette of formatting choices drops down with a variety of color schemes, as depicted in Figure 19-15.

4. **Roll the mouse over a theme and Access will apply that theme to the report in the background. To lock in a choice, click the theme you want.**

Access updates your report with the new look.

TIP

If you don't like any of the prebuilt themes on the drop-down list, use the Colors and Fonts buttons in the Themes group on the Ribbon to design your own. If you like what you created, click Save Current Theme (via the Themes button drop-down menu) to record your creation for posterity.

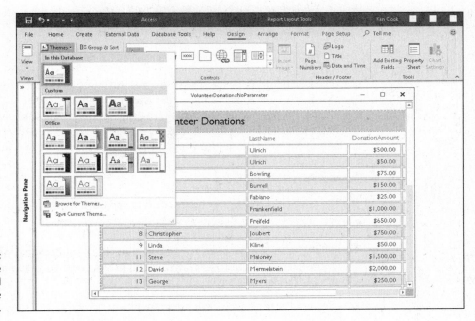

FIGURE 19-15: Choose the look you like and apply it to the entire report.

Adding More Design Elements

Use the controls discussed in this section to enhance the appearance of your report. You'll see suggestions for the control's use in each section.

Drawing lines

An easy way to make your report a bit easier to read is to add lines that divide the sections. Lines can be *added* only in Design view.

Use the Shape Outline button (discussed earlier in this chapter) to dress up your lines.

Straight lines

To add straight lines to your report, follow these steps:

1. Click the Line button (the one with the diagonal line on it) on the Controls button menu in the Controls group of buttons on the Design tab.

Your cursor changes to a crosshairs with a line trailing off to the right.

2. Repeat these steps for each line you want:

   a. Click where you want to start the line.

   b. Drag to the location where you want to end the line.

   c. Release the mouse button.

TIP

It's often difficult to get a perfectly straight line when following Step 2 as just described. It's easy to fix though. Just click on the line to select it, open the Property Sheet (Property Sheet button on the Design tab of the Ribbon), click the Format tab of the Property Sheet, and change the Height property to 0 (zero) for a horizontal line and the Width property to 0 (zero) for a vertical line.

Rectangular boxes

The Rectangle button draws boxes around separate items on your report. You can add rectangles only in Design view. Follow these steps:

1. Click the Rectangle button (the one shaped like a rectangle with a white interior) on the Controls button menu in the Controls group of buttons on the Design tab.

2. Repeat these steps for each rectangle you want:

   a. Click where you want to start the upper left corner of the rectangle.

   b. Drag the rectangle shape down to the lower right corner.

   c. Release the mouse button.

Pretty as a picture

You can add some flair to a report by adding a logo. This, of course, also helps identify that the printed document is from your organization. Use the Logo button to add a logo to the report. After you click the button, you will be prompted to select a logo file. By default, Access places the logo on the upper left corner of the report.

TECHNICAL STUFF

The Logo button places an Image control on your report. You can find this button on the Design tab's Header/Footer group.

Adding a logo

You can add a logo in both Layout and Design views.

WARNING

Pages that contain logos take longer to print. Use your logos wisely:

>> *Headers* and *footers* are the best places for logos.

>> The *Detail* section is not a good place for logos.

In the Detail section, you get one copy of the logo for each record on the report. This could greatly slow the printing of your report and, one could argue, add a few too many logos to the report!

TIP

If you have a report title on the upper left corner of your report, move the title to the right to make room for the logo before you insert it.

If you want to add a logo to your report, switch to Design or Layout view and follow these steps:

1. Select the Design tab on the Ribbon, if necessary.

The Design buttons appear, including the Header/Footer group.

2. Click the Logo button from the Header/Footer group.

The Insert Picture dialog box opens.

3. Navigate to the folder that contains your logo, and select the logo file. (See Figure 19-16.)

4. Click OK.

The logo is placed on the upper left part of the report.

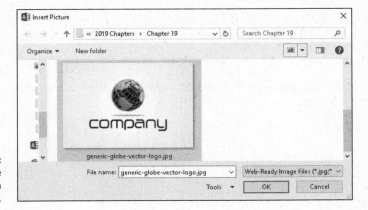

FIGURE 19-16:
The Insert Picture dialog box with a logo file selected.

HITTING THE OFFICE LINKS

You can do a lot with Access, but sometimes you may want to use a different program because Access cannot do what you need. For example, you may need to calculate a median on a report. Access does not contain a built-in median function. To resolve this issue, you can export your data via the Excel button to Excel and use Excel's Median function to perform your calculation.

Access provides tools for converting reports to file formats that can be opened and modified in other programs (including other Office programs) or emailed as attachments:

1. **In the Navigation pane, locate and then right-click the report.**

2. **Choose Print Preview from the shortcut menu that appears.**

   The Data group of buttons on the Print Preview tab has a button for each file format to which you can export your data.

3. **Click the button for your desired format.**

   An Export dialog box will appear.

4. **Use the Browse button to assist you in entering a filename in the File Name box.**

   The File Name box should contain a path and filename when you're finished.

5. **Check the Open the Destination File after the Export Operation is Complete check box.**

   Do this so you won't have to remember where you stored the exported file and what you called it.

6. **Click OK to begin the export process.**

   The report will be exported to your selected file format and then opened in the exported format's application.

TIP

After you add a logo, you can size, move, or delete the logo as described earlier in this chapter.

Chapter **20**

Groups and Page Breaks, Headers and Footers

The Report Wizard takes much of the stress and decision-making out of creating reports. This is also true of the Report tool, which asks no questions at all and just turns your table into a report — bang, zoom, no fuss, no muss. The Report Wizard is almost that simple; it asks just a few simple questions that you won't have any trouble answering.

Well, *maybe* no trouble. A few of the questions, which I address in this chapter, may give you a moment's pause, if only because you may not understand what's being asked or how your answer can affect your report. Given that this book is all about eliminating any stress or concern for the Access user, my goal is to explain those questions — and to help you make the Report Wizard even more wizardly.

In addition to simplifying the already-simple Report Wizard, this chapter also covers the use of two very convenient and powerful report features — headers and footers. These stalwart additions appear at the top and/or bottom of your reports, performing whatever role you dictate — from eye candy to outright informers.

They can be very spare and simply tell your readers what the name of the report is, or they can be really useful and tell people when the report was created, when it was last printed, or that the data within it is proprietary or confidential. What you include in your headers and footers is entirely up to you.

A Place for Everything and Everything in Its Place

The secret to successful report organization lies in the way you set up the information included in the report. Access enables you to choose how your fields are laid out on the report, allowing you to achieve the most effective layout for the data in question.

A report is effective when the reader can glance at it and see exactly what information is offered:

>> What data is included

>> How much detail is available

>> Where to look on the page to find specific pieces of information

Achieving an effective layout is simple; the automatic reporting tools in Access create a very basic, no-confusion-here layout by default.

Layout basics

Reports can be laid out in any of several preset layouts. The layouts available through the Report Wizard vary based on the table/s involved in the report and whether or not the data in the report is grouped by any particular field.

The layout that's right for your report is totally subjective. You can preview your report in the available layouts and make your decision accordingly.

In any layout, each of the fields you choose to include in your report appears in two parts:

>> Fields

>> Labels (a name for the field, essentially)

TIP

This chapter shows how you can take the default layouts that Access's automatic reporting features give you and tweak them by working in Design view. You can drag labels and fields around to achieve a completely custom report layout.

Here's the skinny on how the two most commonly used layouts — Columnar and Tabular — look and work:

>> **Columnar layout:**

- Field descriptions print with every record's data (side by side), as shown in Figure 20-1.

  The layout behaves this way because both the field descriptions and data area are in the report's Detail section.

- The report title prints only once, at the very beginning of the report (because the title is in the Report Header section).

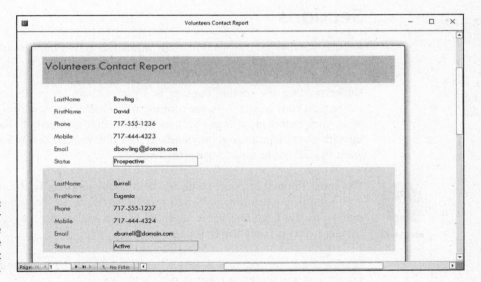

FIGURE 20-1: In a Columnar report, labels are to the left of the fields and repeat for each record.

>> **Tabular layout:**

- Field descriptions (labels) print once per page in the Page Header section, as shown in Figure 20-2.

- The data areas are in the Detail section.

- The title prints only at the top of the report.

Volunteers: Contact Report

Volunteers: Contact Report

LastName	FirstName	Phone	Mobile	Email	Status
Bowling	David	717-555-1236	717-444-4323	dbowling@domain.com	Prospective
Burrell	Eugenia	717-555-1237	717-444-4324	eburrell@domain.com	Active
Fabiano	Jenna	717-555-1238	717-444-4325	jfabiano@domain.com	Active
Frankenfield	Daniel	717-555-1239	717-444-4326	dfrankenfield@domain.com	Active
Freifeld	Iris	717-555-1240	717-444-4327	ifreifeld@domain.com	Active
Joubert	Christopher	717-555-1241	717-444-4328	cjoubert@domain.com	Active
Kline	Linda	717-555-1242	717-444-4329	lkline@domain.com	Active
Maloney	Steve	717-555-1244	717-444-4331	smaloney@domain.com	Active
Mermelstein	David	717-555-1245	717-444-4332	dmermelstein@domain.com	Active
Myers	George	717-555-1246	717-444-4333	gmyers@domain.com	Active
O'Neill	Karen	717-555-1247	717-444-4334	koneill@domain.com	Active
Patrick	Kyle	717-555-1248	717-444-4335	kpatrick@domain.com	Active
Pederzani	Bruce	717-555-1249	717-444-4336	bpederzani@domain.com	Inactive

FIGURE 20-2: In a Tabular report, labels become column headings.

Sections

Reports are divided into sections. The information that appears in each section is dictated by your chosen layout.

Understanding the section concept is a prerequisite for performing any serious surgery on your report — or for running off to build a report from scratch. Otherwise, your report groupings don't work right, fields are out of place, and you end up with a very frustrating, unfriendly report that neither you nor anyone else will want to read (or be able to use effectively).

REMEMBER

The most important point to understand about sections is that the contents of each section are printed *only* when certain events occur. For example, the information in the Page Header is repeated at the top of each page, but the Report Header prints on only the first page.

Getting a grip on sections is easy when you look at the *innermost section* of your report first and work your way outward, like so:

>> **Detail:** Access prints items in this section each time it moves to a new record. Your report includes a copy of the Detail section for each record in the table.

>> **Group headers and footers:** You may have markers for one or more *group sections.*

In Figure 20-3, information in the report is grouped by Status. (You can tell by the section bar labeled *Status Header* — the section bar identifies which field is used for grouping.)

Group sections may contain:

- The *group header* section is above the Detail section in the report design.

- The *group footer* is always below Detail.

Information in these sections repeats for every unique value in the groups' fields. For example, the report shown in Figure 20-3 reprints everything in the Status Header for each volunteer in the database, grouped by Status. Within the section for each status, Access repeats the information for each volunteer.

>> **Page Header and Page Footer:** These sections appear at the top and bottom, respectively, of every page. They're among the few sections not controlled by the contents of your records.

TIP

Use the information in the Page Header and Footer sections to mark the pages of your report.

>> **Report Header and Footer:** These sections appear at the start and end of your report. They each make only one appearance in your report — unlike the other sections, which may pop up many times.

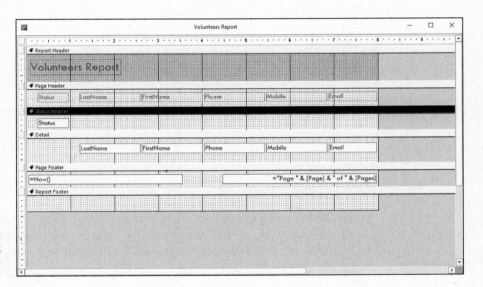

FIGURE 20-3:
Grouping volunteer records by Status.

REPORTING, STEP-BY-STEP

When Access produces a report, what does it do with all these sections? The process goes this way:

1. Access begins by printing the Report Header at the top of the first page.

2. Access then prints the Page Header, if you choose to have the Page Header appear on the first page. (Otherwise, Access reprints this header at the top of every page except the first one.)

3. If your report has groups, the Group Headers for the first set of records appear next.

4. When the headers are in place, Access prints the Detail lines for each record in the first group.

5. After it's finished with all the Detail lines for this group, Access prints that group's Group Footer.

6. If you have more than one group, Access repeats Steps 3, 4, and 5 for each group.

7. At the end of each page, Access prints the Page Footer.

8. When it finishes with the last group, Access prints the Report Footer — which, like the Report Header, appears only once in a given report.

Here's what you can do with headers and footers:

>> The Report Header provides general information about the report. This is a good place to add the report title, printing date, and version information.

>> The Page Header contains any information you want to appear at the top of each page (such as the date or your company logo). If your report layout is set to Tabular, the column headings (field names) for the data included in the report are found in this section.

>> The headers for each group usually identify the contents of that group and the field names.

>> The footers for each group generally contain summary information, such as counts and calculations. For example, the footer section of the Department group may hold a calculation that totals the minimum bids.

>> The Page Footer, which appears at the bottom of every page, traditionally holds fields for the page number and the report date.

>> The Report Footer in your report can be a good place to put things like these:

- Confidentiality statements
- Information regarding the timeliness of the data in the report
- The name(s) of the report's author(s)
- An email address or phone number to contact the person who made the report

Grouping your records

When the Report Wizard creates a report for you, it includes a header and footer section for each group you want. If you tell the Report Wizard to group by the State field, for example, it automatically creates both the State Header and the State Footer sections. You aren't limited to what the wizard does, though. If you're a little adventuresome, you can augment the wizard's work with your own grouping sections.

Before making any big adjustments to the report, take a minute to save the report (choose Save from the Quick Access Toolbar). That way, if something goes wrong and the report becomes horribly chewed up, just close it (click the X at the end of the report's tab) without saving your changes. Ahhh. Your original report is safe and sound.

The key to creating your own grouping sections is the Group, Sort, and Total panel — which is available after you've created a report with the Report Wizard or while you're in Design view working on a customized report. To display the panel (shown in Figure 20-4), click the Ribbon's Design tab and then click the Group & Sort button in the Grouping & Totals section.

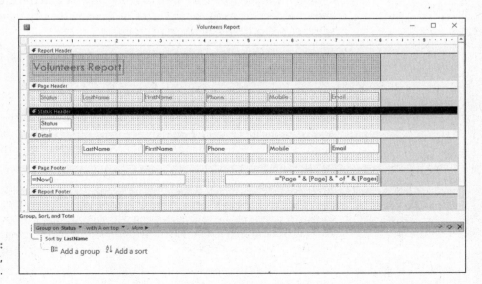

FIGURE 20-4:
The Group, Sort, and Total panel.

This panel allows you to control how Access organizes the records in your report — augmenting the sorting and grouping you may have already set up, whether through the Report Wizard dialog box or while building a report from scratch in Design view.

You can completely customize how your report's records are grouped and sorted and sort by multiple fields quickly and easily. The next set of steps shows you how.

To build your own groupings and add sorting with the Group, Sort, and Total panel, follow these steps:

1. **Click the Design tab in the Report Design Tools tab group.**

2. **Click the Group & Sort button in the Grouping & Totals section.**

   The Group, Sort, and Total panel appears beneath your report's sections.

3. **View any existing grouping or sorting, each represented by a Sort By or Group On bar, as shown in Figure 20-5.**

   The tree-like display shows the hierarchical groups and sorting currently set up for your report.

4. **Click Add a Group (you may need to scroll down within the Group, Sort, and Total Section, as shown in Figure 20-6); when the pop-up menu appears, select a field by which to group.**

   Access displays a list of available fields you can choose and use to group your report's records.

5. **Click Add a Sort and select a field by which to sort from the pop-up menu.**

   Again, a list of fields appears. You can click a field to choose a new field on which to sort your records. If you can't see these boxes (Add a Group and Add a Sort), scroll down, using the scroll bar on the right side of the Group, Sort, and Total panel.

TIP

   If you've already sorted by a field within the report, your subsequent sorting will be applied to the sort already applied. Here's an example using the employee database: If you already elected to sort by Department (say, while you were setting up the report in the Report Wizard), that sort will appear in the panel. If you click Add a Sort, your next logical field on which to sort might be JobTitle or LastName. The resulting sort would then put the list — already in order by Department — in further order: putting the departments in order by field chosen for the added sort. All the Accounting department people will be ordered by that second field, all the Operations people, and so on. It's a lot like the phone book (remember those?) — all the records in that book are in order by last name, and for those listings with the same last name, the records are in order by first name. If the first names are the same, a third order — by Street — is applied; if there are two John Smiths, the one on Elm Street comes before the one on Walnut Street.

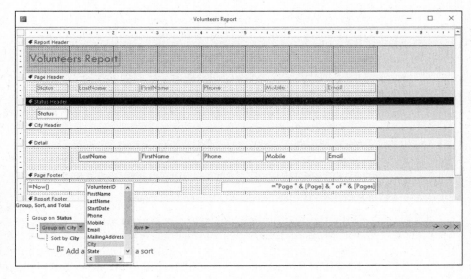

FIGURE 20-6: Choose the field you want to use for further grouping of your records in the report.

6. **To change the settings for an existing group or sort, click the Group On or Sort By bar and change the sort order or pick a different field by which to sort.**

   Your sorting and grouping options are determined by the nature of the existing sort or group. For example, when the sort is based on a field that's a Short or Long Text data type, you can sort alphabetically.

7. **Close the Group, Sort, and Total panel.**

   You can close the panel after you've finished using it by

   ● Clicking the X in its upper right corner.

   ● Clicking the Group & Sort button again (in the Grouping & Totals section of the Design tab).

TIP

To remove a group, click the X on the far right end of the Group On or Sort By bar (visible in Figure 20-6). There is no confirming prompt; when you click that X, your group or sort is gone. Of course, you can re-group or re-sort by using the Add a Group or Add a Sort buttons.

So you want more?

In addition to adding and removing groups and sorts with the Group, Sort, and Total panel, you can make the following adjustments/selections:

» **On the Sort By bar, click More** and view a list of options, including "By Entire Value", "With No Totals", "With Title" (click the Click to Add link to insert a title), and options for adding headers and footers for the sorted records.

To hide these options, click Less.

» **On the Group On bar, click More** to make the same choices as to how to group the records, whether to include totals, and how to use headers and footers.

Click Less to hide the options on the bar when you've finished using them.

If you don't see the More button, be sure to click the Group On bar to activate it.

With the appropriate fields in the correct header, footer, and detail sections, you've successfully finished the biggest step in building your report. Now you're down to the little things — tweaking, adjusting, and touching up the details of how your report presents itself. The properties described in the following sections govern the visual aspect — the look and feel — of your report.

TECHNICAL STUFF

Some of the stuff in the coming paragraphs looks a little technical at first glance because these settings dig deep into the machinery of report-making. Don't let the high-tech look scare you. By organizing your headers, footers, and detail rows, you've already conquered the hard part of building the report. This other stuff's just the window dressing.

Customizing Properties

In an amazing stroke of usability, Access keeps all property settings for your report in a single panel — the Property Sheet, which appears with your report (as shown in Figure 20-7, which shows the daunting All tab) in Layout or Design view. But before you can start using the Property Sheet, you have to have it on your screen:

>> To start adjusting the details of any component of your report, either

- Click the item you want to modify.

- If the Property Sheet isn't showing, right-click the item and choose Properties from the pop-up menu that appears.

- You can also display the Property Sheet by clicking the Property Sheet button, found in the Tools section of the Design tab. The Design tab is one of four tabs available in the Report Design Tools section of the Ribbon.

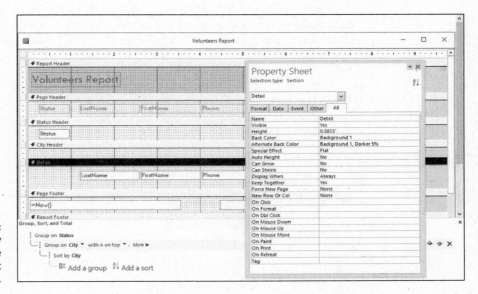

FIGURE 20-7:
Double-click any piece of the report to see that item's properties.

TIP

When displayed, you can widen the Property Sheet panel by pointing to its left side. Your mouse pointer turns to a two-headed arrow; click and drag to the left — essential if you want to use the second column in the panel (which shows values and settings for each property).

>> To display the Property Sheet for the report, double-click the little box where the two rulers meet, just to the left of the Report Header.

>> You can also double-click any part of the report to display the Property Sheet, focused on the part you double-clicked.

When the Property Sheet appears, its Selection Type drop-down list indicates which part of the report you're about to tweak. You can also click the drop-down list (which repeats the name of the currently displayed portion of the report's properties) and choose a different component to work with.

The Property Sheet is very long and a bit scary-looking — but don't worry about it. Regardless of which report component you choose to tweak (or if you're looking at the properties for the entire report), some of the settings won't need to be tweaked, and you'll probably have no idea *how* to tweak them anyway. And that's fine at this stage of the game. Seasoned Access users often leave many of these properties in their default state, because default settings are the defaults for a reason — they're effective in most situations (and suit most users' needs) without adjustment.

The Property Sheet has five tabs along the top of the list of properties — *Format, Data, Event, Other,* and *All* (which is the active tab in Figure 20-7). The only tab that's really worth looking at is Format; the others are really only of interest to programmers, and All is just plain frightening because it lists every possible property you can adjust.

So, with the Format tab clicked, as shown in Figure 20-8, feel free to tweak away. Change the caption, decide whether you want scroll bars on the report when viewed onscreen, decide which pages should have a header or footer, and so on. Most of the properties' names are pretty self-explanatory, so you should be fine.

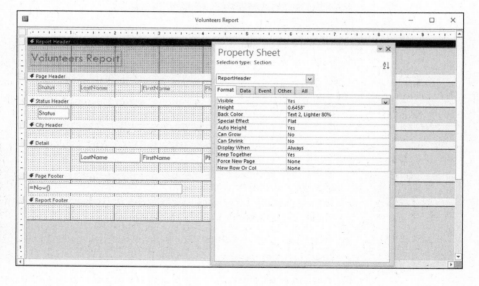

FIGURE 20-8:
The Format tab's Properties list varies depending on which report component you're working with; (here it's the Report Header label).

If you're at a loss as to what one of the properties does or means, click the setting to its right and see the drop-down arrow (as shown in Figure 20-9); then you can use the drop-down list to see the options for the chosen property. In many cases, seeing those options clarifies what the property is and does. (Note that if there's a numerical value in the column, no drop-down arrow appears — instead, you can simply edit the value.)

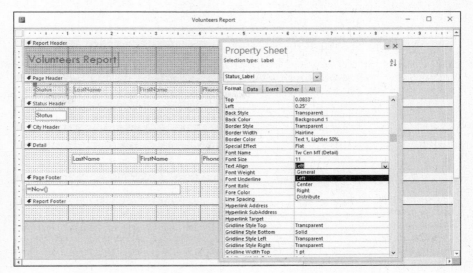

FIGURE 20-9:
Find out more about a property (Text Align is shown here) by using its drop-down list to make alternative selections.

Controlling report and page headings

To adjust when various headings appear in your report, start with the Property Sheet. After the panel appears (open it by double-clicking the report component of your choice), try these settings:

» The default Visible setting for both the Page Header and the Page Footer is Yes (or All Pages when Report is selected at the top of the Property Sheet) — meaning that Access prints a header and footer on every page in the report.

Choose Display When to tell Access to:

- Always show the header.

- Show the header when the report is printed.

- Only show the header onscreen.

The Keep Together option allows you to decide if a given part of the report should be kept with the adjacent parts. The default is Yes, with your alternative being No. Note that this option is not listed in the Property Sheet for the Page Header and Page Footer.

» The Page Header section of the Property Sheet panel comes with a bunch of options, too. Double-click the Page Header to display the PageHeaderSection panel, as shown in Figure 20-10.

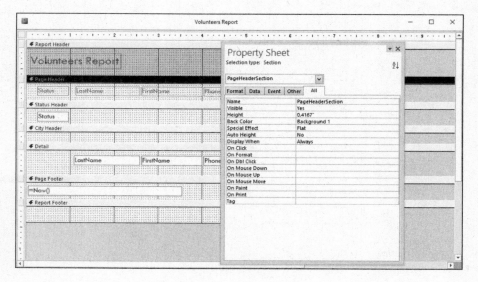

TIP

FIGURE 20-10:
Use the Property
Sheet drop-down
list to display
PageHeaderSec-
tion properties.

>> Click the Format tab on the Property Sheet for the following options:

- **Visible:** Controls whether the Page Header appears at all.

- **Height:** Access sets this property automatically as you click and drag the section header up and down on the screen.

  To specify an exact size, type the size in this section. (Access automatically uses the units of measurement you choose for Windows itself.)

>> **Back Color:** If you want to adjust the section's color, follow these steps:

  1. *Click the currently selected color.*

  2. *Click the small gray button with three dots (the Ellipsis button) that appears to the right of the entry.*

     This button displays a color palette.

  3. *Click your color choice.*

     Let Access worry about the obnoxious color number that goes into the Back Color box.

>> **Special Effect:** This property adjusts the visual effect for the section heading, much as the Special Effect button does for the markers in the report itself — though in this case your choices are limited. Click the Special Effect box and then click the down arrow to list what's available. Choose Flat (the default setting), Raised, or Sunken.

» **Auto Height:** This option is set to Yes, but you can choose No if you'd prefer not to have an automatic height setting applied to your page heading.

» **Display When:** This is set to Always by default, but allows you to choose from Print Only or Screen Only, should those options appeal to you.

Adjusting individual sections

If you want to change the format for just one section of the report, double-click the header for that section to display its GroupHeader properties in the Property Sheet, as shown in Figure 20-11. (You can also choose the associated GroupHeader item from the drop-down menu at the top of the Property Sheet panel.

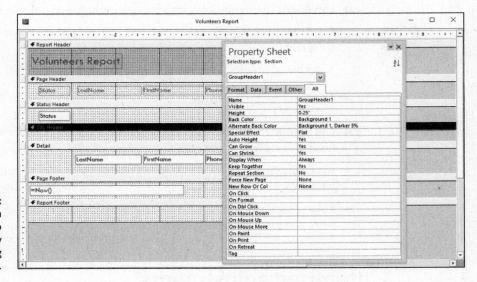

FIGURE 20-11:
Choose a section of your report to adjust by double-clicking the section.

TECHNICAL STUFF

If your report doesn't include any groups, GroupHeader won't be in the list of components for which you can view properties, nor will there be a Group heading to double-click in Design view.

If your report does have a group (or groups) in it, you can tweak 13 different Group Header settings. The settings you're most likely to want to adjust include the following:

» **Force New Page:** This option controls whether the change for that group automatically forces the information to start on a new page. When you set this option, you can determine whether this page break occurs

- Only before the header

- Only after the footer

- In both places

  or

- None, to insert no page break at all

You can control the way in which section beginnings and endings are handled for multiple-column reports (such as having the group always start in a separate column). You can control whether:

- The group is kept together (Keep Together)

- The section is visible (Visible)

>> **Can Grow:** The section expands as necessary, based on the data in it.

Can Grow is particularly useful when you're printing a report that contains a Long Text field:

1. *Set the width of the field so it's as wide as you want.*

2. *Use the Can Grow property to enable Access to adjust the height available for the information.*

>> **Can Shrink:** The section can become smaller if, for example, some of the fields are empty.

To use the Can Grow and Can Shrink properties, you have to set them for both the section and the items in the section that can grow or shrink.

>> **Repeat Section:** Controls whether Access repeats the heading on each page when a group is split across pages or columns.

Itemized adjustments

Double-clicking works for more than sections. When you want to adjust the formatting of any item of your report — a field, a label, or something you've drawn on your report — just double-click that item in Design view. Access again leads you to the Property Sheet, from which you can do all manner of technical nitpicking.

Customizing headers and footers

Although Access includes several default settings for headers and footers, those settings aren't personalized or imaginative. You can do much more with headers and footers than simply display labels for your data. Why not build expressions in these sections — or insert text that introduces or summarizes your data? (Now, *that's* a header or footer that impresses your friends, influences your co-workers, and wins over your boss. In a perfect world, anyway.)

A good header on your report's shoulders

How you place the labels in the report's header sections controls how the final report both looks and works, so you really need to put some thought into your headers. You want to make sure that all your headings are easy to understand and that they add useful information to the report.

When you're setting up a report, feel free to play around with the header layouts. Experiment with your options and see what you can come up with — the way the information repeats through the report may surprise you.

For example, when you use a wizard to create a grouped report, Access puts labels for your records in the page header by default. Figure 20-12 shows such a report in action. Notice that the Status accompanies the volunteers' actual status (the data). This appears at the top of each and every page because that label is in the Page Header section.

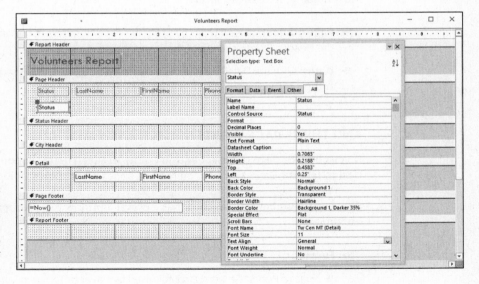

FIGURE 20-12: The Status field has been promoted within the report to Page Header content.

If you want to promote other labels to the page header, simply drag those labels to the Page Header section. You can do this in Layout view (as shown in Figure 20-13). Also in Figure 20-13, the Status label is in transit.

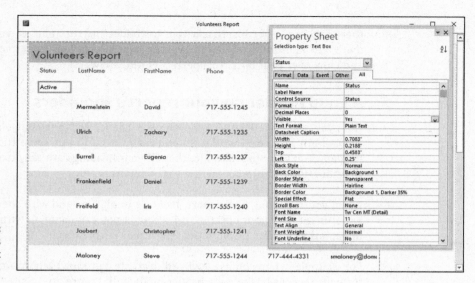

FIGURE 20-13:
Dragging labels is
easy in Layout
view.

Solid footing with page numbers and dates

Access can insert certain information for you in either the header or the footer. Most notably, Access can insert:

>> **Page numbers:** Insert them by using the Page Numbers command found in the Header/Footer section of the Design tab.

>> **Dates:** Click the Date and Time command, also found in the Header/Footer section of the Design tab.

AND THIS IS PAGE WHAT?

If you click the Page Numbers button on the Header/Footer section of the Ribbon's Design tab, the Page Numbers dialog box appears (as shown in Figure 20-14).

The Page Numbers dialog box has several options for your page-numbering excitement:

>> **Format:**

- *Page N:* Prints the word *Page* followed by the appropriate page number

- *Page N of M:* Counts the total number of pages in the report and prints that number with the current page number (as in *Page 2 of 15*)

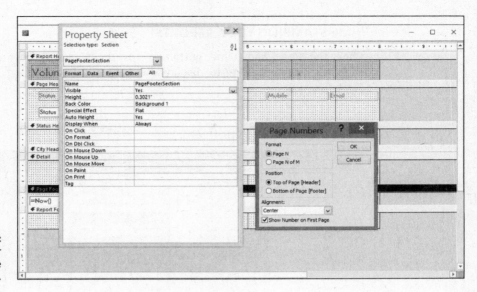

FIGURE 20-14:
Control your report's page numbers.

TIP

>> **Position:** Tells Access whether to print the page number in the Page Header or the Page Footer.

>> **Alignment:** Sets the position of the page number on the page.

Click the arrow at the right edge of the list box to see your options.

>> **Show Number on First Page:**

- Select this option to include a page number on the first page of your report.

- Deselect this option to keep your first page unnumbered.

TIP

To change how the page numbers work on your report, follow these steps:

1. Manually delete the existing page number field.

To delete the field, click it (you should be in Report view at the time) and press the Delete key.

2. Click the Page Numbers button in the Header/Footer section of the Design tab.

3. Set up new page numbers.

TIME-STAMPING YOUR REPORTS

Click the Date and Time button — in the Header/Footer section of the Ribbon's Design tab — to display the Date and Time dialog box (shown in Figure 20-15).

Date and Time button

FIGURE 20-15:
Choose dates and times here.

The most important options are:

>> Include Date

>> Include Time

Select the exact format of your date and/or time from the set of choices. The dialog box displays a sample of your settings in the section cleverly marked *Sample*.

TIP

Including the date and time makes a *huge* difference with information that changes regularly. By printing the information at the bottom of your report pages, Access automatically documents when the report came out. It never hurts to include a date stamp (or a time *and* date stamp) in report footers.

You probably noticed the Logo and Title buttons in the Header/Footer section of the Design tab, too. The Logo button opens an Insert Picture dialog box, where you can choose an image to add to the report (such as your company logo or a photo of the people or objects your report is about). The Title button inserts the report's name (the name that appears on the report's tab).

When inserted, the logo or title can be dragged to any position on the report. Figure 20-16 shows an image on the report, to the right of the report's header.

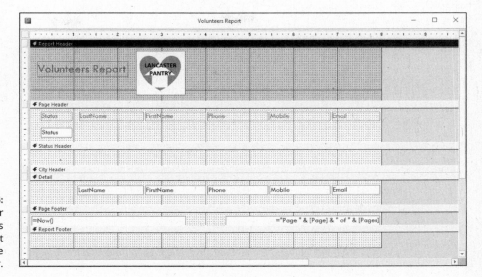

FIGURE 20-16:
Your organization's logo is a great addition to the report header.

As shown in Chapter 19, you can add images (like your logo) to any report, and not just by adding them to a header or footer. Check it out!

Chapter **21**

Mailings to the Masses

The Report Wizard (covered in Chapters 18 and 20) is just the tip of the Access reporting iceberg. If you're so inclined, you can use Access to generate useful printouts that you probably never thought of as reports — mailing or product labels. So grab your basket (and your little dog, too), because we're off to see the wizard again, as Access provides friendly and magical helpers to see you through.

Massive Mailings with the Label Wizard

So you have 5,000 catalogs, postcards, or some other mailable items printed and ready to go out to your adoring (or soon-to-be adoring) public. You also have a big Access database full of names and addresses. How can you introduce these two and get them started on what will surely be a wonderful relationship? Although e-blasts have become even more common as ways to mass "mail" your clients and potential customers, there are still marketing and informative items that (a) require printing, and (b) have to be put in the actual mail.

With the Access Label Wizard, your sheets of labels and your database will be hooked up in no time flat. With the Label Wizard, you can (almost instantly!) generate labels that work with just about any commercial label product on the market. If your local stationery or office-supply store carries them, Access can print your data on them. All you need to know is what kind of label you have, which data should go on the labels, and who's going to slap the labels on the mailings after you've finished your part of the job.

TIP

The names and addresses on labels are just part of the story. You can also print product labels, with product names, numbers, and inventory locations on them, helping your warehouse personnel find and put away products. If you have the data — whatever it might be — and the blank labels, you can bring the two together to print labels for just about any purpose.

TIP

Microsoft engineers put the specifications for hundreds of labels from popular label manufacturers right in the Label Wizard. If you happen to use labels from Avery, Herma, Zweckform, or any other maker listed in the wizard's manufacturer list — it's a long, long list, so yours is probably in there — just tell the wizard the manufacturer's product number. The wizard sets up the report dimensions for you according to the maker's specifications. Life just doesn't get much easier than that.

Before firing up the Label Wizard, decide on the information you'll need for the labels:

>> The Label Wizard uses the active table's fields by default.

>> You can create a query that includes only those fields you want to print, drawing those fields from the tables that currently house them.

TIP

Chapters 12 through 15 show the procedures for creating queries. It can be as simple as selecting the table that contains the data destined for your label, querying for all the records, and choosing to include only some of the fields. Or you can query for certain records — again, specifying which fields to include — and you're good to go. Call it one more great reason to check out the query chapters — especially Chapter 13 — for the basics before you embark on this process.

Of course, if your label information can all be found in a single table, make sure that table is open or selected in the All Access Objects panel — and follow these steps to build a label report:

1. **In the database window, click the Ribbon's Create tab and then make your way over to the Reports section of the tab.**

   The Create tab's many tools appear, including the Report and Report Wizard buttons discussed in Chapters 18 and 20.

2. **Click the Report section's Labels button to start the Label Wizard.**

   The Label Wizard dialog box opens, as shown in Figure 21-1.

3. **Click the Filter by Manufacturer drop-down list and select your label manufacturer.**

   Access assumes you have Avery labels; if you do, there's no need to perform this step — just move on to Step 4.

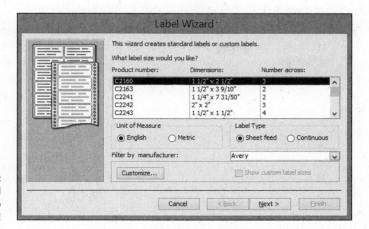

FIGURE 21-1:
The Label Wizard is prepared to make label magic!

4. **Scroll through the list of label types and find your label's product number — and when you locate it, click it to select it.**

The three-column list includes Product Number, Dimensions, and Number Across information.

TIP

Find the product number on your package of labels in the list. If you don't see it, check the packaging for an equivalent product number that the manufacturer recommends. If you buy a generic or store brand of labels, often the Avery equivalent is printed right on the packaging; you can look for that number in the list. If that fails, you can use the Customize button in the wizard to name your custom label, set your label's dimensions, and indicate how many labels there are per sheet. Click OK to proceed, which also saves the custom label for future use.

5. **Click Next.**

The Label Wizard asks you for your font choices, as in Figure 21-2.

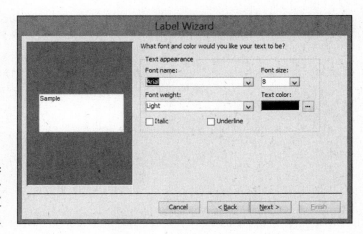

FIGURE 21-2:
Choose font, size, weight, and text color for your labels.

6. Choose the font, size, font weight (to determine whether you want your text to be light or very bold — click the drop-down list to see your choices for the font you've chosen), and the text color you want for your labels; then click Next.

The next page of the Label Wizard appears; here's where you choose which fields from the active table you want to include in your labels.

7. Double-click the first field you want to include on the labels.

As shown in Figure 21-3, there are two boxes — Available Fields and Prototype Label. When fields from the left-hand box are double-clicked, they end up in the right-hand box.

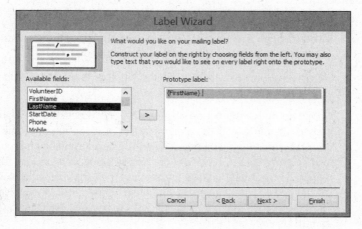

FIGURE 21-3:
Choose fields from the Available Fields box.

8. After the field name appears in the Prototype Label box, type a space after it so there's a space between the first field and the second one. If the field needs to be on the next line, you can press Enter.

9. Double-click the next field to insert it into your label and place a space or press Enter after the field (to advance to the next line), as in Step 8.

Continue double-clicking fields to add them to the Prototype — being careful to put spaces between fields and to press the Enter key to move to a new line in the Prototype box, as needed. Figure 21-4 shows a completed address label.

10. Click Next.

Now the dialog box changes to offer choices for sorting your labels.

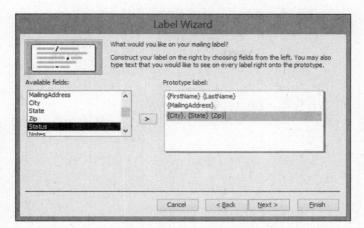

FIGURE 21-4:
Space your fields,
place them on
separate lines,
and include
commas and
other symbols
between fields.

11. **Select the field by which to sort your labels — such as by last name or by postal code.**

As shown in Figure 21-5, you can sort by more than one field; the order in which you add fields to the Sort By box dictates the sort order.

TIP

If you plan a bulk mailing with discounted postage, check with your local postal authority for details about how to organize your mail. Post offices often want the mail presorted by zip or postal code; check first because each post office may handle things differently. Rather than drive your friendly postal workers over the edge, bring your mail sorted the way *they* want it.

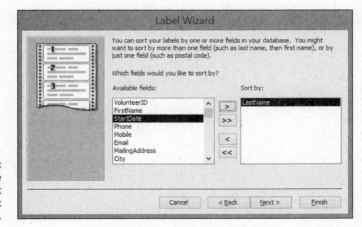

FIGURE 21-5:
Choose the
field(s) you want
to use to sort
your labels.

12. **Click Next.**

The next step in the wizard process appears, as shown in Figure 21-6.

FIGURE 21-6:
Name your Labels
report.

13. **Type a name for your Labels report.**

14. **Leave the default option chosen (See the Labels as They Will Look Printed) and click Finish.**

    The Labels report appears onscreen, as shown in Figure 21-7, and you can print as desired (by using the Print command, as usual). You can also save your work for future reprintings of the same report.

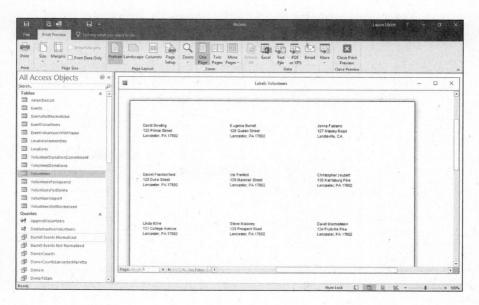

FIGURE 21-7:
You can print
your labels now
and save them
for later.

SO YOU WANT TO CREATE A CHART?

Although Access 2019, like its predecessors, offers the Chart Wizard (you'll find the Chart tool in the Controls group while you're in Design view of your report), I don't recommend using Access to turn your data into charts (or graphs, depending on your terminology preference). You'll be much better off building them in other applications within the Office suite, which also means you can use the same charts in the applications used to make them:

- **PowerPoint, the presentation application in Microsoft Office:** If you want to use PowerPoint, you can use the datasheet that appears automatically in a PowerPoint chart slide, and you can type your chart data (such as department names and total salary expenses for a given time period) into that datasheet. Alternatively, you can paste your data from an Access table into the PowerPoint chart.

- **Excel, the Microsoft Office spreadsheet application:** You can paste or import your Access table data into Excel and then use Excel's charting tools to create a chart based on those numbers.

If you're feeling discouraged that I've dissed one of the tools in Access you may have counted on using to make charts, don't be. If you have Office, then you already have much better charting tools in PowerPoint and Excel; these two applications use charting more naturally than a database application ever could. A PowerPoint presentation is a perfect place for charts — as is an Excel workbook, where rows and rows of numeric data are often better explained with pictures, in the form of a nice, clear pie chart. Because you can easily use your Access table data to populate a PowerPoint datasheet or an Excel worksheet (and therefore base a chart on the data), you could say that the charting capability has simply been confined to the application where it belongs.

6

The Parts of Tens

Contents at a Glance

> » **Resolving data-entry problems**
>
> » **Consoling query woes**
>
> » **Sending the Parameter dialog box back where it belongs**
>
> » **Tuning up performance troubles**
>
> » **Importing spreadsheet data with less mess**
>
> » **Dealing with corruption**

Chapter **22**

Ten Common Problems

Yes, even so-called "experts" have problems with computers. I've chosen ten of the most common Microsoft Access problems and presented them to you in this chapter — with their solutions, of course!

Don't give up hope if your problem is not on this list. I find many solutions to my computing problems by searching online. Chances are, if you're having the problem, someone else has already had it and figured out the solution. That's why the Internet is a valuable resource. The Appendix at the back of this book lists a few more valuable help resources.

Speaking of valuable resources, check out the ten problems in this chapter.

That's Just Not Normal

One of the hardest things to do (yet most important when building a database) is building the table structures properly. This process is known as *normalization*. A properly normalized database should never have just one table containing redundant information. Consider the following table:

Customer	Address	City	State	Zip	Telephone
Jones	125 Main Street	Jonestown	NJ	08000	609–555–1244
Jones	125 Main Street	Jonestown	NJ	08000	609–555–7890
Smith	1542 Jones Hwy	Laramie	WY	82051	307–555–5412
Wilson	78 Smith Circle	Jones	CA	90000	451–555–8645

Do you see the redundant information? Right you are. It's the customer name and address. What is causing the redundancy? Right again! It's the two phone numbers for customer Jones. The correct way to normalize this table would be to split it into two tables — one for customer name and address information and the second for phone numbers. This would eliminate the need to repeat the second Jones record in the Customers table. For more on normalization, see Chapter 4.

TIP

If you're having trouble normalizing empty tables, fill each table with five to ten records. Viewing the tables with data usually makes it easier to spot normalizing issues.

Here's how to get started normalizing your tables:

1. **Examine each table as it is currently structured.**

   Are you repeating any information unnecessarily (as you saw with the address and customer name earlier)?

2. **If you have duplicate information, determine why you're repeating it (for example, the multiple phone numbers for one customer).**

3. **Break the one table into two tables to eliminate the redundancy.**

4. **Repeat Steps 1 through 3 for each table until all redundancy is eliminated.**

TIP

You may find that splitting one table into two still does not eliminate all redundancy in a table. In that case, keep splitting the tables until all redundancy is gone.

You Type 73.725, but It Changes to 74

Automatic rounding can frustrate the living daylights out of you, but correcting it is easy. By default, Access sets all number fields to accept *long integers*. As you may remember from your high school math days, an integer is a negative or positive *whole number*. To accommodate decimals, you change the field-size setting so it accepts decimals. Here's how:

1. **Open the table in Design view and then click the field that's not cooperating.**

2. **On the General tab of the Properties area at the bottom of the screen, click the Field Size box.**

3. **Click the down arrow at the end of the box, and then select Single, Double, or Decimal from the drop-down menu that appears.**

4. **Save the table, and your automatic rounding problem is over.**

TIP

For details about the difference between Single, Double, and Decimal field sizes, press the F1 key while in the Field Size property box. The Help screen gives a detailed description of each field size, the numbers it will hold, and the amount of space reserved for that size. Access requires an Internet connection to use its help system.

The Words They Are A-Changing

Sometimes those "helpful" features in Access can become a nuisance. One such feature is called AutoCorrect. You may be familiar with it from Microsoft Word, where it is often a great thing. Databases, however, often contain acronyms, part numbers, and the like. AutoCorrect can have a field day with such "words". You may not even realize it as you enter your data.

You have two choices to resolve this problem.

>> **Undo AutoCorrect's effects as they occur.** Press Ctrl+Z right after AutoCorrect has botched your data entry. Access puts the data back to the way you typed it. Unfortunately, for this to work you actually have to notice that Access has changed what you entered.

>> **Turn AutoCorrect off entirely.** To turn off AutoCorrect, follow these steps:

1. *Click the File tab in the upper left corner of the Access screen.*

2. *Click the Options button in the menu down the left side of the screen.*

   The Access Options dialog box appears.

3. *Click Proofing from the list on the left.*

   Your proofing choices appear.

4. *Click the AutoCorrect Options button.*

   The AutoCorrect dialog box appears.

5. *Uncheck some or all of the check boxes in the AutoCorrect dialog box.*

   You can disable some or all of the AutoCorrect features, depending on what AutoCorrect is doing to annoy you at present. Uncheck the Replace Text as You Type option if you no longer want Access to "fix" your "spelling errors" for you.

6. *Click OK two times to save your changes.*

   You can now type your problem text correctly, without AutoCorrect's interference, and have it stay as you typed it.

Was There and Now It's Gone

You might've heard this one a lot over the years: "The database deleted my record!" Well, I've got news for you: The database doesn't do anything without us humans commanding it. And humans can make a couple of mistakes:

WARNING

>> **Accidental deletion:** There are several ways to delete a record accidentally. Usually a keyboard shortcut for Delete is pressed, such as Ctrl+− (delete record) or Ctrl+X (cut).

The Undo command (Ctrl+Z) will not reverse the deletion of a record.

>> **Data error:** A record may *appear* deleted if someone inadvertently changes a particularly vital piece of information. For example, suppose the record in question contains an order date of 12/15/19, and someone inadvertently changes the date to 12/15/09. The order date isn't what's expected, so the record may seem to have been deleted.

>> If a data error makes the record seem deleted, there are several possible fixes, as outlined in the following sections.

Undo

REMEMBER

Don't panic. Before doing anything else, press Ctrl+Z. That's the Undo command. If the record comes back, you're in luck. Undo reverses data-entry errors that may cause the record to appear deleted. However, this will work only if you Undo right after the data-entry error takes place.

Search for the missing record

If you try the Undo command and the record doesn't come back, there's still a chance that a data-entry error is hiding it by putting it where you don't expect it to be. Open the table that contained the record and search for it in some way other than you normally would. Look for anything out of the ordinary on similar records. Here are some examples:

>> If you normally search for orders by date, search by client. See whether an order similar to the missing one exists for that client *and* has an unusual date (say, the same month and day as the missing order but with the wrong year).

>> Try looking at all orders on the date in question to see whether the client on each order seems to be correct. It could be that the client was changed inadvertently on the missing order.

Backup recovery

If you can't find the record anywhere, copy the record from a backup of the database file.

TECHNICAL STUFF

This solution works only if you've backed up your database since the record was originally added. If you back up at night and the record was entered during the same day it went missing, that record will not be in your backup.

You Run a Query, but the Results Aren't What You Expect

Query-writing is an art form. Even the experts mess up every now and then. Here are some common solutions to unexpected query results:

» **Check criteria for accuracy.** A single misplaced keystroke is all it takes to turn your query into a dud. Check your criteria for spelling or syntax errors — and then run the query again.

» **Try the Unique Values property.** Ever see two copies of each record in your query results when you were expecting just one? A quick fix often comes from using the Unique Values property. This property tells Access to stop with the doubling, already — and, if the query results contain a group of exact duplicates, to return only one row from the group. Here's how to use this property:

1. *Open the problem query in Design view.*

   The Design tab on the Ribbon appears.

2. *Click the Property Sheet button from the tab's Show/Hide Ribbon group.*

   The Property Sheet window opens to the right of the query grid.

3. *Click in the gray area between the field lists in the top half of the query grid.*

   The Property Sheet should now display Query Properties. (Look right under the Property Sheet's title bar to confirm this.)

4. *Click in the Unique Values row of the Property Sheet.*

   A drop-down list arrow appears at the end of the Unique Values row.

5. *Select Yes from the drop-down list and run the query.*

   The doubling should disappear.

» **Correct the selection logic.** Juggling a bunch of AND and OR connections in a query can quickly mess up even the hardiest of database designers. Chapter 14 has tips on untangling the mess.

» **Fix table relationships.** If your query results show *way* too many records, and the query uses two or more tables, improper relationships (also called joins) are the likely cause. Flip back to Chapter 5 for more about relating one table to another.

» **Check table relationship types.** If your query involves two or more tables, and you get fewer records than you expected, incorrect table relationships are the likely cause. For example, if you have an order entry database and run a query listing all customers and their orders, by default, you'll see only those customers who have placed an order. To see all customers, whether or not they've placed orders, do the following:

1. *In Design view, right-click the join (the line connecting the two tables) and choose Join Properties from the menu that appears.*

2. *Examine the types of joins offered and choose the one that says something like "Include ALL records from 'Customers' and only those records from 'Orders' where the joined fields are equal".*

   The actual text you see differs according to the names of your tables. To query aficionados, this is called an *outer join.* Very cool.

3. *Click OK and run the query.*

   You should now have all records from the Customers table whether or not there are corresponding records in the Orders table.

TIP

» If your query involves several criteria, some calculated fields, and numerous relationships, try breaking the task into several smaller steps instead of trying to solve the problem all at once. The step-by-step approach lets you focus on each piece, one at a time, making sure each works perfectly before moving on to the next one.

TIP

If your query still doesn't work no matter what you do, ask someone else to take a look. I've often worked on a tough query problem for hours, shown it to someone else, and heard those magical words: "That's simple. Just do this." And the problem is solved. Getting a fresh pair of eyes on the problem often solves things fast.

The Dreaded Parameter Dialog Box

At some point, when opening a query, form, or report, you'll see a Parameter dialog box when you don't want to see a Parameter dialog box. Do you throw your hands in the air and curse the universe? Of course not! Whenever you see a Parameter dialog box unexpectedly (you can set them on purpose — see Chapter 16 for details), it means that Access can't find a field referenced by either the form or report or the query behind the form or report. Say that the problem is with a report. To troubleshoot, start with the query behind the report. Open that query in Datasheet view and see if you get the parameter. If you do, what field is it asking for? That field is the one Access can't find. So, switch the query to Design view and find the column with the field that Access can't find. The problem field is usually a Calculated field that references other fields. Is each field and table name spelled correctly? If not, correct the spelling errors. Is each field in the table it's supposed to be in? For example, if your reference reads `Orders.LastName` and the `LastName` field is in the Customers table, correct the error by typing **Customers.LastName**.

If the query runs without a parameter, then the problem is on the report. So, open the report in Design view and check each control on the report that is bound to a field. If Access can't find one of the fields the control is supposed to display, it'll put a green triangle in the upper left corner of the control. Check each one for the green triangle. If you find the green triangle, check the spelling of the field referenced by the control. For example, if the control is supposed to display `LastName` (no space) and the reference in the control says Last Name (space), then remove the space so that the control on the report matches the field name from the query. Also check the report's underlying query to confirm the problem field is selected in the query.

The Slowest Database in Town

An Access database may end up on the shared drive of a business so it's available to everyone who needs it. The problem with placing the entire Access database on the shared drive is that it often runs slowly on each user's workstation (that's a fancy word for an individual computer). You'll also likely run into errors if multiple people attempt to use the database at the same time. The complaints start rolling in, and you don't know what to do.

The solution to this problem lies in splitting the Access database file into two separate files:

>> **Front end:** Contains all the database objects *except* the tables

   The front end resides on the user workstation.

>> **Back end:** Contains just the tables

   The back end resides on the shared server.

   The front end is linked to tables in the back end. (See Chapter 9 for more on table linking.)

TIP

All you're really sharing is the data — so the data is all that should go on the shared drive. By setting things up this way, the only information that *must* travel across the network is the data requested by the user. Such a setup dramatically speeds database performance and allows multiple users to enter and edit data at the same time.

Splitting the dataset is not as hard as you might think. Access makes it a snap with the Database Splitter Wizard. Follow these steps to split your database:

1. **Back up the database you want to split.**

   If anything goes wrong (unlikely, but hey, you can never be too safe when it comes to data!), you can try again with the backup copy.

2. **If necessary, move the database you want to split to a folder on your shared drive.**

   This step allows the Database Splitter to set up table links properly for you.

3. **Open the database file you want to split from the shared folder.**

   Make sure you have a backup copy of this database before going any further. Also make sure all database objects are closed.

4. **Click the Database Tools tab on the Ribbon.**

   The Move Data group appears on the Ribbon. It contains a button called Access Database.

5. **Click the Access Database button.**

   The Database Splitter Wizard dialog box appears.

6. **Click the Split Database button and let the wizard do its thing.**

   You will be prompted for a back-end database filename. Enter a name, sit back, and watch the fun unfold before your very eyes.

7. **Copy the front-end file (the original file you split) to each user's workstation.**

   Have the users open the file from their workstations — and see how they marvel at the improved speed of the database! You are a hero. Yea!

TIP

Don't have a shared drive or want to get rid of your share? You can still have multiple users in your database at one time by placing your data in the cloud. For details, check out Chapter 11.

Your Database File Is as Big as a House

As time goes by, you find your database file growing larger and larger. This is a result of deleting objects and records over time. If, for example, you create a query and then later delete it because it's no longer needed, Access doesn't automatically remove the space occupied by that query from the database file. The same is true for records. As you delete records from a table, the space that those records occupied in the database file remains. Eventually, the file can become four or five times the size required to hold the data and objects within it.

Why should you care if the file size increases? Here are two reasons:

>> **A smaller database file runs faster.** Performance is a key component to happy database users. You want your forms to load quickly and your queries and reports to run as fast as possible.

>> **A regularly compacted database is more stable.** If the database is used often, compacting regularly helps keep file and table corruption from occurring.

The Compact and Repair command removes the excess. It is good practice to compact your database regularly (once a week is usually fine). Always compact it after making any design changes. Here's how:

1. **Open the bloated database and click the Database Tools tab on the Ribbon.**

   The Tools group appears at the very left of the Ribbon.

2. **Click the Compact and Repair Database button from the Tools group.**

   The status bar (lower right of your screen) displays a progress bar that notifies you of how the compact process is progressing. When the progress bar disappears, compacting is complete — and you'll be left with a much trimmer (faster and more stable) database file. If you've split your database, don't forget to compact both the front- and back-end files.

TIP

Want a database file to compact each time you close it? Follow these steps:

1. **Click the File tab on the Ribbon.**

2. **Click the Access Options button in the menu bar down the left side of the screen.**

   The Access Options dialog box appears.

3. **Click Current Database from the list on the left.**

   Options for the current database appear.

4. **Check the Compact on Close check box.**

5. **Click OK to save your changes.**

6. **Click OK from the resulting message box.**

7. **Close the database and note the lower right status bar.**

   The database is compacting before it closes!

WARNING

Compact on close is used best on the front-end file only. Compacting the back end on close may cause corruption of the back-end file should another user be in it when you close out of it. Do not turn on Compact on Close on the back-end file.

You Get a Mess When Importing Your Spreadsheet

It's common practice to upgrade a collection of spreadsheets to an Access database after the spreadsheet solution no longer suits your needs. It's also common to find the imported spreadsheet (now table) data in a state of disarray. The easiest way to solve this problem is by cleaning up the spreadsheet *before* you import it. Here are a few tips for a tidy import:

» **Double-check information coming from any spreadsheet program to be sure that it's *consistent* and *complete*.** Above all, make sure that all entries in each column (field) are the same data type (all numbers, all text, or all whatever).

» **Remove any titles and blank rows from the top of the spreadsheet.** An ideal spreadsheet for import will have field names (column headings) in row 1 and data starting in row 2.

» **Make sure your spreadsheet column headings are short and unique so Access can easily translate them to field names during import.**

We're Sorry; Your Database File Is Corrupt

It started out as a day just like any other. However, on this day, you are getting an error when you open the front end of your split Access database. You can't seem to open any forms or reports. It's funny how a few little messages can ruin your day. You start wondering if you backed up the data file last night and when the file was actually corrupted. Then you start wondering how you'll get out of this mess.

Fear not. There is a simple solution to a corrupt database. Here are the steps:

1. **Browse to the folder that contains the back-end file.**

2. **Double-click the file to open it.**

   Access will launch and attempt to repair the file. You should see a repair progress bar on the right part of the status bar. If all goes well, the file opens.

3. **Close the back-end data file.**

4. **Reopen the front-end file and everything should be working normally.**

TIP

If, after following the preceding directions, the corrupted file still doesn't open, you have a serious problem that could take some effort to clean up. The next step is to resort to a backup copy of the database. Check what data is missing between the backup and your recollection of the corrupted file. Yes, you'll have to reenter any missing data. Sorry!

If you don't have a backup, all hope is not lost. You can buy software designed specifically to repair corrupted Access database files. Try searching the web for *repair corrupt Microsoft Access database files.* Make sure the software works with Microsoft Access 2019 and it is from a legitimate company.

Chapter **23**

Ten Uncommon Tips

Technical experts — the people who know Access inside and out — might be a little intimidating, but they're important — and they (we?) in no way intend to intimidate. They're important to average Access users because they provide invaluable advice, and they're important to Access itself because they drive the way Microsoft continuously improves its products. These men and women are the people who test Office products before new versions are released to the public, and they're the ones who write books (like this one and more advanced books for more advanced users) to help users of all levels make the most of the software.

So the people who develop databases for a living are an essential resource to the average user, to the "power user," and to the software manufacturer as well. This chapter is a compilation of some of the best advice gathered from a long list of Access experts. Knowing they were offering suggestions for new users, they offered advice to fit your needs and to help ensure that, after reading this book, you really can use Access confidently and effectively. By the time you finish, you'll have given your efforts the right amount of planning and organizing — and you'll have solid plans for moving forward with your development and use of the databases you build with Access.

So here's the sage advice — in ten quick bites.

Document Everything as Though One Day You'll Be Questioned by the FBI

Don't skimp on the time spent documenting your database. Why? Because you'll be glad later on that you *didn't* skimp. You'll have all your plans, your general information, and all your ideas — those you acted on and those that remained on the drawing board — ready the next time you need to build a database. You'll also have them to refer to when or if something goes wrong with your current database. You accidentally deleted a saved query? No problem. Refer to your documentation. Forgot how your tables were related? Check the documentation and rebuild the relationships. Need to explain to someone why or how you set something up? Refer to your notes and wow them with your forethought and careful consideration.

So what should this glorious documentation include? Well, everything. But here's a list to get you started:

>> **General information about the database:**

- File/data locations (with specific network paths or Internet URLs)
- Explanation of what the database does
- Information on how it works

>> **Table layouts:**

- Include field names, sizes, contents, and sample contents.
- If some of the data comes from esoteric or temporary sources (say, the credit card data that you download monthly online), note that fact in the documentation.

>> **Summary of reports:**

- Report names
- An explanation of the information on the report

TIP

If you need to run some queries before creating a report, document the process. (Better yet, get a friendly nerd to help you automate the work.)

>> **Queries and logic:** For every query, provide a detailed explanation of how the query works, especially if it involves multiple tables or data sources outside Access (such as SQL tables or other big-time information-storage areas).

>> **Answer the question "Why?":** As you document your database, focus on *why* your design works the way it works. Why do the queries use those particular tables? Granted, if you work in a corporate environment, you may not *know* why the system works the way it does, but it never hurts to ask.

>> **Disaster-recovery details:**

- The backup process and schedule

- Where backups are located (you *are* making backups, right?) and how to restore a backed-up file

- What to do if the database stops working

TIP

If your database runs an important organizational function — such as accounting, inventory, contact management, or order entry — make sure that a manual process is in place to keep the organization going if the database malfunctions — and remember to document the process!

If you need help with any of these items, *ask someone!* Whether you borrow someone from your Information Technology department or rent a computer geek, get the help you need. Treat your documentation like insurance — no organization should run without it.

REMEMBER

Every 6 to 12 months, review your documentation to see whether updates are needed. Documentation is useful only if it's up to date *and* if someone other than you can understand it. Likewise, make sure you (or your counterparts in the office) know where the documentation is located. If you have an electronic version, keep it backed up and have a printout handy — something you'll be glad you did if you or someone else attempts to recycle your database parts using the Application Parts feature.

Keep Your Fields as Small as Possible

As you build tables, make your text fields the appropriate sizes for the data you keep in them. By default, Access sets up text (known as Short Text) fields to hold 255 characters — a pretty generous setting, particularly if the field holds measly two-letter state abbreviations.

A hundred or more extra spaces — that go unused in most text fields — wouldn't seem like anything to lose sleep over, but multiply that space across a table with 100,000 customer addresses in it, and you end up with lots of megabytes of storage space that are very busy holding nothing.

TIP

Adjust the field size with the Field Size setting on the General tab in Design view. For more information, see Chapter 4.

Use Number Fields for Real Numbers

Use number fields for numbers used in calculations, not for text pretending to be a number. Software applications perceive a huge difference between the postal code 47999 and the number 47,999. The application views a postal code as a series of characters that all happen to be digits, but the *number* is treated as an actual number that you can use for math and all kinds of other fun numeric stuff. The other reason a zip code isn't a Number field? If you're in the U.S. and your zip code starts with zero, the application cuts off the leading zero and stores just the non-zero digits in the field – 01234 becomes 1234. Not good!

TIP

When choosing the type for a new field with numbers in it, ask yourself a simple question: Are you *ever* going to make a calculation or do anything math-related with that field?

>> If you'll calculate with the field, use a *Number* type.

>> If you won't calculate with the field, store the field as *Short Text*.

Validate Your Data

Validations can help prevent bad data from getting close to your tables. Validations are easy to make, quick to set up, and ever-vigilant (even when you're so tired you can't see straight). If you aren't using validations to protect the integrity of your database, you really should start. Flip back to Chapter 7 and have a look at the topic.

Use Understandable Names to Keep Things Simple

When building a table or creating a database, think about the database file, field, and table names you use:

>> Will you remember what the names mean three months from now? Six months from now?

>> Are the names intuitive enough that someone else can look at the table and figure out what it does, long after you've moved on to bigger and better things?

This becomes even more important as you start using the tools for putting your Access tables and databases online and sharing them via SharePoint — potentially you're bringing millions of users "to the table". Also, with the Application Parts feature, the components of your databases can be recycled to help speed the creation of a new database. You don't want mysterious names for the parts of your database to spread to a new database — to create nightmarish mysteries there too — right?

Delete with Great Caution

Whenever you're deleting field values from a table, make sure you're killing the values in the right record — check again, and *then* only when you're sure, delete the original. Even then, you can still do a quick Ctrl+Z and recover the offending item provided you undo right after catching the mistake.

WARNING

Why all the checking and double-checking? Because after you delete a field value *and do anything else in the table,* Access completely forgets about your old value. It's gone, just as though it never existed. If you delete a record from a table, the record is really gone — because there is no Undo available for an entire record. If that record happened to be important and you didn't have a current backup file when the record went away, you're out of luck. Sorry!

Backup, Backup, Backup

Did I make that clear enough? Always keep a backup of your work! There's no substitute for a current backup of your data — particularly if the data is vital to your personal or professional life. Effective strategies often include maintaining backup copies at another location in case a disaster destroys your office, be it at a different office or in the cloud.

If you're thinking that you've never needed a backup before so why bother, think about floods. Think about newscasters saying that an area currently underwater has never flooded before. Picture people's lives floating down the street. Whether you're faced with a real disaster of hurricane proportions, a fire, or your computer's hard drive deciding to die (and that does happen — even if it has never happened to you before), you'll be much happier if you have a backup of your database.

Think, Think, and Think Again

You know the carpenter's slogan, "Measure twice, cut once"? The same can be said for thinking when it comes to your database. Don't just think about something, come to a quick conclusion, and then dive in. Wait, think it through again, and then maybe think about it a third time. *Then* draw a conclusion and begin acting on it. With all the power Access gives you, coupled with the capability to store thousands upon thousands of records in your database, a relatively simple mistake can be quite costly because of the potential ramifications in terms of data loss or an "un-undoable" action taken in error.

Get Organized and Stay Organized

Although the suggestions to get organized and to keep it simple may seem to be at odds, these two pieces of advice are really companions. Keeping things simple can often be a way to avoid the need for a lot of organization after the fact. Whereas you probably got tired of hearing your parents remind you that "there's a place for everything, and everything in its place" (or if they were less poetic, "*Clean your room!!!*"), they were right.

If you keep your database organized, you'll save yourself time and grief. A well-planned, well-organized table will be easier to query, report on, and include in a form. It'll also sort and filter like lightning.

TIP

Yes, you can get *too* organized. In fact, over-organizing is altogether too easy. Temper your desire to organize by cultivating another passion: working with as few steps as possible. Limit the number of folders and subfolders you use — a maximum of five levels of folders is more than enough for just about anybody.

If you go much beyond five levels, your organization starts bumping into your productivity (and nobody likes a productivity loss, least of all the people who come up with those silly little slogans for corporate feel-good posters).

There's No Shame in Asking for Help

If you're having trouble with something, swallow your ego and ask for help. Saying "I don't know" — and then trying to find out about what you don't yet know — holds no shame. This rule is especially important when you're riding herd on thousands of records in a database. Small missteps quickly magnify and multiply a small problem into a huge crisis. Ask for help before the situation becomes dire.

TIP

Not sure how to ask for help? Check the Appendix in this book, which offers you ways to get help through the installed Office suite, through Microsoft's online help, and through third-party sources that offer help on the Internet 24/7. Crying "Uncle!" has never been easier.

Appendix **A**

Getting Help

L ike all Office applications, help is available within Access — represented by a question mark in the upper right corner of the application window. This, when clicked, opens a panel that runs down the right side of the Access window, and gives you a Search box and a list of general topics you can click on and drill down within to hone in on the topic you need help with. You can also press the F1 key for context-sensitive help on what you're doing, or whatever's going on at the time, in terms of the windows open, the tools in use, displayed dialog boxes, and so on.

In that right-hand panel there's also an ellipsis that, when clicked, displays a short menu containing three options:

» **Home:** Choosing this takes you right back to the view you were just in, before displaying the menu.

» **Office Help Center:** This opens a browser window and takes you to a website: https://support.office.com/.

» **Contact Us:** This option takes you to an interactive panel within the help panel through which you can type your question and ask to be routed to the correct support department/source. Click Get Help to commence the search for that correct source. You can also try this web address to get to a list of contact sources:

https://support.microsoft.com/en-us/contactus/

While all this help from Microsoft seems rather comprehensive, we've found that it can also be faster and more effective to tap into various third-party online sources for help. The reasons that alternative sources can be as or more helpful than Microsoft's help is because your situation isn't likely to be unique (even though it probably feels that way) and will no doubt have been experienced by someone else. A lot of those Someone Else's have written blogs, articles, and created videos explaining how and when a tool or feature is used within the application.

You'll also find plenty of forums when you search online — typing your question into a Google or Bing search box. Most of them are used and fed by programmers and more advanced users, but from time to time, even new users with no coding ability will find a tip that helps solve a problem they're having or something they don't understand.

TIP

Access 2019 For Dummies saves you from a lot of that searching — within the application's help as well as online. The information you need is probably found in the pages of this book, and at the very least, this book enables you to understand Access features well enough to find and grasp the more advanced assistance you may eventually need.

TIP

If you are deaf or hearing-impaired and have a TDD or TT modem, call this number for all questions about Access (and all other Microsoft products):

800-892-5234

WARNING

Unless you (or your company) have a Microsoft support contract, TDD/TT help calls incur a fee per *incident*, just like the technical voice line.

Index

Symbols
+ (addition), 260
& (ampersand), 114, 263
@ (at sign), 114
/ (division), 260
= (equals) operator, 218, 234, 238
^ (exponents), 260
> (greater-than) symbol, 114, 218, 234, 238
>= (greater than or equal to) symbol, 218
< (less-than) symbol, 114, 218, 234
<= (less than or equal to) symbol, 218
* (multiplication), 260
<> (not equal to) symbol, 218
(pound sign), 237
- (subtraction), 260

A
Access. *See also specific topics*
  connecting Office 365 to, 181–190
  how it works, 18–23
  new features in, 16
  opening, 18–19
  uses for, 8–16
Access files, 155
accessing
  context-sensitive tools, 33
  panels, 33
  panes, 33
  properties, 110–112
accidental deletion, 364
action queries, 269–270
ad hoc queries, 227–229

Add a Place option (Open command), 28
adding
  buttons to Quick Access toolbar, 35–37
  color in reports, 313–314
  design elements to reports, 325–328
  Hyperlink field to desktop database table, 187–188
  indexes, 91
  logos to reports, 326–328
  tables, 57–60
  Total row to queries, 245–246
  words with text formulas, 262–263
addition (+), 260
adjusting
  borders in reports, 318–321
  field content, 102–103
  field-size setting, 363
  fonts in reports, 321–322
  items in reports, 311
  join types, 249
  line type in reports, 320–321
  lines in reports, 318–321
  queries, 227
  records, 102–103, 177
  records in tables, 102–103
  relationships, 87
  sections in reports, 343–344
  tabular settings for reports, 286
  text in reports, 321–322
  thickness for lines in reports, 320
Adobe Acrobat files (PDF), 162
Advanced Filter/Sort option, 201, 212–213, 215

properties
  about, 109–110
  accessing, 110–112
  customizing, 338–349
  Default Value, 110, 131–132
  Format, 110, 112–121
  Input Mask, 110, 121–126, 121–128
  Required, 110, 128–129
  Unique Values, 366
  Validation Rule, 110, 129–131
Property Sheet panel, 285, 338–349
protocol codes, 186
punctuation, in Text fields, 114–115

Q

queries. *See also* action queries
  about, 209–210, 212, 235
  action, 269–270
  ad hoc, 227–229, 227–234
  adding Total Row to, 245–246
  Advanced Filter/Sort tool, 214–219
  Append, 269–270, 274–276
  automating editing with, 173–178
  compared with filters, 212
  creating, 173, 222–225, 256
  creating Calculated fields in, 256
  creating with Query Wizard, 222–225
  criteria for, 210
  defined, 9
  documenting, 375
  exporting data from, 163–164
  files, 211
  Filter window, 213–214
  filters/filtering, 201–202, 210–213
  modifying, 227
  multiple-table, 228–229
  parameter, 261–262

resizing columns for, 257–258
  running, 233
  saving, 231–233
  Select query, 220–227
  sorting results from, 230–231
  summary, 249
  troubleshooting, 234, 366–367
  using, 227
Query Design grid, 214, 227, 232
Query Design window, 228
Query Wizard
  about, 173–174
  running, 221–227
  running Find Duplicates Query Wizard,
    174–178
Quick Access toolbar
  adding buttons to, 35–37
  location of, 33
  moving, 34
  removing buttons from, 37
  repositioning, 34–35
Quick Launch toolbar, opening Access
    from, 18–19

R

ranges, data in, 237–238
rearranging columns in reports, 287
Recent option (Open command), 28
records
  about, 45
  changing in tables, 102–103
  deleting, 178
  duplicate, 173–174
  editing, 177
  finding, 150–151
  grouping, 335–338
  inserting in tables, 97–98

About the Author

Laurie Ann Ulrich has been writing about and teaching people to use computers and software in general, and Microsoft Office in particular, for more than 20 years. She's been there through every new version of Access as Office has evolved to meet the needs of users from all walks of life — from individuals to huge corporations, from growing businesses to non-profit organizations.

In the meantime, Laurie has personally trained more than 20,000 people to make better, more creative use of their computers, and has written and co-written 30+ internationally published books on computers and software — including several titles on Microsoft Office. In the last few years, she's also created several online training courses, teaching online students to use Microsoft Office, Adobe Photoshop, and Google Analytics.

Laurie's own firm, Limehat & Company, offers instructional design, training, and educational materials as well as graphic design, marketing, promotions, and web development services. She invites you to contact her with your Office-related questions at `mailto:help@limehat.com` and to visit her website at `www.limehat.com`.

Ken Cook built and manages a successful computer consulting business (called Cook Software Solutions, LLC) located in Pennsylvania. He began as a trainer — training numerous users on a variety of software packages — specializing in Microsoft Office and proprietary software applications. He still does some training, but his main focus is creating expert Microsoft Office solutions and Microsoft Access database solutions for small to mid-sized business clients.

Ken is also a published contributing author of several books on Microsoft Excel and Microsoft Office. Ken coauthored all the previous editions of this book starting with *Access 2010 For Dummies* (Wiley).

Ken is a graduate of Syracuse University with a bachelor's degree in Marketing. He can be contacted through his website (`www.kcookpcbiz.com`) or by email (`mailto:ken@kcookpcbiz.com`).

Publisher's Acknowledgments

Executive Editor: Steve Hayes
Development/Copy Editor: Scott Tullis
Technical Editor: Guy Hart-Davis

Production Editor: Siddique Shaik
Project Manager: Maureen Tullis
Cover Image: © Digital Genetics/Shutterstock

Leverage the power

Dummies is the global leader in the reference category and one of the most trusted and highly regarded brands in the world. No longer just focused on books, customers now have access to the dummies content they need in the format they want. Together we'll craft a solution that engages your customers, stands out from the competition, and helps you meet your goals.

Advertising & Sponsorships

Connect with an engaged audience on a powerful multimedia site, and position your message alongside expert how-to content. Dummies.com is a one-stop shop for free, online information and know-how curated by a team of experts.

- Targeted ads
- Video
- Email Marketing
- Microsites
- Sweepstakes sponsorship

20 MILLION PAGE VIEWS EVERY SINGLE MONTH

15 MILLION UNIQUE VISITORS PER MONTH

43% OF ALL VISITORS ACCESS THE SITE VIA THEIR MOBILE DEVICES

700,000 NEWSLETTER SUBSCRIPTIONS TO THE INBOXES OF *300,000* UNIQUE INDIVIDUALS EVERY WEEK

Custom Publishing

Reach a global audience in any language by creating a solution that will differentiate you from competitors, amplify your message, and encourage customers to make a buying decision.

- Apps
- Books
- eBooks
- Video
- Audio
- Webinars

Brand Licensing & Content

Leverage the strength of the world's most popular reference brand to reach new audiences and channels of distribution.

For more information, visit dummies.com/biz

PERSONAL ENRICHMENT

     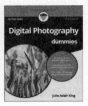

Staying Sharp	Facebook	Guitar	Investing	Beekeeping	Digital Photography
9781119187790	9781119179030	9781119293354	9781119293347	9781119310068	9781119235606
USA $26.00	USA $21.99	USA $24.99	USA $22.99	USA $22.99	USA $24.99
CAN $31.99	CAN $25.99	CAN $29.99	CAN $27.99	CAN $27.99	CAN $29.99
UK £19.99	UK £16.99	UK £17.99	UK £16.99	UK £16.99	UK £17.99

Meditation	Pregnancy	Samsung Galaxy S7	iPhone	Crocheting	Nutrition
9781119251163	9781119235491	9781119279952	9781119283133	9781119287117	9781119130246
USA $24.99	USA $26.99	USA $24.99	USA $24.99	USA $24.99	USA $22.99
CAN $29.99	CAN $31.99	CAN $29.99	CAN $29.99	CAN $29.99	CAN $27.99
UK £17.99	UK £19.99	UK £17.99	UK £17.99	UK £16.99	UK £16.99

PROFESSIONAL DEVELOPMENT

Windows 10	AutoCAD	Excel 2016	QuickBooks 2017	macOS Sierra	LinkedIn	Windows 10
9781119311041	9781119255796	9781119293439	9781119281467	9781119280651	9781119251132	9781119310563
USA $24.99	USA $39.99	USA $26.99	USA $26.99	USA $29.99	USA $24.99	USA $34.00
CAN $29.99	CAN $47.99	CAN $31.99	CAN $31.99	CAN $35.99	CAN $29.99	CAN $41.99
UK £17.99	UK £27.99	UK £19.99	UK £19.99	UK £21.99	UK £17.99	UK £24.99

SharePoint 2016	Fundamental Analysis	Networking	Office 2016	Office 365	Salesforce.com	Coding
9781119181705	9781119263593	9781119257769	9781119293477	9781119265313	9781119239314	9781119293323
USA $29.99	USA $26.99	USA $29.99	USA $26.99	USA $24.99	USA $29.99	USA $29.99
CAN $35.99	CAN $31.99	CAN $35.99	CAN $31.99	CAN $29.99	CAN $35.99	CAN $35.99
UK £21.99	UK £19.99	UK £21.99	UK £19.99	UK £17.99	UK £21.99	UK £21.99

dummies.com

dummies®
A Wiley Brand

Learning Made Easy

ACADEMIC

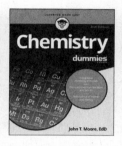

9781119293576
USA $19.99
CAN $23.99
UK £15.99

9781119293637
USA $19.99
CAN $23.99
UK £15.99

9781119293491
USA $19.99
CAN $23.99
UK £15.99

9781119293460
USA $19.99
CAN $23.99
UK £15.99

9781119293590
USA $19.99
CAN $23.99
UK £15.99

9781119215844
USA $26.99
CAN $31.99
UK £19.99

9781119293378
USA $22.99
CAN $27.99
UK £16.99

9781119293521
USA $19.99
CAN $23.99
UK £15.99

9781119239178
USA $18.99
CAN $22.99
UK £14.99

9781119263883
USA $26.99
CAN $31.99
UK £19.99

Available Everywhere Books Are Sold

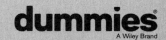

Small books for big imaginations

GETTING STARTED WITH Coding

Get Creative with Code!

Camille McCue, PhD

9781119177173
USA $9.99
CAN $9.99
UK £8.99

MODDING Minecraft™

Build Your Own Minecraft Mods!

Sarah Guthals, PhD
Stephen Foster, PhD
Lindsey Handley, PhD

9781119177272
USA $9.99
CAN $9.99
UK £8.99

MAKING YouTube VIDEOS

Star in Your Own Video!

Nick Willoughby

9781119177241
USA $9.99
CAN $9.99
UK £8.99

DESIGNING Digital Games

Create Games with Scratch™!

Derek Breen

9781119177210
USA $9.99
CAN $9.99
UK £8.99

GETTING STARTED WITH Raspberry Pi™

Program Your Raspberry Pi™!

Richard Wentk

9781119262657
USA $9.99
CAN $9.99
UK £6.99

EXPERIMENTING WITH Science

Think, Test, and Learn!

9781119291336
USA $9.99
CAN $9.99
UK £6.99

CREATING Digital Animations

Animate Stories with Scratch™!

Derek Breen

9781119233527
USA $9.99
CAN $9.99
UK £6.99

GETTING STARTED WITH Engineering

Think Like an Engineer!

Camille McCue, PhD

9781119291220
USA $9.99
CAN $9.99
UK £6.99

WRITING Computer Code

Learn the Language of Computers!

Chris Minnick and Eva Holland

9781119177302
USA $9.99
CAN $9.99
UK £8.99

Unleash Their Creativity

dummies.com

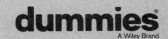